5/15/13
$16.00

Praise for

Flourish

"This is particularly helpful for people who want to know why learned optimism works and the variety of venues in which it has been successful."

—*Library Journal*

"Repaves the path to true happiness. Seligman parlays his 20-year experience studying and applying theories about personal contentment into an instructional book on personal growth through affirmative, upbeat reinforcement. Utilizing interactive exercises, case histories and examples from everyday life (health and wealth factors), the author energetically coaches those interested in self-improvement and personal growth. Graphs, charts and tables offer refreshingly visual proof of the success of his model, including a reprint of his 'Signature Strengths Test.' A relentlessly optimistic guidebook on finding and securing individual happiness."

—*Kirkus*

"Important."

—*Publishers Weekly*

"No psychologist in history has done more than Martin Seligman to discover the keys to flourishing and then give them away to the world. *Flourish* is full of specific techniques you can use to change yourself, your relationships, and your organization. More important, Seligman teaches you how to look at life and see possibilities, rather than constraints. If you lead people, work with people, or know any people, you should read this book."

—Jonathan Haidt, author of *The Happiness Hypothesis*

"This book is a guide to a state of truly flourishing, reaching our max, getting to the sweetness of life, which comes with our being engaged and committed to people and our own self-care. *Flourish* will help you get the most out of life. A great book to be sure—a must for every bookshelf."

—John Ratey, MD, author of *Spark*

"You might think you know about well-being and positive psychology, but there's so much more you can learn in *Flourish*. With flashes of brilliance, rigorous research, and stories so absorbing that they're impossible to put down, Seligman's new book contains wisdom garnered over a long and storied career. If you liked *Authentic Happiness*, you will like *Flourish* ten times more. This book is not only a source of knowledge, but a fount of inspiration."

—Sonja Lyubomirsky, professor of psychology at the University of California, Riverside, and author of *The How of Happiness*

"Brilliant, beautiful, useful, and true. How many books can you say that about? Well, you can say it for sure about *Flourish*. Written by a master of research as well as a thoroughly joyful man, *Flourish* will allow you to flourish if you simply read the book and follow its sane, sage, groundbreaking advice. Skeptics, beware! This book will prove you wrong. You actually can plan your way to a joyful and fulfilling life. Read and rejoice!"

—Edward Hallowell, M.D., author of *Shine*

"One of the leading psychologists in the world has applied his wisdom and experience to the task of increasing wellness, resilience, and happiness for everyone. He also offers a blueprint for policy makers at the national level to promote better performance in the classroom, mental fitness in the military, and health orientation in the practice of medicine. This volume is written in the lucid style characteristic of Seligman and represents a landmark in positive psychology."

—Aaron T. Beck, M.D., founder of Cognitive Therapy

"The spread of positive psychology is a key development in world culture. This book tells the remarkable story, including its adoption by the U.S. Army."

—Richard Layard, author of *Happiness: Lessons from a New Science*

"Seligman is a rational optimist . . . his recipes for increasing well-being are founded on empirical tests."

—*New Scientist*

"I greatly enjoyed the book! It's another Positive Psychology classic!"

—Yakov Smirnoff

ALSO BY MARTIN E. P. SELIGMAN

*Authentic Happiness: Using the New Positive Psychology
to Realize Your Potential for Lasting Fulfillment*

*The Optimistic Child: A Proven Program to Safeguard Children
Against Depression and Build Lifelong Resilience*

*What You Can Change and What You Can't:
The Complete Guide to Successful Self-Improvement*

Learned Optimism: How to Change Your Mind and Your Life

Helplessness: On Development, Depression & Death

Flourish

A VISIONARY NEW UNDERSTANDING
OF HAPPINESS AND WELL-BEING

Martin E. P. Seligman

FREE PRESS

NEW YORK   LONDON   TORONTO   SYDNEY   NEW DELHI

*f*P

Free Press
A Division of Simon & Schuster, Inc.
1230 Avenue of the Americas
New York, NY 10020

First Free Press trade paperback edition February 2012

FREE PRESS and colophon are trademarks of Simon & Schuster, Inc.

For information about special discounts for bulk purchases,
please contact Simon & Schuster Special Sales
at 1-866-506-1949 or business@simonandschuster.com.

The Simon & Schuster Speakers Bureau can bring authors to
your live event. For more information or to book an event contact
the Simon & Schuster Speakers Bureau at 1-866-248-3049
or visit our website at www.simonspeakers.com.

Designed by Julie Schroeder

Manufactured in the United States of America

8   10   9   7

The Library of Congress has cataloged the hardcover edition as follows:

Seligman, Martin E. P.
Flourish: A visionary new understanding of happiness and well-being /
Martin E. P. Seligman.
p.   cm.
Includes bibliographical references and index.
1. Positive psychology.   2. Well-being.   3. Satisfaction.   I. Title.
BF204.6.S45 2011
150.19'88—dc22   2010033642

ISBN 978-1-4391-9075-3
ISBN 978-1-4391-9076-0 (pbk)
ISBN 978-1-4391-9077-7 (ebook)

This book is dedicated to my two youngest daughters,

Carly Dylan Seligman
and
Jenny Emma Seligman

With all of a father's love.

CONTENTS

Flourish

PREFACE

This book will help you flourish.

There, I have finally said it.

I have spent my professional life avoiding unguarded promises like this one. I am a research scientist, and a conservative one at that. The appeal of what I write comes from the fact that it is grounded in careful science: statistical tests, validated questionnaires, thoroughly researched exercises, and large, representative samples. In contrast to pop psychology and the bulk of self-improvement, my writings are believable because of the underlying science.

My thinking about the goal of psychology has changed since I published my last book (*Authentic Happiness*, 2002) and, even better, psychology itself is also changing. I have spent most of my life working on psychology's venerable goal of relieving misery and uprooting the disabling conditions of life. Truth be told, this can be a drag. Taking the psychology of misery to heart—as you must when you work on depression, alcoholism, schizophrenia, trauma, and the panoply of suffering that makes up psychology-as-usual's primary material—can be a vexation to the soul. While we do more than our bit to increase the well-being of our clients, psychology-as-usual typically does not do much for the well-being of its practitioners. If anything changes in the practitioner, it is a personality shift toward depression.

I have been part of a tectonic upheaval in psychology called positive psychology, a scientific and professional movement. In 1998, as president of the American Psychological Association (APA), I urged psychology to supplement its venerable goal with a new goal: exploring what makes life worth living and building the enabling conditions of a life worth living. The goal of understanding well-being and building the enabling conditions of life is by no means identical with the goal of understanding misery and undoing the disabling conditions of life. At this moment, several thousand people around the world work in this field and are striving to further these goals. This book narrates their story, or at least the public face of their story.

The private face also needs to be shown. Positive psychology makes people happier. Teaching positive psychology, researching positive psychology, using positive psychology in practice as a coach or therapist, giving positive psychology exercises to tenth graders in a classroom, parenting little kids with positive psychology, teaching drill sergeants how to teach about post-traumatic growth, meeting with other positive psychologists, and just reading about positive psychology all *make people happier*. The people who work in positive psychology are the people with the highest well-being I have ever known.

The content itself—happiness, flow, meaning, love, gratitude, accomplishment, growth, better relationships—constitutes human flourishing. Learning that you can have more of these things is life changing. Glimpsing the vision of a flourishing human future is life changing.

And so this book will increase your well-being—and it will help you flourish.

PART 1

A New Positive
Psychology

Chapter 1

—————

What Is Well-Being?

The real way positive psychology got its start has been a secret until now. When I was president-elect of the American Psychological Association in 1997, my email tripled. I rarely answer phone calls, and I never do snail mail anymore, but because there is a twenty-four-hour-a-day bridge game on the Internet, I answer my email swiftly and diligently. My replies are just the length that fits the time it takes for my partner to play the hand when I am the dummy. (I am seligman@psych.upenn.edu, and you should feel free to email me if you don't mind one-sentence answers.)

One email that I received in late 1997, however, puzzled me, and I put it into my "huh?" folder. It said simply, "Why don't you come up to see me in New York?" and was signed with initials only. A couple of weeks later, I was at a cocktail party with Judy Rodin, then the president of the University of Pennsylvania, where I have taught for forty years. Judy, now the president of the Rockefeller Foundation, was a senior at Penn when I was a first-year graduate student, and we both worked in psychology professor Richard Solomon's animal lab. We became fast friends, and I watched with admiration and more than a little envy when Judy zoomed at an astonishingly young age from president of the Eastern Psychological Association, to chairman of psychology at Yale University, to dean, and to provost at Yale, and then to president at Penn. In between, we even managed to collaborate on a study investigating the correlation of optimism with a stronger immune system in senior citizens when Judy headed the MacArthur Foundation's massive project on psychoneuroimmunology—the pathways through which psychological events influence neural events which in turn influence immune events.

"Do you know a 'PT' who might have sent me an email inviting me to New York?" I asked Judy, who knows everybody who is anybody.

"Go see him!" she gasped.

So two weeks later, I found myself at an unmarked door on the eighth floor of a small, grimy office building in the bowels of lower Manhattan. I was ushered into an undecorated, windowless room in which sat two gray-haired, gray-suited men and one speakerphone.

"We are the lawyers for an anonymous foundation," explained one of them, introducing himself as PT. "We pick winners, and you are a winner. We'd like to know what research and scholarship you want to do. We don't micromanage. We should warn you at the outset, however, that if you reveal our identity, any funding we give you will stop."

I briefly explained to the lawyers and the speakerphone one of my APA initiatives, ethnopolitical warfare (most assuredly not any kind of positive psychology), and said that I would like to hold a meeting of the forty leading people who work in genocide. I wanted to find out when genocides do or do not occur, by comparing the settings surrounding the dozen genocides of the twentieth century to the fifty in settings so rife with hatred that genocide should have occurred but did not. Then I would edit a book about how to avoid genocide in the twenty-first century.

"Thanks for telling us," they said after just five minutes. "And when you get back to your office, would you send us a one-pager about this? And don't forget to include a budget."

Two weeks later, a check for over $120,000 appeared on my desk. This was a delightful shock, since almost all the academic research I had known is funded through tedious grant requests, annoying peer reviews, officious bureaucracy, unconscionable delays, wrenching revisions, and then rejection or at best heart-stopping budget cuts.

I held the weeklong meeting, choosing Derry in Northern Ireland as its symbolic location. Forty academics, the princes and princesses of ethnopolitical violence, attended. All but two knew one another from the social-science circuit. One was my father-in-law, Dennis McCarthy, a retired British industrialist. The other was the treasurer of the anonymous foundation, a retired engineering professor from Cornell University. Afterward, Dennis commented to me that people have never been so nice to him. And the volume *Ethnopolitical Warfare*, edited by Daniel Chirot and me, was indeed published in 2002. It's worth reading, but that is not what this story is about.

I had almost forgotten this generous foundation, the name of which I still did not know, when I got a call from the treasurer about six months later.

"That was a super meeting you held in Derry, Marty. I met two brilliant people there, the medical anthropologist Mel Konner and that McCarthy chap. What does he do, by the way? And what do you want to do next?"

"Next?" I stammered, wholly unprepared to solicit more funding. "Well, I am thinking about something I call 'positive psychology.'" I explained it for about a minute.

"Why don't you come visit us in New York?" he said.

The morning of this visit, Mandy, my wife, offered me my best white shirt. "I think I should take the one with the worn collar," I said, thinking of the modest office in lower Manhattan. The office building, however, had changed to one of Manhattan's swankiest, and now the top-floor meeting room was large and windowed—but still with the same two lawyers and the speakerphone, and still no sign on the door.

"What is this positive psychology?" they asked. After about ten minutes of explanation, they ushered me out and said, "When you get back to your office, would you send us a three-pager? And don't forget to include a budget."

A month later, a check for $1.5 million appeared.

This tale has an ending as strange as its beginning. Positive psychology began to flourish with this funding, and the anonymous foundation must have noted this, since two years later, I got another one-line email from PT.

"Is the Mandela-Milosevic dimension a continuum?" it read.

"Hmmm . . . now what could that mean?" I wondered. Knowing, however, that this time I was not dealing with a crank, I made my best guess and sent PT a long, scholarly response, outlining what was known about the nature and nurture of saints and of monsters.

"Why don't you come visit us in New York?" was his response.

This time I wore my best white shirt, and there was a sign on the door that read "Atlantic Philanthropies." The foundation, it turned out, was the gift of a single generous individual, Charles Feeney, who had made his fortune in duty-free shops and donated it all—$5 billion—to these trustees to do good work. American law had forced it to assume a public name.

"We'd like you to gather together the leading scientists and scholars and answer the Mandela-Milosevic question, from the genetics all the way up to the political science and sociology of good and evil," they said. "And we intend to give you twenty million dollars to do it."

That is a lot of money, certainly way above my pay grade, and so I bit. Hard. Over the next six months, the two lawyers and I held meetings with scholars and drafted and redrafted the proposal, to be rubber-stamped the following week by their board of directors. It contained some very fine science.

"We're very embarrassed, Marty," PT said on the phone. "The board turned us down—for the first time in our history. They didn't like the genetics part. Too politically explosive." Within a year, both these wonderful custodians of good works—figures right out of *The Millionaire* (a 1950s television series, on which I had been imprinted as a teenager, in which a person shows up on your doorstep with a check for a million dollars)—had resigned.

I followed the good work that Atlantic Philanthropies did over the next three years—funding Africa, aging, Ireland, and schools—and I decided to phone the new CEO. He took the call, and I could almost feel him steeling himself for yet another solicitation.

"I called only to say thank you and to ask you to convey my deepest gratitude to Mr. Feeney," I began. "You came along at just the right time and made just the right investment in the offbeat idea of a psychology about what makes life worth living. You helped us when we were newborn, and now we don't need any further funding because positive psychology is now self-supporting. But it would not have happened without Atlantic."

"I never got this sort of call before," the CEO replied, his voice puzzled.

The Birth of a New Theory

My encounter with that anonymous foundation was one of the high points of the last ten years in positive psychology, and this book is the story of what this beginning wrought. To explain what positive psychology has become, I begin with a radical *re*thinking of what positivity and flourishing are. First and most important, however, I have to tell you about my new thoughts of what happiness is.

Thales thought that everything was water.
Aristotle thought that all human action was to achieve
    happiness.
Nietzsche thought that all human action was to get power.
Freud thought that all human action was to avoid anxiety.

All of these giants made the grand mistake of monism, in which all human motives come down to just one. Monisms get the most mileage from the fewest variables, and so they pass with flying colors the test of "parsimony," the philosophical dictum that the simplest answer is the right answer. But there is also a lower limit on parsimony: when there are too few variables to explain the rich nuances of the phenomenon in question, nothing at all is explained. Monism is fatal to the theories of these four giants.

Of these monisms, my original view was closest to Aristotle's—that everything we do is done in order to make us happy—but I actually detest the word *happiness,* which is so overused that it has become almost meaningless. It is an unworkable term for science, or for any practical goal such as education, therapy, public policy, or just changing your personal life. The first step in positive psychology is to dissolve the monism of "happiness" into more workable terms. Much more hangs on doing this well than a mere exercise in semantics. Understanding happiness requires a theory, and this chapter is my new theory.

"Your 2002 theory can't be right, Marty," said Senia Maymin when we were discussing my previous theory in my Introduction to Positive Psychology for the inaugural class of the Master of Applied Positive Psychology in 2005. A thirty-two-year-old Harvard University summa in mathematics who is fluent in Russian and Japanese and runs her own hedge fund, Senia is a poster child for positive psychology. Her smile warms even cavernous classrooms like those in Huntsman Hall, nicknamed the "Death Star" by the Wharton School business students of the University of Pennsylvania who call it their home base. The students in this master's program are really special: thirty-five successful adults from all over the world who fly into Philadelphia once a month for a three-day feast of what's at the cutting edge in positive psychology and how they can apply it to their professions.

"The 2002 theory in the book *Authentic Happiness* is supposed to be a theory of what humans choose, but it has a huge hole in it: it omits success and mastery. People try to achieve just for winning's own sake," Senia continued.

This was the moment I began to rethink happiness.

When I wrote *Authentic Happiness* a decade ago, I wanted to call it *Positive Psychology*, but the publisher thought that "happiness" in the title would sell more books. I have been able to win many skirmishes with editors, but never over titles. So I found myself saddled with the word. (I also dislike *authentic*, a close relative of the overused term *self*, in a world of overblown selves.) The primary problem with that title and with "happiness" is not only that it underexplains what we choose but that the modern ear immediately hears "happy" to mean buoyant mood, merriment, good cheer, and smiling. Just as annoying, the title saddled me with that awful smiley face whenever positive psychology made the news.

"Happiness" historically is not closely tied to such hedonics—feeling cheerful or merry is a far cry from what Thomas Jefferson declared that we have the right to pursue—and it is an even further cry from my intentions for a positive psychology.

The Original Theory: Authentic Happiness

Positive psychology, as I intend it, is about what we choose for its own sake. I chose to have a back rub in the Minneapolis airport recently because it made me feel good. I chose the back rub for its own sake, not because it gave my life more meaning or for any other reason. We often choose what makes us feel good, but it is very important to realize that often our choices are not made for the sake of how we will feel. I chose to listen to my six-year-old's excruciating piano recital last night, not because it made me feel good but because it is my parental duty and part of what gives my life meaning.

The theory in *Authentic Happiness* is that happiness could be analyzed into three different elements that we choose for their own sakes: positive emotion, engagement, and meaning. And each of these elements is better defined and more measurable than happiness. The first is positive emotion; what we feel: pleasure, rapture, ecstasy, warmth, comfort, and the like. An entire life led successfully around this element, I call the "pleasant life."

The second element, engagement, is about flow: being one with the music, time stopping, and the loss of self-consciousness during an absorbing activity. I refer to a life lived with these aims as the "engaged life." Engagement is different, even opposite, from positive emotion; for if you ask people who are in flow what they are thinking and feeling, they usually say, "nothing." In flow we merge with the object. I believe that the concentrated attention that flow requires uses up all the cognitive and emotional resources that make up thought and feeling.

There are no shortcuts to flow. On the contrary, you need to deploy your highest strengths and talents to meet the world in flow. There are effortless shortcuts to feeling positive emotion, which is another difference between engagement and positive emotion. You can masturbate, go shopping, take drugs, or watch television. Hence, the importance of identifying your highest strengths and learning to use them more often in order to go into flow (www.authentichappiness.org).

There is yet a third element of happiness, which is meaning. I go into flow playing bridge, but after a long tournament, when I look in the mirror, I worry that I am merely fidgeting until I die. The pursuit of engagement and the pursuit of pleasure are often solitary, solipsistic endeavors. Human beings, ineluctably, want meaning and purpose in life. The Meaningful Life consists in belonging to and serving something that you believe is bigger than the self, and humanity creates all the positive institutions to allow this: religion, political party, being green, the Boy Scouts, or the family.

So that is authentic happiness theory: positive psychology is about happiness in three guises—positive emotion, engagement, and meaning. Senia's challenge crystallized ten years of teaching, thinking about, and testing this theory and pushed me to develop it further. Beginning in that October class in Huntsman Hall, I changed my mind about *what positive psychology is*. I also changed my mind about *what the elements of positive psychology are* and *what the goal of positive psychology should be*.

Authentic Happiness Theory	Well-Being Theory
Topic: happiness	Topic: well-being
Measure: life satisfaction	Measures: positive emotion, engagement, meaning, positive relationships, and accomplishment
Goal: increase life satisfaction	Goal: increase flourishing by increasing positive emotion, engagement, meaning, positive relationships, and accomplishment

From Authentic Happiness Theory to Well-Being Theory

I used to think that the topic of positive psychology was happiness, that the gold standard for measuring happiness was life satisfaction, and that the goal of positive psychology was to increase life satisfaction. I now think that the topic of positive psychology is well-being, that the gold standard for measuring well-being is flourishing, and that the goal of positive psychology is to increase flourishing. This theory, which I call well-being theory, is very different from authentic happiness theory, and the difference requires explanation.

There are three inadequacies in authentic happiness theory. The first is that the dominant popular connotation of "happiness" is inextricably bound up with being in a cheerful mood. Positive emotion is the rock-bottom meaning of happiness. Critics cogently contend that authentic happiness theory arbitrarily and preemptively redefines happiness by dragging in the desiderata of engagement and meaning to supplement positive emotion. Neither engagement nor meaning refers to how we feel, and while we may desire engagement and meaning, they are not and can never be part of what "happiness" denotes.

The second inadequacy in authentic happiness theory is that life satisfaction holds too privileged a place in the measurement of happiness. Happiness in authentic happiness theory is operationalized by the gold standard of life satisfaction, a widely researched self-report measure that asks on a 1-to-10 scale how satisfied you are with your life, from terrible (a score of 1) to ideal (10). The goal of positive psychology follows from the gold standard—to increase the amount of life satisfaction on the planet. It turns out, however, that how much life satisfaction people report is itself determined by how good we *feel* at the very moment we are asked the question. Averaged over many people, the mood you are in determines more than 70 percent of how much life satisfaction you report and how well you *judge* your life to be going at that moment determines less than 30 percent.

So the old, gold standard of positive psychology is disproportionately tied to mood, the form of happiness that the ancients snobbishly, but rightly, considered vulgar. My reason for denying mood a privileged place is not snobbishness, but liberation. A mood view of happiness consigns the 50 percent of the world's population who are "low-positive affectives" to the hell of unhappiness. Even though they lack cheerfulness, this low-mood half may have more engagement and meaning in life than merry people. Introverts are much less cheery than extroverts, but if public policy is based (as we shall inquire in the final chapter) on maximizing happiness in the mood sense, extroverts get a much greater vote than introverts. The decision to build a circus rather than a library based on how much additional happiness will be produced counts those capable of cheerful mood more heavily than those less capable. A theory that counts increases in engagement and meaning along with increases in positive emotion is morally liberating as well as more democratic for public policy. And it turns out that life satisfaction does not take into account how much meaning we have or how engaged we are in our work or how engaged we are with the people we love. *Life satisfaction essentially measures cheerful mood, so it is not entitled to a central place in any theory that aims to be more than a happiology.*

The third inadequacy in authentic happiness theory is that positive emotion, engagement, and meaning do not exhaust the elements that people choose for their own sake. "Their own sake" is the operative phrase: to be a basic element in a theory, what you choose must serve no other master. This was Senia's challenge; she asserted that many people live to achieve, just for achievement's sake. A better theory will more completely specify the elements of what people choose. And so, here is the new theory and how it solves these three problems.

Well-Being Theory

Well-being is a construct, and happiness is a thing. A "real thing" is a directly measurable entity. Such an entity can be "operationalized"— which means that a highly specific set of measures defines it. For instance, the windchill factor in meteorology is defined by the combination of temperature and wind at which water freezes (and frostbite occurs). Authentic happiness theory is an attempt to explain a *real thing*—happiness—as defined by life satisfaction, where on a 1-to-10 ladder, people rate their satisfaction with their lives. People who have the most positive emotion, the most engagement, and the most meaning in life are the happiest, and they have the most life satisfaction. Well-being theory denies that the topic of positive psychology is a real thing; rather the topic is a *construct*—well-being—which in turn has several measurable elements, each a real thing, each contributing to well-being, *but none defining well-being.*

In meteorology, "weather" is such a construct. Weather is not in and of itself a real thing. Several elements, each operationalizable and thus each a real thing, contribute to the weather: temperature, humidity, wind speed, barometric pressure, and the like. Imagine that our topic were not the study of positive psychology but the study of "freedom." How would we go about studying freedom scientifically? Freedom is a construct, not a real thing, and several different elements contribute to it: how free the citizens feel, how often the press is censored, the frequency of elections, the ratio of representatives to population, how many officials are corrupt, among other factors. Each of these elements, unlike the construct of freedom itself, is a measurable thing, but only by measuring these elements do we get an overall picture of how much freedom there is.

Well-being is just like "weather" and "freedom" in its structure: no single measure defines it exhaustively (in jargon, "defines exhaustively" is called "operationalizes"), but several things contribute to it; these are the *elements* of well-being, and each of the elements is a measurable thing. By contrast, life satisfaction operationalizes happiness in authentic happiness theory just as temperature and wind speed define windchill. Importantly, the elements of well-being are themselves different kinds of things; they are not all mere self-reports of thoughts and feelings of positive emotion, of how engaged you are, and of how much meaning you have in life, as in the original theory of authentic happiness. So the construct of well-being, not the entity of life satisfaction, is the focal topic of positive psychology. Enumerating the elements of well-being is our next task.

The Elements of Well-Being

Authentic happiness theory comes dangerously close to Aristotle's monism because happiness is operationalized, or defined, by life satisfaction. Well-being has several contributing elements that take us safely away from monism. It is essentially a theory of uncoerced choice, and its five elements comprise what free people will choose for their own sake. And each element of well-being must itself have three properties to count as an element:

1. It contributes to well-being.
2. Many people pursue it for its own sake, not merely to get any of the other elements.
3. It is defined and measured independently of the other elements (exclusivity).

Well-being theory has five elements, and each of the five has these three properties. The five elements are positive emotion, engagement, meaning, positive relationships, and accomplishment. A handy mnemonic is PERMA. Let's look at each of the five, starting with positive emotion.

Positive emotion. The first element in well-being theory is positive emotion (the pleasant life). It is also the first in authentic happiness theory. But it remains a cornerstone of well-being theory, although with two crucial changes. Happiness and life satisfaction, as subjective measures, are now demoted from being the goal of the entire theory to merely being one of the factors included under the element of positive emotion.

Engagement. Engagement remains an element. Like positive emotion, it is assessed only subjectively ("Did time stop for you?" "Were you completely absorbed by the task?" "Did you lose self-consciousness?"). Positive emotion and engagement are the two categories in well-being theory where all the factors are measured only subjectively. As the hedonic, or pleasurable, element, positive emotion encompasses all the usual subjective well-being variables: pleasure, ecstasy, comfort, warmth, and the like. Keep in mind, however, that thought and feeling are usually absent during the flow state, and only in retrospect do we say, "That was fun" or "That was wonderful." While the subjective state for the pleasures is in the present, the subjective state for engagement is only retrospective.

Positive emotion and engagement easily meet the three criteria for being an element of well-being: (1) Positive emotion and engagement contribute to well-being. (2) They are pursued by many people for their own sake, and not necessarily to gain any of the other elements (I want this back rub even if it brings no meaning, no accomplishment, and no relationships). (3) They are measured independently of the rest of the elements. (There is, in fact, a cottage industry of scientists that measures all the subjective well-being variables.)

Meaning. I retain meaning (belonging to and serving something that you believe is bigger than the self) as the third element of well-being. Meaning has a subjective component ("Wasn't that all-night session in the dormitory the most meaningful conversation ever?"), and so it might be subsumed into positive emotion. Recall that the subjective component is *dispositive* for positive emotion. The person who has it cannot be wrong about his own pleasure, ecstasy, or comfort. What he feels settles the issue. Not so for meaning, however: you might think that the all-night bull session was very meaningful, but when you remember its gist years later and are no longer high on marijuana, it is clear that it was only adolescent gibberish.

Meaning is not solely a subjective state. The dispassionate and more objective judgment of history, logic, and coherence can contradict a subjective judgment. Abraham Lincoln, a profound melancholic, may have, in his despair, judged his life to be meaningless, but we judge it pregnant with meaning. Jean-Paul Sartre's existentialist play *No Exit* might have been judged meaningful by him and his post–World War II devotees, but it now seems wrongheaded ("Hell is other people") and almost meaningless, since today it is accepted without dissent that connections to other people and relationships are what give meaning and purpose to life. Meaning meets the three criteria of elementhood: (1) It contributes to well-being. (2) It is often pursued for its own sake; for example, your single-minded advocacy for AIDS research annoys others, makes you miserable subjectively, and has gotten you fired from your writing job on the *Washington Post,* but you persist undaunted. And (3) meaning is defined and measured independently of positive emotion or engagement and independent of the other two elements—accomplishment and relationships—to which I now turn.

Accomplishment. Here is what Senia's challenge to authentic happiness theory—her assertion that people pursue success, accomplishment, winning, achievement, and mastery for their own sakes—has wrought. I have become convinced that she is correct and that the two transient states above (positive emotion and meaning, or the pleasant life and the meaningful life in their extended forms) do not exhaust what people commonly pursue for their own sakes. Two other states have an adequate claim on "well-being" and need not be pursued in the service of either pleasure or meaning.

Accomplishment (or achievement) is often pursued for its own sake, even when it brings no positive emotion, no meaning, and nothing in the way of positive relationships. Here is what ultimately convinced me: I play a lot of serious duplicate bridge. I have played with and against many of the greatest players. Some expert bridge players play to improve, to learn, to solve problems, and to be in flow. When they win, it's great. They call it "winning pretty." But when they lose—as long as they played well—it's almost as great. These experts play in the pursuit of engagement or positive emotion, even outright joy. Other experts play only to win. For them, if they lose, it's devastating no matter how well they played; if they win, however, it's great, even if they "win ugly." Some will even cheat to win. It does not seem that winning for them reduces to positive emotion (many of the stonier experts deny feeling anything at all when they win and quickly rush on to the next game or play backgammon until the next bridge game assembles), nor does the pursuit reduce to engagement, since defeat nullifies the experience so easily. Nor is it about meaning, since bridge is not about anything remotely larger than the self.

Winning only for winning's sake can also be seen in the pursuit of wealth. Some tycoons pursue wealth and then give much of it away, in astonishing gestures of philanthropy. John D. Rockefeller and Andrew Carnegie set the model, and Charles Feeney, Bill Gates, and Warren Buffett are contemporary paragons of this virtue: Rockefeller and Carnegie both spent the second half of their lives giving away to science and medicine, to culture and education much of the fortunes they had made in the first half of their lives. They created meaning later in their lives after early lives of winning only for winning's sake.

In contrast to these "donors," there are the "accumulators" who believe that the person who dies with the most toys wins. Their lives are built around winning. When they lose, it's devastating, and they do not give away their toys except in the service of winning more toys. It is undeniable that these accumulators and the companies they build provide the means for many other people to build lives, have families, and create their own meaning and purpose. But this is only a side effect of the accumulators' motive to win.

So well-being theory requires a fourth element: accomplishment in its momentary form, and the "achieving life," a life dedicated to accomplishment for the sake of accomplishment, in its extended form.

I fully recognize that such a life is almost never seen in its pure state (nor are any of the other lives). People who lead the achieving life are often absorbed in what they do, they often pursue pleasure avidly and they feel positive emotion (however evanescent) when they win, and they may win in the service of something larger. ("God made me fast, and when I run, I feel His pleasure," says the actor portraying the real-life Olympic runner Eric Liddell in the film *Chariots of Fire*.) Nevertheless, I believe that accomplishment is a fourth fundamental and distinguishable element of well-being and that this addition takes well-being theory one step closer to a more complete account of what people choose for its own sake.

I added accomplishment pursued for its own sake because of one of the most formative articles I ever read. In the early 1960s, I was working in psychology professor Byron Campbell's rat lab at Princeton University, and at that time the umbrella theory of motivation was "drive-reduction" theory: the notion that animals acted only to satisfy their biological needs. In 1959 Robert White had published a heretical article, "Motivation Reconsidered: The Concept of Competence," which threw cold water on the entire drive-reduction enterprise by arguing that rats and people often acted simply to exert mastery over the environment. We pooh-poohed it as soft-headed then, but White, I discovered on my own long and winding road, was right on target.

The addition of the achieving life also emphasizes that the task of positive psychology is to *describe,* rather than *prescribe,* what people actually do to get well-being. Adding this element in no way endorses the achieving life or suggests that you should divert your own path to well-being to win more often. Rather I include it to better describe what human beings, when free of coercion, choose to do for its own sake.

Positive Relationships. When asked what, in two words or fewer, positive psychology is about, Christopher Peterson, one of its founders, replied, "*Other people.*"

Very little that is positive is solitary. When was the last time you laughed uproariously? The last time you felt indescribable joy? The last time you sensed profound meaning and purpose? The last time you felt enormously proud of an accomplishment? Even without knowing the particulars of these high points of your life, I know their form: all of them took place around other people.

Other people are the best antidote to the downs of life and the single most reliable up. Hence my snide comment about Sartre's "Hell is other people." My friend Stephen Post, professor of Medical Humanities at Stony Brook, tells a story about his mother. When he was a young boy, and his mother saw that he was in a bad mood, she would say, "Stephen, you are looking piqued. Why don't you go out and help someone?" Empirically, Ma Post's maxim has been put to rigorous test, and we scientists have found that doing a kindness produces the single most reliable momentary increase in well-being of any exercise we have tested.

Kindness Exercise

"Another one-penny stamp increase!" I fumed as I stood in an enormous, meandering line for forty-five minutes to get a sheet of one hundred one-cent stamps. The line moved glacially, with tempers rising all around me. Finally I made it to the front and asked for ten sheets of one hundred. All of ten dollars.

"Who needs one-penny stamps?" I shouted. "They're free!" People burst into applause and clustered around me as I gave away this treasure. Within two minutes, everyone was gone, along with most of my stamps. It was one of the most satisfying moments of my life.

Here is the exercise: find one wholly unexpected kind thing to do tomorrow and just do it. Notice what happens to your mood.

There is an island near the Portuguese island of Madeira that is shaped like an enormous cylinder. The very top of the cylinder is a several-acre plateau on which are grown the most prized grapes that go into Madeira wine. On this plateau lives only one large animal: an ox whose job is to plow the field. There is only one way up to the top, a very winding and narrow path. How in the world does a new ox get up there when the old ox dies? A baby ox is carried on the back of a worker up the mountain, where it spends the next forty years plowing the field alone. If you are moved by this story, ask yourself why.

Is there someone in your life whom you would feel comfortable phoning at four in the morning to tell your troubles to? If your answer is yes, you will likely live longer than someone whose answer is no. For George Vaillant, the Harvard psychiatrist who discovered this fact, the master strength is the capacity to *be* loved. Conversely, as the social neuroscientist John Cacioppo has argued, loneliness is such a disabling condition that it compels the belief that the pursuit of relationships is a rock-bottom fundamental to human well-being.

There is no denying the profound influences that positive relationships or their absence have on well-being. The theoretical issue, however, is whether positive relationships qualify as an *element* of well-being. Positive relationships clearly fulfill two of the criteria of being an element: they contribute to well-being and they can be measured independently of the other elements. But do we ever pursue relationships for *their own sake,* or do we pursue them only because they bring us positive emotion or engagement or meaning or accomplishment? Would we bother pursuing positive relationships if they did not bring about positive emotion or engagement or meaning or accomplishment?

I do not know the answer to this with any certainty, and I do not even know of a crucial experimental test, since all positive relationships that I know about are accompanied either by positive emotion or engagement or meaning or accomplishment. Two recent streams of argument about human evolution both point to the importance of positive relationships in their own right and for their own sake.

What is the big human brain for? About five hundred thousand years ago, the cranial capacity of our hominid ancestors' skulls doubled in size from 600 cubic centimeters to its present 1,200 cubic centimeters. The fashionable explanation for all this extra brain is to enable us to make tools and weapons; you have to be really smart to deal instrumentally with the physical world. The British theoretical psychologist Nick Humphrey has presented an alternative: the big brain is a social problem solver, not a physical problem solver. As I converse with my students, how do I solve the problem of saying something that Marge will think is funny, that won't offend Tom, and that will persuade Derek that he is wrong without rubbing his nose in it? These are extremely complicated problems—problems that computers, which can design weapons and tools in a trice, cannot solve. But humans can and do solve social problems, every hour of the day. The massive prefrontal cortex that we have is continually using its billions of connections to simulate social possibilities and then to choose the optimal course of action. So the big brain is a relationship simulation machine, and it has been selected by evolution for exactly the function of designing and carrying out harmonious but effective human relationships.

The other evolutionary argument that meshes with the big brain as social simulator is *group selection.* The eminent British biologist and polemicist Richard Dawkins has popularized a selfish-gene theory which argues that the individual is the sole unit of natural selection. Two of the world's most prominent biologists, unrelated but both named Wilson (Edmund O. and David Sloan), have recently amassed evidence that the group is a primary unit of natural selection. Their argument starts with the social insects: wasps, bees, termites, and ants, all of which have factories, fortresses, and systems of communication and dominate the insect world just as humans dominate the vertebrate world. Being social is the most successful form of higher adaptation known. I would guess that it is even more adaptive than having eyes, and the most plausible mathematization of social insect selection is that selection is done by groups and not by individuals.

The intuition for group selection is simple. Consider two primate groups, each made up of genetically diverse individuals. Imagine that the "social" group has the emotional brain structures that subserve love, compassion, kindness, teamwork, and self-sacrifice—the "hive emotions"—and cognitive brain structures, such as mirror neurons, which reflect other minds. The "nonsocial" group, equally intelligent about the physical world and equally strong, does not have these hive emotions. These two groups are now put into a deadly competition that can have only one winner, such as war or starvation. The social group will win, being able to cooperate, hunt in groups, and create agriculture. The unrelated set of genes of the entire social group is preserved and replicated, and these genes include the brain mechanisms for the hive emotions and for the belief in other minds—the ability to understand what others are thinking and feeling.

We will never know if social insects have hive emotions and if arthropods have found and exploited nonemotional ways to sustain group cooperation. But positive human emotion we know well: it is largely social and relationship oriented. We are, emotionally, creatures of the hive, creatures who ineluctably seek out positive relationships with other members of our hive.

So the big social brain, the hive emotions, and group selection persuade me that positive relationships are one of the five basic elements of well-being. The important fact that positive relationships always have emotional or engagement or meaning or accomplishment benefits does not mean that relationships are conducted just for the sake of receiving positive emotion or meaning or accomplishment. Rather, so basic are positive relationships to the success of *Homo sapiens* that evolution has bolstered them with the additional support of the other elements in order to make damn sure that we pursue positive relationships.

SUMMARY OF WELL-BEING THEORY

Here then is well-being theory: well-being is a construct; and well-being, not happiness, is the topic of positive psychology. Well-being has five measurable elements (PERMA) that count toward it:

- Positive emotion (of which happiness and life satisfaction are all aspects)
- Engagement
- Relationships
- Meaning
- Achievement

No one element defines well-being, but each contributes to it. Some aspects of these five elements are measured subjectively by self-report, but other aspects are measured objectively.

In authentic happiness theory, by contrast, happiness is the centerpiece of positive psychology. It is a real thing that is defined by the measurement of life satisfaction. Happiness has three aspects: positive emotion, engagement, and meaning, each of which feeds into life satisfaction and is measured entirely by subjective report.

There is one loose end to clarify: in authentic happiness theory, the strengths and virtues—kindness, social intelligence, humor, courage, integrity, and the like (there are twenty-four of them)—are the supports for engagement. You go into flow when your highest strengths are deployed to meet the highest challenges that come your way. In well-being theory, these twenty-four strengths underpin all five elements, not just engagement: deploying your highest strengths leads to more positive emotion, to more meaning, to more accomplishment, and to better relationships.

Authentic happiness theory is one-dimensional: it is about feeling good and it claims that the way we choose our life course is to try to maximize how we feel. Well-being theory is about all five pillars, the underpinnings of the five elements is the strengths. Well-being theory is plural in method as well as substance: positive emotion is a subjective variable, defined by what you think and feel. Engagement, meaning, relationships, and accomplishment have both subjective and objective components, since you can believe you have engagement, meaning, good relations, and high accomplishment and be *wrong,* even deluded. The upshot of this is that well-being cannot exist just in your own head: well-being is a combination of feeling good as well as actually having meaning, good relationships, and accomplishment. The way we choose our course in life is to maximize all five of these elements.

This difference between happiness theory and well-being theory is of real moment. Happiness theory claims that the way we make choices is to estimate how much happiness (life satisfaction) will ensue, and then we take the course that maximizes future happiness. Maximizing happiness is the final common path of individual choice. As economist Richard Layard argues, that is how individuals choose and in addition maximizing happiness should become the gold standard measure for all policy decisions by government. Richard, the advisor to both prime ministers Tony Blair and Gordon Brown on unemployment, and my good friend and teacher, is a card-carrying economist, and his view— for an economist—is remarkable. It sensibly departs from the typical economist's view of wealth: that the purpose of wealth is to produce more wealth. For Richard, the only rationale for increasing wealth is to increase happiness, so he promotes happiness, not only as the criterion by which we choose what to do as individuals, but as the single outcome measure that should be measured by government in order to decide what policies to pursue. While I welcome this development, it is another naked monism, and I disagree with the idea that happiness is the be-all and end-all of well-being and its best measure.

The final chapter of this book is about the politics and economics of well-being, but for now I want to give just one example of why happiness theory fails abysmally as the sole explanation of how we choose. It is well established that couples with children have on average lower happiness and life satisfaction than childless couples. If evolution had to rely on maximizing happiness, the human race would have died out long ago. So clearly either humans are massively deluded about how much life satisfaction children will bring or else we use some additional metric for choosing to reproduce. Similarly, if personal future happiness were our sole aim, we would leave our aging parents out on ice floes to die. So the happiness monism not only conflicts with the facts, but it is a poor moral guide as well: from happiness theory as a guide to life choice, some couples might choose to remain childless. When we broaden our view of well-being to include meaning and relationships, it becomes obvious why we choose to have children and why we choose to care for our aging parents.

Happiness and life satisfaction are one element of well-being and are useful subjective measures, but well-being cannot exist just in your own head. Public policy aimed only at subjective well-being is vulnerable to the *Brave New World* caricature in which the government promotes happiness simply by drugging the population with a euphoriant called "soma." Just as we choose how to live by plural criteria, and not just to maximize happiness, truly useful measures of well-being for public policy will need to be a dashboard of both subjective and objective measures of positive emotion, engagement, meaning, good relationships, and positive accomplishment.

Flourishing as the Goal of Positive Psychology

The goal of positive psychology in authentic happiness theory is, like Richard Layard's goal, to increase the amount of happiness in your own life and on the planet. The goal of positive psychology in well-being theory, in contrast, is plural and importantly different: it is to increase the amount of *flourishing* in your own life and on the planet.

What is flourishing?

Felicia Huppert and Timothy So of the University of Cambridge have defined and measured flourishing in each of twenty-three European Union nations. Their definition of flourishing is in the spirit of well-being theory: to flourish, an individual must have all the "core features" below and three of the six "additional features."

Core features	Additional features
Positive emotions Engagement, interest Meaning, purpose	Self-esteem Optimism Resilience Vitality Self-determination Positive relationships

They administered the following well-being items to more than two thousand adults in each nation in order to find out how each country was doing by way of its citizens' flourishing.

Positive emotion	Taking all things together, how happy would you say you are?
Engagement, interest	I love learning new things.
Meaning, purpose	I generally feel that what I do in my life is valuable and worthwhile.
Self-esteem	In general, I feel very positive about myself.
Optimism	I'm always optimistic about my future.
Resilience	When things go wrong in my life, it generally takes me a long time to get back to normal. (Opposite answers indicate more resilience.)
Positive relationships	There are people in my life who really care about me.

Denmark leads Europe, with 33 percent of its citizens flourishing. The United Kingdom has about half that rate, with 18 percent flourishing; and Russia sits at the bottom, with only 6 percent of its citizens flourishing.

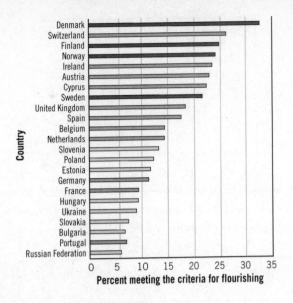

This kind of study leads to the "moon-shot" goal for positive psychology, which is what the final chapter is about and what this book is really aimed at. As our ability to measure positive emotion, engagement, meaning, accomplishment, and positive relations improves, we can ask with rigor how many people in a nation, in a city, or in a corporation are flourishing. We can ask with rigor when in her lifetime an individual is flourishing. We can ask with rigor if a charity is increasing the flourishing of its beneficiaries. We can ask with rigor if our school systems are helping our children flourish.

Public policy follows only from what we measure—and until recently, we measured only money, gross domestic product (GDP). So the success of government could be quantified only by how much it built wealth. But what is wealth for, anyway? The goal of wealth, in my view, is not just to produce more wealth but to engender flourishing. We can now ask of public policy, "How much will building this new school rather than this park increase flourishing?" We can ask if a program of vaccination for measles will produce more flourishing than an equally expensive corneal transplant program. We can ask by how much a program of paying parents to take extra time at home raising their children increases flourishing.

So the goal of positive psychology in well-being theory is to measure and to build human flourishing. Achieving this goal starts by asking what really makes us happy.

Chapter 2

___

Creating Your Happiness:
Positive Psychology Exercises
That Work

Here's a brief exercise that will raise your well-being and lower your depression:

The Gratitude Visit

Close your eyes. Call up the face of someone still alive who years ago did something or said something that changed your life for the better. Someone who you never properly thanked; someone you could meet face-to-face next week. Got a face?

Gratitude can make your life happier and more satisfying. When we feel gratitude, we benefit from the pleasant memory of a positive event in our life. Also, when we express our gratitude to others, we strengthen our relationship with them. But sometimes our thank-you is said so casually or quickly that it is nearly meaningless. In this exercise, called the "Gratitude Visit," you will have the opportunity to experience what it is like to express your gratitude in a thoughtful, purposeful manner.

Your task is to write a letter of gratitude to this individual and deliver it in person. The letter should be concrete and about three hundred words: be specific about what she did for you and how it affected your life. Let her know what you are doing now, and mention how you often remember what she did. Make it sing!

Once you have written the testimonial, call the person and tell her you'd like to visit her, but be vague about the purpose of the meeting; this exercise is much more fun when it is a surprise. When you meet her, take your time reading your letter. Notice her reactions as well as yours. If she interrupts you as you read, say that you really want her to listen until you are done. After you have read the letter (every word), discuss the content and your feelings for each other.

You will be happier and less depressed one month from now.

Can Well-Being Be Changed?

If positive psychology aims to build well-being on the planet, well-being must be buildable. That sounds trivial, but it is not. The behaviorists of the first half of the twentieth century were optimists: they believed that if you could rid the world of the disabling conditions of life—poverty, racism, injustice—human life would be transformed for the better. Contrary to their insouciant optimism, it turns out that many aspects of human behavior do not change lastingly. Your waistline is a prime example. Dieting is a scam, one that bilks Americans out of $50 billion annually. You can follow any diet on the bestseller list and within a month lose 5 percent of your body weight. I did the watermelon diet for thirty days and lost twenty pounds. I had diarrhea for a month. But like 80 percent to 95 percent of dieters, I regained all that weight (and more) within three years. Similarly, as we will see in the next chapter, much psychotherapy and many drugs are merely cosmetic, relieving the symptoms for a short time, followed by a dismaying return to square one.

Is well-being like your waistline—just a temporary boost followed by relapse to your usual curmudgeonliness—or can it be lastingly changed? Before positive psychology started a decade ago, most psychologists had become pessimistic about lasting changes in happiness. The hope that better externalities could make people lastingly happier was discouraged by a study of lottery winners, who were happier for a few months after their windfall but soon fell back to their habitual level of grouchiness or cheerfulness. We adapt rapidly to windfall, job promotion, or marriage, so theorists argue, and we soon want to trade up to yet more goodies to raise our plummeting happiness. If we trade up successfully, we stay on the hedonic treadmill, but we will always need yet another shot.

Not a pretty picture for the pursuit of well-being.

If well-being could not be lastingly increased, then the aim of positive psychology would have to be abandoned, but I believe that well-being can be robustly raised. So this chapter is about my search for exercises that actually make us lastingly happier. From the Buddha to modern pop psychology, there have been at least two hundred endeavors proposed that allegedly do this. Which—if any—of these really produce lasting increases in well-being, which are temporary boosts, and which are just bogus?

I am a "naughty thumb of science" person—an empiricist, in other words, who prods and pokes people to get at truth that we cannot see otherwise—and some of my earlier work involved testing therapies and drugs that make people less depressed. There is a gold standard for testing therapies—random-assignment, placebo-controlled studies: randomly assigning some volunteers to the treatment group (to receive the therapy under investigation) and other subjects to what's called the control group (which is given either an inactive treatment or the current standard therapy). The random assignment of some individuals to the treatment and the others to the control group controls for internal, confounding factors, such as being highly motivated to get better: the really unmotivated and the really motivated people should in principle get spread equally into both groups by randomization. And the placebo nature of the control group controls for external factors: an equal number of individuals in each group will do each treatment when it is raining or when it is sunny. So if the treatment works, and the experimental group improves more than the randomly assigned placebo-controlled group, the treatment is gold-standard "efficacious" and is indeed the actual cause of the improvement.

The same logic holds for testing exercises that purport to increase well-being. So starting in 2001, the Positive Psychology Center at the University of Pennsylvania (which I direct; visit the website at www.ppc.sas.upenn.edu/) began to ask what actually makes us happier. In these studies, we did not measure all the elements of well-being, but only the emotional element—increases in life satisfaction and decreases in depression.

Here's a second exercise to give you the flavor of the interventions that we have validated in random-assignment, placebo-controlled designs:

What-Went-Well Exercise
(Also Called "Three Blessings")

We think too much about what goes wrong and not enough about what goes right in our lives. Of course, sometimes it makes sense to analyze bad events so that we can learn from them and avoid them in the future. However, people tend to spend more time thinking about what is bad in life than is helpful. Worse, this focus on negative events sets us up for anxiety and depression. One way to keep this from happening is to get better at thinking about and savoring what went well.

For sound evolutionary reasons, most of us are not nearly as good at dwelling on good events as we are at analyzing bad events. Those of our ancestors who spent a lot of time basking in the sunshine of good events, when they should have been preparing for disaster, did not survive the Ice Age. So to overcome our brains' natural catastrophic bent, we need to work on and practice this skill of thinking about what went well.

Every night for the next week, set aside ten minutes before you go to sleep. *Write down three things that went well today and why they went well.* You may use a journal or your computer to write about the events, but it is important that you have a physical record of what you wrote. The three things need not be earthshaking in importance ("My husband picked up my favorite ice cream for dessert on the way home from work today"), but they can be important ("My sister just gave birth to a healthy baby boy").

Next to each positive event, answer the question "Why did this happen?" For example, if you wrote that your husband picked up ice cream, write "because my husband is really thoughtful sometimes" or "because I remembered to call him from work and remind him to stop by the grocery store." Or if you wrote, "My sister just gave birth to a healthy baby boy," you might pick as the cause "God was looking out for her" or "She did everything right during her pregnancy."

Writing about why the positive events in your life happened may seem awkward at first, but please stick with it for one week. It will get easier. The odds are that you will be less depressed, happier, and addicted to this exercise six months from now.

Aside from being a naughty-thumb type, I take my own medicine. When I did experiments with electric shock and dogs forty-five years ago, I first gave myself the shock, and I tasted the Purina Dog Chow the dogs fed on—which was worse than the shock. So when I thought up the what-went-well exercise, I first tried it on myself. It worked. Next I tried it on my wife and my children. It worked again. Next my students got it.

Over the last forty-five years, I've taught almost every topic in psychology. But I have never had so much fun teaching, nor have my teaching ratings ever been so high as when I have taught positive psychology. When I taught abnormal psychology for twenty-five years, I could not assign my students meaningful, experiential homework: they couldn't become schizophrenic for a weekend! It was all book learning, and they could never know craziness itself. But in teaching positive psychology, I can assign my students to make a gratitude visit or to do the what-went-well exercise.

Many of the exercises that work actually began in my courses. For example, after we had read the scholarly literature on gratitude, I asked the students to devise a gratitude homework exercise: hence, the gratitude visit, which was dreamed up by Marisa Lascher. In five courses on positive psychology, I assigned students to carry out in their own lives the exercises we had thought up. What ensued was remarkable. I have never seen so much positive life change in my students or heard the sweetest words a teacher can hear—*life changing*—used so often to describe the course.

I then tried a new departure. Instead of teaching university students, I taught professional mental health workers from all over the world about positive psychology. I gave four live telephone courses under the auspices of Dr. Ben Dean, who has made a profession of giving telephone courses on coaching for continuing education to licensed clinical psychologists. Each course was two hours per week for six months, and more than eight hundred professionals (including psychologists, life coaches, counselors, and psychiatrists) took my course. Each week I gave a live lecture, and then I assigned one out of about a dozen positive psychology exercises for them to do with their patients and clients, as well as to practice in their own lives.

Positive Psychology Interventions and Cases

I was astonished by how well these interventions "took" even with very depressed patients. I know that testimonials are suspect, but, for what it's worth, as a therapist and trainer of therapists for thirty years and director of clinical training for fourteen years, I had never encountered such a mass of positive reports. Here are three from the therapists who were new to positive psychology and were trying the exercises for the first time:

CASE STORY

The client is a thirty-six-year-old female who is currently under out-patient counseling and medication for depression (and is working full-time). I have been working with her for eight weeks and have basically been walking her through the telephone course in generally the same sequence we have followed. One assignment that worked especially well:

"Three happy moments" (what-went-well). She mentioned that she had forgotten all of these positives from the past. We used this to transition to "blessings," which we described as "happy moments every day," which have helped her to see her daily life more positively.

In short, everything has "worked" very well. Her scores on the scales from the website are much more positive than before, and she credits the coaching process very strongly.

CASE STORY

The client is a depressed woman, middle-aged, morbidly obese, with underlying depression and blocks to her health and weight reduction. Among other interventions, she took the "approaches to happiness" test (AHI, available online at www.authentichappiness .org) about three months into therapy. She was working on balancing her life using the ideas of flow, meaning, and pleasantries. She noted that she knew from the start that she had no flow in her life and that all of the meaning was defined by helping others and certainly not at all about herself and her needs and wishes (pleasantries). After working hard for the three months, she took the test and was pleased to note that the three areas were quite in balance at about 3.5 on the scale of 5. She was thrilled and encouraged that there was a measure available to feedback her progress. She summarily made more plans to work with the three areas, adding all sorts of new ways to add more flow and meaning into her life.

Therapists reported to me that getting their patients in touch with their strengths, rather than just trying to correct their weaknesses, was particularly beneficial. The crucial step in this process is systematic: it begins when patients take the Values in Action Signature Strengths (VIA) test (available in a short version in the Appendix and in the full version on the Authentic Happiness website, at www.authentic happiness.org).

CASE STORY

I've been working with Emma for about six years, with an interruption of one year. She came back two years ago following the death of one of her few friends. I have recently used a few positive psychology exercises/interventions with Emma, a severely depressed, suicidal client who has been abused in every way possible since she was a baby, up to and including present-day abuse. In the past few months, I have decided to use some of the positive psychology material. I started her with the VIA Signature Strengths test in an effort to help her see the truth of who she is at her core, rather than who she has believed she is (no better than "pond scum"). This survey was the launch pad and foundation upon which to build a clear reflection. It was a tool in which I used the metaphor of a clear image being reflected back from a clear mirror that I was holding up for her. It was slow going, but soon she was able to talk about each strength, see each strength as "true" about her, see how some of the strengths get her into trouble, see where she uses the strengths to her benefit and the benefit of others, and see what strengths could help her to develop less-developed strengths. Three days later, she came for her appointment with two pages in hand . . . with seven items and the steps she was willing to take. I cried all the way through the reading of those two pages, and she smiled the entire time. This is a woman who rarely if ever smiles! It was a moment of celebration, and beyond that, she was leaping over some of the most salient and challenging "stuck places" having to do with learned helplessness and all her other personal issues that have been a part of her work in therapy.

I want you to take the test Emma took, the Values in Action Signature Strengths test, either in the Appendix or on my website and then we will do the exercise that started Emma on the road to recovery.

Let me first tell you about why I constructed the website, which has all the major validated tests of the positive side of life, with feedback on where you stand. This website is free and is intended as a public service. It is also a gold mine for positive psychology researchers, much better for obtaining valid results than asking questions, as researchers usually do, of college sophomores or clinic volunteers.

At this writing 1.8 million people have registered at the website and taken the tests. Between 500 and 1,500 new people register every day, and every so often I put up a link. One link is about exercises. People who go to this link are invited to help us test new exercises. First they take depression and happiness tests, such as the Center for Epidemiological Studies depression scale and the authentic happiness inventory, which are both on www.authentichappiness.org. Next we randomly assign them to a single exercise that is either active or a placebo. All exercises require two to three hours over the course of one week. In our first web study, we tried six exercises, including the gratitude visit and what-went-well.

Of the 577 participants who completed the baseline questionnaires, 471 completed all five follow-up assessments. We found that participants in all conditions (including the placebo-control condition, which was to write up a childhood memory every night for a week) were happier and less depressed one week after they received their assigned exercise. Thereafter, people in the control condition were no happier or less depressed than they were at baseline.

Two of the exercises—what-went-well and the signature strengths exercise below—markedly lowered depression three months and six months later. These two exercises also substantially increased happiness through six months. The gratitude visit produced large decreases in depression and large increases in happiness one month later, but the effect faded three months later. Not surprisingly, we found that the degree to which participants actively continue their assigned exercise beyond the prescribed one-week period predicted how long the changes in happiness last.

Signature Strengths Exercise

The purpose of this exercise is to encourage you to own your signature strengths by finding new and more frequent uses for them. A signature strength has the following hallmarks:

- A sense of ownership and authenticity ("This is the real me")
- A feeling of excitement while displaying it, particularly at first
- A rapid learning curve as the strength is first practiced
- A sense of yearning to find new ways to use it
- A feeling of inevitability in using the strength ("Try to stop me")

- Invigoration rather than exhaustion while using the strength
- The creation and pursuit of personal projects that revolve around it
- Joy, zest, enthusiasm, even ecstasy while using it

Now please take the strengths survey. If you do not have access to the web, you can go to the Appendix and take a brief version of this test. On the website, you will get your results immediately and can print them out if you like. This questionnaire was developed by Chris Peterson, a professor at the University of Michigan, and has been taken by more than a million people from two hundred nations. You will have the benefit of being able to compare yourself to other people like you.

As you complete the questionnaire, pay most attention to the rank order of your own strengths. Were there any surprises for you? Next, take your five highest strengths one at a time and ask yourself, "Is it a *signature* strength?"

After you have completed the test, perform the following exercise: this week I want you to create a designated time in your schedule when you will exercise one or more of your signature strengths in a new way either at work or at home or in leisure—just make sure that you create a clearly defined opportunity to use it. For example:

- If your signature strength is creativity, you may choose to set aside two hours one evening to begin working on a screenplay.
- If you identify hope/optimism as a strength, you might write a column for the local newspaper in which you express hope about the future of the space program.
- If you claim self-control as a strength, you might choose to work out at the gym rather than watch TV one evening.
- If your strength is an appreciation of beauty and excellence, you might take a longer, more beautiful route to and from work, even though it adds twenty minutes more to your commute.

The best thing to do is to create the new way of using your strength yourself. Write about your experience. How did you feel before, during, and after engaging in the activity? Was the activity challenging? Easy? Did time pass quickly? Did you lose your sense of self-consciousness? Do you plan to repeat the exercise?

These positive psychology exercises worked on me, they worked on my family, they worked on my students, and they were taught to professionals and then worked on their clients—even very depressed clients. And the exercises even worked in the gold-standard testing of placebo-controlled, random assignment.

Positive Psychotherapy

We positive psychologists continued our work on these single exercises with normal people, and about a dozen proved effective. I include some of these at appropriate places throughout this book.

Our next step in our research, however, was to test the best of these exercises on depressed people. Acacia Parks, then my graduate student, now teaching at Reed College, created a six-week package of six exercises, delivered in group therapy, as a means of treating depressive symptoms in mildly to moderately depressed young adults. We found dramatic effects: the exercises lowered their depression markedly into the nondepressed range, relative to randomly assigned depressed controls. And they stayed nondepressed for the year that we tracked them.

Finally Dr. Tayyab Rashid created positive psychotherapy (PPT) for depressed patients seeking treatment at Counseling and Psychological Services at the University of Pennsylvania. As with other psychotherapies, positive psychotherapy is a set of techniques that are most effectively delivered with basic therapeutic essentials such as warmth, accurate empathy, basic trust and genuineness, and rapport. We believe that these essentials allow for tailoring the techniques to the individual needs of depressed clients. We first conduct a careful assessment of the client's depressive symptoms and the well-being scores from www.authentichappiness.org. We then discuss how depressive symptoms are potentially explained by lack of well-being: lack of positive emotion, engagement, and meaning in life. As shown by the following outline, thirteen more sessions follow in which we tailor positive psychology exercises to the client. The details can be found in my book *Positive Psychotherapy: A Treatment Manual* co-authored with Dr. Rashid (Rashid and Seligman, 2011):

AN OVERVIEW OF FOURTEEN SESSIONS OF PPT
(Rashid and Seligman, 2011)

Session 1: The absence or lack of positive resources (positive emotions, character strengths, and meaning) can cause and maintain depression and can create an empty life. Homework: The client writes a one-page (roughly three hundred words) "positive introduction," in which she tells a concrete story showing her at her best and illustrating how she used her highest character strengths.

Session 2: The client identifies his character strengths from the positive introduction and discusses situations in which these character strengths have helped him previously. Homework: The client completes the VIA questionnaire online to identify his character strengths.

Session 3: We focus on specific situations in which character strengths may facilitate cultivation of pleasure, engagement, and meaning. Homework (starting now and continuing through the entire course of therapy): The client starts a "blessings journal," in which she writes, every night, three good things (big or small) that happened that day.

Session 4: We discuss the roles of good and bad memories in maintaining depression. Holding on to anger and bitterness maintains depression and undermines well-being. Homework: The client writes about feelings of anger and bitterness and how they feed his depression.

Session 5: We introduce forgiveness as a powerful tool that can transform feelings of anger and bitterness into neutrality, or even, for some, into positive emotions. Homework: The client writes a forgiveness letter describing a transgression and related emotions and pledges to forgive the transgressor (only if appropriate) but does not deliver the letter.

Session 6: Gratitude is discussed as enduring thankfulness. Homework: The client writes a gratitude letter to someone she never properly thanked and is urged to deliver it in person.

Session 7: We review the importance of cultivating positive emotions through writing in the blessings journal and the use of character strengths.

Session 8: We discuss the fact that "satisficers" ("This is good enough") have better well-being than "maximizers" ("I must find the perfect wife, dishwasher, or vacation spot"). Satisficing is encouraged over maximizing. Homework: The client reviews ways to increase satisficing and devises a personal satisficing plan.

Session 9: We discuss optimism and hope, using explanatory style: the optimistic style is to see bad events as temporary, changeable, and local. Homework: The client thinks of three doors that closed on her. What doors opened?

Session 10: The client is invited to recognize character strengths of significant other(s). Homework: We coach the client to respond actively and constructively to positive events reported by others, and the client arranges a date that celebrates his character strengths and those of his significant other(s).

Session 11: We discuss how to recognize the character strengths of family members and where the client's own character strengths originated. Homework: The client asks family members to take the VIA questionnaire online and then draws a tree that includes the character strengths of all members of the family.

Session 12: Savoring is introduced as a technique to increase the intensity and duration of positive emotion. Homework: The client plans pleasurable activities and carries them out as planned. The client is provided with a list of specific savoring techniques.

Session 13: The client has the power to give one of the greatest gifts of all—the gift of time. Homework: The client is to give the gift of time by doing something that requires a fair amount of time and calls on her character strengths.

Session 14: We discuss the full life integrating pleasure, engagement, and meaning.

In our one test of positive psychotherapy with severe depression, the patients were randomly assigned to either individual positive psychotherapy following the outline above or treatment as usual. A matched but nonrandomized group of equally depressed patients underwent treatment as usual plus antidepressant medication. (I don't think randomly assigning patients to medication is ethical, so we matched on demographics and intensity of depression.) Positive psychotherapy relieved depressive symptoms on all outcome measures better than treatment as usual and better than drugs. We found that 55 percent of patients in positive psychotherapy, 20 percent in treatment as usual, and only 8 percent in treatment as usual plus drugs achieved remission.

Positive psychotherapy is only at its very beginning stages of practice and application, and these results are preliminary and much in need of replication. It will be important to tailor the order and duration of the exercises to clients' reactions. Even though they are new as a package, however, the individual exercises themselves have been well validated.

Probably the most striking result of the exercises happened in January 2005. *Time* magazine ran a cover story on positive psychology, and anticipating a flood of requests, we opened a website offering one free exercise: what-went-well. Thousands of people registered. My particular interest was in the fifty most severely depressed people who came to the website, took the depression and happiness tests, and then did the what-went-well exercise. These fifty people had an average depression score of 34, which put them in the "extremely" depressed category of people who barely get out of bed, go to their computer, and then go back to bed. They each did what-went-well—recording three things that went well each day for one week and then reporting back to the website. On average, their depression score plummeted from 34 to 17, from extreme to the cusp of mild-moderate, and their happiness score jumped from the 15th percentile to the 50th percentile. Forty-seven of the fifty were now less depressed and happier.

This was by no means a controlled study, like the two studies above; there was no random assignment, no placebo, and there was potential bias because the people mostly came to the website in the first place wanting to get better. On the other hand, I've worked with psychotherapy and drugs in depression for forty years, and I've never seen results like this. All of which brings me to the dirty little secret of psychotherapy and drugs.

Chapter 3

The Dirty Little Secret of Drugs and Therapy

I am an old hand at cultivating funding for science. I have spent much of the last forty years as a supplicant for government funding, and my knees are just about worn out. I have been funded continuously for forty years by the National Institute of Mental Health (NIMH), however, and I know an important breakthrough when I see it. The findings presented in the last chapter are such a breakthrough: not conclusive, of course, but easily intriguing enough to merit the big bucks in the effort to find out if such inexpensive treatments of depression work reliably.

According to the World Health Organization (WHO), depression is the most costly disease in the world, and the treatments of choice are drugs and psychotherapy. On average, treating a case of depression costs about $5,000 per year, and there are around ten million such cases annually in America. Antidepressant drugs are a multibillion-dollar industry. Imagine a treatment—giving positive psychology exercises on the web—that is dirt cheap, massively disseminated, and at least as effective as therapy and drugs. So I was shocked when I applied for funding from the NIMH three times to pursue these findings, and the proposals were rejected unreviewed each time. (This chapter is not special pleading for personal funding, which I am happy to say that I have more of than I know what to do with. Rather it is about misplaced government and industry priorities.) For you to understand why this proposal was rejected, I have to tell you a bit about the hammerlock that two industries—the drug companies and the Psychotherapy Guild—have over the treatment of mood disorders, including depression.

Cure Versus Symptom Relief

The first dirty little secret of biological psychiatry and of clinical psychology is that they both have given up the notion of cure. Cure takes too long if it can be done at all, and only brief treatment is reimbursed by insurance companies. So therapy and drugs are now entirely about short-term crisis management and about dispensing cosmetic treatments.

There are two kinds of medications: cosmetic drugs and curative drugs. If you take an antibiotic long enough, it cures by killing the bacterial invaders. When you're done taking it, the disease will not recur because the pathogens are dead. Antibiotics are curative drugs. On the other hand, if you take quinine for malaria, you get only temporary suppression of symptoms. When you stop taking quinine, malaria returns full-blown. Quinine is a cosmetic drug—a palliative—and all medications can be classified either as curative in intention or cosmetic in intention. Palliation is a good thing (I wear hearing aids), but it is not the highest good, nor is it the ultimate end of intervention. Symptom relief should be a way station on the road to cure.

But the road has come to a dead end at symptom relief. *Every single drug on the shelf of the psychopharmacopoeia is cosmetic.* There are no curative drugs, and no drug is in development that I know of that aims at cure. Biological psychiatry has given up on cure. I am by no means a Freudian, but one thing that I find exemplary about Freud is that he was after a cure. Freud wanted a psychotherapy that worked like an antibiotic; his talking cure was an attempt to cure the patient by ridding her of the symptoms forever by using insight and catharsis. Freud was not after symptom relief—some symptom relief can even be seen as a defense called "flight into health," which preserves the disease intact—and palliation is not a significant goal in psychodynamic psychotherapy. The stringencies of managed care, far more than the decline of the Freudian influence, has seduced psychology and psychiatry into working only on symptom relief, not on cure.

The 65 Percent Barrier

I've spent a good part of my life measuring the effects of psychotherapy and of drugs, and here's the second dirty little secret. Almost always, the effects are what is technically called "small." Depression is typical. Consider two treatments that are certified by vast literatures to "work": cognitive therapy for depression (which changes how you think about bad events) and selective serotonin reuptake inhibitors (SSRIs, such as Prozac, Zoloft, Lexapro, to name a few). Taking an average over the entire huge literature, for each you get a 65 percent relief rate, accompanied by a placebo effect that ranges from 45 percent to 55 percent. The more realistic and elaborate the placebo, the higher the placebo percentage: so high is the placebo response that in half the studies on which the U.S. Food and Drug Administration (FDA) based its official approval of the antidepressant drugs, there was no difference between placebo and drug.

Recent studies of the antidepressant drugs are even more discouraging. A prestigious consortium of psychologists and psychiatrists took the data from all 718 patients together from the six best-done studies of drug versus placebo, dividing the patients by severity of depression. For very severe depression (if you have depression this severe, you likely would not be reading a paragraph as challenging as this one), the drugs showed reliable effects, but for moderate or mild depression, the effects were nonexistent. The vast majority of prescriptions for antidepressant drugs, unfortunately, are written for just these patients—moderate and mild depressives. So a 20 percent drug edge over placebo would be a generous, maximum estimate of their benefit. This 65 percent number crops up over and over, whether you're looking at the percentage of patients that gain relief or at the percentage of symptom relief within patients. I call this problem the "65 percent barrier."

Why is there a 65 percent barrier, and why are the effects so small?

From the first day I took up skiing until five years later when I quit, I was always fighting the mountain. Skiing was never easy. Every form of psychotherapy I know, every exercise, is a "fighting the mountain" intervention. In other words, these therapies are not self-reinforcing, and so the benefits fade over time. In general, talk therapy techniques all share the property of being difficult to do, no fun at all, and difficult to incorporate into your life. In fact, the way we measure how efficacious talk therapies are is by how long they last before they "melt" once treatment ends. Every single drug has exactly the same property: once you stop taking it, you are back to square one, and recurrence and relapse are the rule.

By contrast, try this next positive psychology exercise. It is fun to do and self-maintaining once you catch on.

Active, Constructive Responding

Strangely, marriage counseling usually consists of teaching partners to fight better. This may turn an insufferable relationship into a barely tolerable one. That's not bad. Positive psychology, however, is more interested in how to turn a good relationship into an excellent one. Shelly Gable, professor of psychology at the University of California at Santa Barbara, has demonstrated that how you celebrate is more predictive of strong relations than how you fight. People we care about often tell us about a victory, a triumph, and less momentous good things that happen to them. How we respond can either build the relationship or undermine it. There are four basic ways of responding, only one of which builds relationships:

ACTIVE AND CONSTRUCTIVE RESPONDING

This table illustrates two examples of the four styles.

YOUR PARTNER SHARES POSITIVE EVENT	TYPE OF RESPONSE	YOUR RESPONSE
"I received a promotion and a raise at work!"	Active and Constructive	"That is great! I am so proud of you. I know how important that promotion was to you! Please relive the event with me now. Where were you when your boss told you? What did he say? How did you react? We should go out and celebrate." Nonverbal: maintaining eye contact, displays of positive emotions, such as genuine smiling, touching, laughing.
	Passive and Constructive	"That is good news. You deserve it." Nonverbal: little to no active emotional expression.
	Active and Destructive	"That sounds like a lot of responsibility to take on. Are you going to spend even fewer nights at home now?" Nonverbal: displays of negative emotions, such as furrowed brow, frowning.
	Passive and Destructive	"What's for dinner?" Nonverbal: little to no eye contact, turning away, leaving the room.
"I just won five hundred dollars in a charity raffle!"	Active and Constructive	"Wow, what luck. Are you going to buy yourself something nice? How did you buy that ticket? Doesn't it feel great to win something?" Nonverbal: maintaining eye contact, displays of positive emotions.
	Passive and Constructive	"That is nice." Nonverbal: little to no active emotional expression.
	Active and Destructive	"I bet you are going to have to pay taxes on that. I never win anything." Nonverbal: displays of negative emotions.
	Passive and Destructive	"I had a bad day at work today." Nonverbal: little eye contact, turning away.

ACTIVE AND CONSTRUCTIVE RESPONDING

Here's your assignment for the week: listen carefully each time someone you care about tells you about something good that happened to
them. Go out of your way to respond actively and constructively. Ask
the person to relive the event with you; the more time he or she spends
reliving, the better. Spend lots of time responding. (Laconic is bad.)
Hunt all week long for good events, recording them nightly in the following form:

OTHER'S EVENT	MY RESPONSE (VERBATIM)	OTHER'S RESPONSE TO ME

If you find you are not particularly good at this, plan ahead. Write
down some concrete positive events that were reported to you recently.
Write down how you should have responded. When you wake up in
the morning, spend five minutes visualizing whom you will encounter
today and what good things they are likely to tell you about themselves. Plan your active, constructive response. Use variants of these
active and constructive responses throughout the week.

In contrast to fighting the mountain, this technique is self-
maintaining. But it does not come naturally to most of us, and we need
to practice it with diligence until it becomes a habit.

I was delighted to see my sixteen-year-old son, Darryl, sitting in
the front row of a workshop I gave in Berlin in July 2010. Finally, a
chance to show Darryl what I really do for a living, other than sitting in front of my computer, writing and playing bridge! In the first
hour, I gave the six hundred participants the active-constructive exercise, dividing them into pairs, with person A presenting a good event
and person B responding, then switching. I saw that Darryl found a
stranger and did it as well.

The next day, the whole family went to the enormous flea market
in the Tiergarten. We scattered, buying trinkets and various souve-

nirs of our tour of Eastern Europe. My two little girls, Carly, age nine, and Jenny, age six, were thrilled about this adventure, and they sprinted from booth to booth. It was a record hot day in Berlin—one hundred degrees—and we were out of steam and money before too long, so we reassembled for air-conditioning and iced coffee at the nearest café. Carly and Jenny were both sporting gold tiaras made of plastic and encrusted with costume jewels.

"We got them for thirteen euros," Carly said proudly.

"Didn't you bargain?" I retorted unthinkingly.

"Now, that is a great example of active destructive, Dad," commented Darryl.

So I am still practicing it, and with lots of coaching.

Once you start doing it, however, other people like you better, they spend more time with you, and they share more of the intimate details of their lives. You feel better about yourself, and all this strengthens the skill of active, constructive responding.

Dealing with
Negative Emotions

In the therapeutic century we've just lived through, the therapist's job was to minimize negative emotion: to dispense drugs or psychological interventions that make people less anxious, angry, or depressed. Today, too, the healer's job is minimizing anxiety, anger, and sadness. Parents and teachers have taken on the same job, and I worry about this because there is another, more realistic approach to these dysphorias: learning to function well even if you are sad or anxious or angry—in other words, *dealing with it*.

My posture emerges from the most important (and most politically uncongenial) research discovery in the field of personality of the last quarter of the twentieth century. This rock-solid finding disillusioned an entire generation of environmentalist researchers (me included), but it is true that most personality traits are highly heritable, which is to say that a person may have genetically inherited a strong predisposition to sadness or anxiety or religiosity. Dysphorias often, but not always, stem from these personality traits. Strong biological under-pinnings predispose some of us to sadness, anxiety, and anger. Therapists can modify these emotions but only within limits. It is likely that depression, anxiety, and anger come from heritable personality traits that can only be ameliorated, not wholly eliminated. This means that, as a born pessimist, even though I know and use every therapeutic trick in the book about arguing against my automatic catastrophic thoughts, I still hear the voices frequently that tell me, "I am a failure" and "Life is not worth living." I can usually turn down their volume by disputing them, but they will always be there, lurking in the background, ready to seize on any setback.

What can a therapist do if the heritability of dysphoria is one cause of the 65 percent barrier? Oddly enough, therapists can use information from the way that snipers and fighter pilots are trained. (I'm not endorsing sniping, by the way; I want only to describe how training is conducted.) It can take about twenty-four hours for a sniper to get into position. And then it can take another thirty-six hours to get off the shot. This means that snipers often haven't slept for two days before they shoot. They're dead tired. Now, let's say the army went to a psychotherapist and asked her how she would train a sniper. She would use wake-up drugs (Provigil is a good one) or psychological interventions that relieve sleepiness (a rubber band on the wrist snapping you into temporary alertness is a good one).

That is not how snipers are trained, however. Instead you keep them up for three days and have them practice shooting when they are dead tired. That is, you teach snipers to *deal* with the negative state they're in: to function well even in the presence of fatigue. Similarly, fighter pilots are selected from rugged individuals who do not scare easily. But many things happen to fighter pilots that scare the pants off even the toughest of them. Again, flight instructors don't call on therapists to teach them the tricks of anxiety reduction (which are legion), thereby training candidates to become relaxed fighter pilots. Rather, the trainer sends the jet into a dive straight for the ground until the trainee is terrified, and then the trainee—in a state of terror—must learn to pull up.

Negative emotions and the negative personality traits have very strong biological limits, and the best a clinician can ever do with the cosmetic approach is to get patients to live in the best part of their set range of depression or anxiety or anger. Think about Abraham Lincoln and Winston Churchill, two severe depressives. They were both enormously well-functioning human beings who dealt with their "black dog" and their suicidal thoughts. (Lincoln came close to killing himself in January 1841.) Both learned to function extremely well even when they were massively depressed. So one thing that clinical psychology needs to develop in light of the heritable stubbornness of human pathologies is a psychology of "dealing with it." We need to tell our patients, "Look, the truth is that many days—no matter how successful we are in therapy—you will wake up feeling blue and thinking life is hopeless. Your job is not only to fight these feelings but also to live heroically: functioning well even when you are very sad."

A New
Approach to Cure

So far I've argued that all drugs and most psychotherapy is only cosmetic and that the best they can do is to approach 65 percent relief. One way to do better than 65 percent is to teach patients to deal with it. But more important is the possibility that the positive interventions may break through the 65 percent barrier and move psychotherapy beyond cosmetic symptom relief toward cure.

Psychotherapy and drugs as they now are used are half baked. On the rare occasions when they are completely successful, they rid the patient of suffering, misery, and the negative symptoms. In short, they remove the internal disabling conditions of life. Removing the disabling conditions, however, is not remotely the same as building the enabling conditions of life. If we want to flourish and if we want to have well-being, we must indeed minimize our misery; but in addition, we must have positive emotion, meaning, accomplishment, and positive relationships. The skills and exercises that build these are entirely different from the skills that minimize our suffering.

I am a rose gardener. I spend a lot of time clearing away underbrush and then weeding. Weeds get in the way of roses; weeds are a disabling condition. But if you want to have roses, it is not nearly enough to clear and weed. You have to amend the soil with peat moss, plant a good rose, water it, and feed it nutrients. (In Pennsylvania, you also need to bathe it with the latest wonder drugs of modern horticochemistry.) You have to supply the enabling conditions for flourishing.

Similarly, as a therapist, once in a while I would help a patient get rid of all of his anger and anxiety and sadness. I thought I would then get a happy patient. But I never did. I got an *empty* patient. And that is because the skills of flourishing—of having positive emotion, meaning, good work, and positive relationships—are something over and above the skills of minimizing suffering.

When I started out as a therapist almost forty years ago, it was common for my patient to tell me, "I just want to be happy, Doctor." I transformed this into "You mean you want to get rid of your depression." Back then I did not have the tools of building well-being at hand and was blinded by Sigmund Freud and Arthur Schopenhauer (who taught that the best humans can ever achieve is to minimize their own misery); the difference had not even occurred to me. I had only the tools for relieving depression. But every person, every patient, just wants "to be happy," and this legitimate goal combines relieving suffering and building well-being. Cure, to my way of thinking, uses the entire arsenal for minimizing misery—drugs and psychotherapy— and adds positive psychology.

Here then is my vision of the therapy of the future, my vision for cure.

First, patients need to be told that the drugs and therapies are temporary symptom relievers only, and that they should expect recurrence when treatment stops. Hence, explicit, successful practice in dealing with it and functioning well even in the presence of the symptoms must be a serious part of therapy.

Second, treatment should not end when suffering is relieved. Patients need to learn the specific skills of positive psychology: how to have more positive emotion, more engagement, more meaning, more accomplishment, and better human relations. Unlike the skills of minimizing misery, these skills are self-sustaining. They likely treat depression and anxiety and they likely help prevent them as well. More important than relieving pathology, these skills are what flourishing is, and they are crucial to everyone's search for well-being.

But who will disseminate these skills to the world?

Applied Psychology Versus Basic Psychology: Problems Versus Puzzles

When the University of Pennsylvania's top administration was debating in 2004 whether to offer a new degree in order to cash in on the public demand for positive psychology, the dean of natural science said, with a touch of venom, "Let's make sure we put an *A* in it. After all, it is the psychology department that does the pure science, and we wouldn't want people to be confused, would we?"

"Will Professor Seligman go along?" wondered the dean of social science. "It is sort of insulting. An *A* for 'applied'—master of applied positive psychology?"

Far from being insulted, I welcomed the *A*. Even though Penn was founded by Benjamin Franklin to teach both the "applied" and the "ornamental," by which he meant "not currently useful," the ornamental has long won out, and I have labored for four decades as the "applied" maverick in an almost solely ornamental department. Pavlovian conditioning, color vision, serial-versus-parallel mental scanning, mathematical models of T-maze learning in rats, the moon illusion—these are the high-prestige enterprises in my home department. Researching the real world has a slightly fetid odor in the high reaches of academic psychology, an odor that wafted through the deans' debate about creating the new degree.

Originally, I went into psychology to relieve human suffering and to increase human well-being. I thought I was well prepared to do this, but I was actually *mis*educated to this task. It took me decades to recover and to work my way out of solving puzzles and into solving problems, as I explain below. Indeed, this is the story of my entire intellectual and professional development.

My miseducation is instructive. I went to Princeton in the early

1960s afire with the hope of making a difference in the world. I got ambushed in a manner so subtle that I did not know I had been ambushed for about twenty years. I was attracted to psychology, but the research in that department seemed pedestrian: laboratory studies of college sophomores and white rats. The world-class heavy hitters at Princeton were in the philosophy department. So I majored in philosophy, and, like so many bright young people, I was seduced there by the ghost of Ludwig Wittgenstein.

Wittgenstein, Popper, and Penn

The overlord of philosophy at Cambridge University, Wittgenstein (1889–1951) was the most charismatic figure in philosophy of the twentieth century. He fathered two major movements. He was born in Vienna, fought gallantly for Austria and was taken prisoner by the Italians. A prisoner of war in 1919, he finished *Tractatus Logico-Philosophicus,* a collection of sequential, numbered epigrams that led to the founding of logical atomism and of logical positivism. Logical atomism is the doctrine that reality can be understood as a hierarchy of ultimate facts, and logical positivism is the doctrine that only tautologies and empirically verifiable statements have meaning. Twenty years later, he changed his mind about what philosophy should do, arguing in *Philosophical Investigations* that the task was not to analyze the building blocks of reality (logical atomism) but rather to analyze the "language games" humans play. This was the trumpet call to ordinary language philosophy, the systematic analysis of words as they are spoken by laymen.

At the heart of both incarnations of the Wittgensteinian movement is analysis. The job of philosophy is to analyze in rigorous and minute detail the basic underpinnings of reality and of language. The larger issues that concern philosophy—free will, God, ethics, beauty—cannot be tackled (if ever) until this preliminary analysis succeeds. "Of what we cannot speak, we must be silent," the *Tractatus* famously concludes.

Just as important as Wittgenstein's ideas was the fact that he was a spellbinding teacher. Crowds of the brightest Cambridge students turned up to watch him pace his bare room, mouthing his epigrams, striving for moral purity, overpowering his students' queries, and all the while demeaning himself for being so inarticulate. The combination of his brilliance, his striking good looks, his magnetic and unusual sexuality, and his exotic otherworldliness (he renounced a huge family fortune) was seductive, and his students fell in love with the man and with his thought. (It is commonplace for students to learn best when they fall in love with their teacher.) These students then fanned out across the intellectual world through the 1950s and ruled English-speaking academic philosophy for the next forty years, passing along their infatuation to their own students. The Wittgensteinians certainly ruled the Princeton philosophy department, and we students were imbued with Wittgensteinian dogma.

I call it dogma because we were rewarded for doing rigorous linguistic analyses. For example, my senior thesis, later the subject of an eerily similar publication by my advisor under his name, was a careful analysis of *same* versus *identical*. We were punished for trying to speak about "what we could not speak about." The students who took Walter Kaufmann, the charismatic teacher of Nietzsche ("the point of philosophy is to change your life"), seriously were dismissed as woolly headed and sophomoric. We did not ask the "naked emperor" questions such as "Why bother to do linguistic analysis in the first place?"

We were assuredly not taught about the historic encounter between Ludwig Wittgenstein and Karl Popper at the Moral Philosophy Club in Cambridge in October 1947. (This event is re-created in David Edmonds and John Eidinow's gripping *Wittgenstein's Poker.*) Popper accused Wittgenstein of suborning an entire generation of philosophers by setting them to work on *puzzles*—the preliminary to the preliminaries. Philosophy, Popper argued, should not be about puzzles but about *problems*: morality, science, politics, religion, and law. So infuriated was Wittgenstein that he brandished a poker at Popper and walked out, slamming the door.

How I wish I had suspected in my college years that Wittgenstein was not the Socrates but the Darth Vader of modern philosophy. How I wish I'd had the sophistication to recognize him as an academic poseur. I did eventually realize that I had been turned in the wrong direction, and I started to correct my course by entering Penn to pursue psychology as a graduate student in 1964, turning down a fellowship to Oxford to study analytic philosophy. Philosophy was a mind-bending game, but psychology was not a game, and it could, I fervently hoped, actually help humanity. I was helped to this realization by Robert Nozick (my undergraduate teacher of René Descartes), to whom I went for advice when I was awarded the fellowship. In the cruelest—and wisest—career advice ever vouchsafed me, Bob said, "Philosophy is a good preparation to something else, Marty." Bob would later, as a professor at Harvard, challenge the Wittgensteinian puzzle parade and carve out his own method of solving philosophical problems rather than unraveling linguistic puzzles. He did it so adroitly, however, that no one threatened him with a poker, and so he helped to nudge high academic philosophy in the direction that Popper urged.

I had also turned down the opportunity to become a professional bridge player for the same reason, because it too was a game. Even though I had changed fields from philosophy to psychology, I was still a Wittgensteinian by training, and as it turned out, I had entered a very congenial department that was and is a shrine to ornamental knowledge and to solving psychological puzzles. Academic prestige at Penn came from working rigorously on the puzzles, but my longing to work on the problems of real life, such as achievement and despair, gnawed incessantly at me.

I did my PhD with white rats, but while it satisfied the puzzle masters who edited the journals, it took hesitant aim at problems: unpredictable shock produced more fear than predictable shock because the rat never knew when it was safe. I had also worked on learned helplessness, the passivity induced by uncontrollable shock. But that too was a laboratory model, acceptable therefore within the high journals but also taking only hesitant aim at a human problem. The turning point came shortly after I had taken the equivalent of a psychiatric residency under psychiatry professors Aaron (Tim) Beck and Albert (Mickey) Stunkard from 1970 to 1971. I had resigned from an assistant professorship at Cornell—my first job after I finished my PhD in 1967—as a political protest and with Tim and Mickey was attempting to learn something of real psychiatric problems in order to tie my puzzle solving closer to real-world problems. Tim and I met for an occasional lunch at Kelly and Cohen, our local deli (Kelly was fictitious), after I rejoined the Penn Psychology Department in 1972.

"Marty, if you keep working as an experimental psychologist with animals, you will waste your life," said Tim, giving me the second best advice I ever got and watching me choke on my grilled Reuben. And so I became an applied psychologist, working explicitly on problems. I knew I was from that moment consigned to the role of maverick, "popularizer," and a wolf in sheep's clothing among my peers. My days as a basic academic scientist were numbered.

To my surprise, Penn nonetheless appointed me associate professor with tenure, with the secret faculty debate, I am told, centered on the awful possibility that my work would drift in an applied direction. It has been an uphill battle for me at Penn ever since, but I never understood just how uphill until I was on a committee to hire a social psychologist in 1995. My colleague Jon Baron made the revolutionary suggestion that we advertise for someone who did research on work, love, or play. "That's what life is about," he said, and I agreed enthusiastically.

Then I had a sleepless night.

I mentally scanned (serially) the tenured faculty in the ten leading psychology departments in the world. Not a single one focused on work or on love or on play. They all worked on "basic" processes: cognition, emotion, decision theory, perception. Where were the scholars who would help guide us about what makes life worth living?

The next day, it happened that I had lunch with psychologist Jerome Bruner. Then in his mideighties and almost blind, Jerry is a walking history of American psychology. I asked him why the entire faculties of the great universities work only on so-called basic processes and not on the real world.

"It happened at a moment in time, Marty," said Jerry, "and I was there. It was at a 1946 meeting of the Society of Experimental Psychologists. [I am a nonattending member of this elite fraternity—now a sorority as well—of ivy-covered professors.] Edwin Boring, Herbert Langfeld, and Samuel Fernberger, the chairmen of Harvard,

Princeton, and Penn, respectively, met at lunch and agreed that psychology should be more like physics and chemistry—doing basic research only—and that they would hire no applied psychologists. All the rest of academia immediately fell into line."

This decision was a momentous error. For an insecure science like psychology in 1946, imitating physics and chemistry might have earned some brownie points with deans, but it made no sense at all scientifically. Physics was preceded by an ancient science of engineering, which actually solved problems, before it grafted on abstract, basic research. Applied physics predicted eclipses, floods, and the motions of heavenly bodies—and it coined money. Isaac Newton ran the British mint in 1696. Chemists made gunpowder and learned an enormous amount of scientific fact even as they pursued what turned out to be the dead-end of trying to turn lead into gold. These real-world problems and applications set the boundaries for the basic puzzles applied physics would then go on to unravel. Psychology, in contrast, had no engineering—nothing that was proven to work in the real world—no underpinning that would guide and constrain what its basic research should be about.

Good science requires the interplay of analysis and synthesis. One never knows if basic research is truly basic until one knows what it is basic to. Modern physics came into its own not because of its theories—which can be enormously counterintuitive and highly controversial (muons, wavicles, superstrings, the anthropic principle, and all that)—but because physicists built the atomic bomb and modern nuclear power plants. Immunology, a backwater enterprise in medical research in the 1940s, came into its own on the back of the Salk and Sabin vaccines against polio. The burgeoning of basic research only followed.

In the nineteenth century, a dispute raged in physics about how birds flew. The controversy was settled in twelve seconds on December 17, 1903, when the Wright brothers flew an airplane they had built. Therefore, many concluded, all birds must fly that way. This is, indeed, the logic of the artificial intelligence endeavor: if basic science can build a computer that can understand language, or speak, or perceive objects, merely by networking binary switching circuits, this must be how humans do these wondrous things. Application often points the way toward basic research, whereas basic research without a clue about how it might be applied is usually just wanking.

The principle that good science necessarily involves the active interplay between application and pure science sits uneasily both with the pure scientists and with the prime appliers. Being a maverick in the Penn Psychology Department to this day gives me weekly reminders of how pure scientists look askance on application, but I did not find out how skeptical the appliers are of science until I became president of the American Psychological Association (APA) in 1998. I was elected by the largest majority in history, and I attribute the landslide to the fact that my work stands squarely between science and application, and so attracted many of both the scientists and the clinicians. The emblematic work that I had done was to help with the 1995 *Consumer Reports* study of the effectiveness of psychotherapy. Using sophisticated statistical tools, *Consumer Reports,* in a massive survey, found good results of psychotherapy generally, but, surprisingly, the benefits were not specific to any one kind of therapy or to any one kind of disorder. This was welcomed by the rank and file of applied psychologists who do all sorts of therapy on all sorts of disorders.

When I arrived in Washington to preside over the American Psychological Association, I found myself in exactly the same situation among the leaders of the applied endeavors that I was in among my pure-scientist colleagues: a wolf in sheep's clothing. My first initiative as president, evidence-based psychotherapy, never got off the ground. Steve Hyman, then the director of the National Institute of Mental Health, told me that he could find about $40 million to support work on this initiative. Greatly heartened, I met with the Committee for the Advancement of Professional Practice, the high council of independent practitioners, which, except for my election, had a hammerlock on the election of APA presidents. I outlined my initiative to an increasingly stone-faced group of these twenty opinion makers, talking up the virtues of basing therapy in scientific evidence of its efficacy. Stan Moldawsky, one of the staunchest of the old-timers, brought down the curtain on my initiative by saying, "What if the evidence doesn't come out in our favor?"

Afterward, Ron Levant, one of Stan's allies, told me over a drink, "You're in deep shit, Marty." Indeed, it was from this bloody nose that positive psychology—an endeavor not quite as inimical to independent practice as evidence-based therapy—was born.

So it was exactly with this tension between application and science in mind that in 2005 I happily consented to direct the Positive Psychology Center at the University of Pennsylvania and to create a new degree—the master of applied positive psychology (MAPP)—that would combine cutting-edge scholarship with the application of the knowledge to the real world as its mission.

Chapter 4

Teaching Well-Being:
The Magic of MAPP

> *. . . I came upon a crossroads*
> *Where I sought only shelter for a brief time.*
> *But as I lay down my sack and kicked off my shoes,*
> *I noticed that this crossroads was like no other I had found.*
>
> *The air in this place held an inviting warmth*
> *And a vibrancy permeated all things.*
> *As I introduced myself to the travelers here,*
> *I felt no hesitation or discouragement*
> *But sincerity and optimism in their place.*
> *In their eyes I saw something I could not name*
> *But that felt very much like home.*
> *In this place, together, we shared and encouraged*
> *And rejoiced in the abundance of life. . . .*
>
> —"Crossroads," Derrick Carpenter

I want a revolution in world education. All young people need to learn workplace skills, which has been the subject matter of the education system in place for two hundred years. In addition, we can now teach the skills of well-being—of how to have more positive emotion, more meaning, better relationships, and more positive accomplishment. Schools at every level should teach these skills, and the next five chapters revolve around this idea. In this chapter, I explain graduate-level education in applied positive psychology and who will teach well-being. Chapter 5 concerns teaching well-being in schools. Chapter 6 is a new theory of intelligence and Chapters 7 and 8 are about teaching well-being to the U.S. Army. The aim is for the young people of the next generation to flourish.

Even though I have taught at the university, grade school, and high school levels, the most extraordinary of all my experiences has occurred in only the last ten years in teaching positive psychology. And it is not just me: others teaching positive psychology around the world relay similar stories of wonder. By narrating these, I am trying to come to grips with why it is so extraordinary and also why run-of-the-mill teaching so often fails. What follows is about the MAPP program, the master of applied positive psychology, and reveals why its ingredients are "magic." These magical components include: First, the *content* is challenging, informative, and uplifting. Second, positive psychology is *personally and professionally transformative*. The third ingredient is that positive psychology is a *calling*.

The First MAPP

In February 2005, the University of Pennsylvania, a little haltingly, officially approved the new master of applied positive psychology. The application deadline was set for March 30, 2005. We were looking not for young people fresh out of their undergraduate degrees or for psychologists but for mature people who had succeeded in the world and who wanted to work positive psychology into their professions. They also needed to display outstanding academic credentials. The format is executive education—nine long weekends a year plus a capstone project—and it is very expensive: more than $40,000 just for the tuition, plus hotels, food, and airfare.

We started with a coup, when Penn lured an outstanding teacher of religion, philosophy, and psychology from Vanderbilt University, Dr. James Pawelski. He in turn recruited Debbie Swick, who was just finishing her MBA there. They direct the MAPP program. Debbie, James, and I optimistically hoped—with only one month's lead time—that we could somehow convince eleven applicants to attend our first program; eleven being the financial break-even point for the program, as the deans had reminded us more than once.

Surprisingly, we had more than 120 applicants—more than five times the number we had expected, with almost no advertising, in such a short time—with about 60 of them meeting Penn's very high Ivy League admission standards. We accepted 36 of them, of which 35 accepted our offer.

At eight in the morning on September 8, the thirty-five gathered in the Benjamin Franklin Room of Houston Hall. This group of students included:

- Tom Rath, best-selling author and a senior executive of the Gallup Corporation
- Shawna Mitchell, a researcher in finance in Tanzania, and a finalist from the reality TV series *Survivor*
- Angus Skinner, the director of social services for the government of Scotland, commuting from Edinburgh
- Yakov Smirnoff, the well-known comic and artist, fresh from his one-man Broadway show
- Senia Maymin, a vivacious Harvard mathematics graduate, and head of her own hedge fund (whom you met in Chapter 1)
- Peter Minich, a neurosurgeon as well as a PhD from Canada
- Juan Humberto Young, commuting from Zurich, Switzerland; the head of a successful finance advisory company

Ingredients of Applied Positive Psychology

INTELLECTUALLY CHALLENGING
APPLICABLE CONTENT

To teach these students, we had lined up the leading faculty in positive psychology from around the world. They, like the students, commute to Philadelphia for the monthly intellectual feast. Barbara Fredrickson, the laboratory genius of positive psychology and the winner of the first $100,000 Templeton Prize for research in positive psychology, is a perennial mainstay of "immersion week," the five-day September introduction to the content of the discipline. The *content* of the discipline of positive psychology is the first ingredient in the alchemy that is the magic of MAPP.

Barb began by detailing her "broaden-and-build" theory of positive emotion. Unlike the negative, firefighting emotions, which identify, isolate, and combat external irritants, the positive emotions broaden and build abiding psychological resources that we can call on later in life. So when we are engrossed in a conversation with our best friend, we are laying down social skills that we can call on and use for the rest of our lives. When a child feels joy in rough-and-tumble play, she is building the motor coordination that will serve her well in school sports. Positive emotion does much more than just feel pleasant; it is a neon sign that growth is under way, that psychological capital is accumulating.

"Here's our latest finding," Barb explained to the thirty-five students and five faculty members, all of us now on the edge of our seats. "We go into companies and transcribe every word that is said in their business meetings. We have done this in sixty companies. One-third of the companies are flourishing economically, one-third are doing okay, and one-third are failing. We code each sentence for positive or negative words, and then we take a simple ratio of positive to negative statements.

"There is a sharp dividing line," Barb continued. "Companies with better than a 2.9:1 ratio for positive to negative statements are flourishing. Below that ratio, companies are not doing well economically. We call this the 'Losada ratio,' named after my Brazilian colleague Marcel Losada, who discovered this fact.

"But don't go overboard with positivity. Life is a ship with sails and rudder. Above 13:1, without a negative rudder, the positive sails flap aimlessly, and you lose your credibility."

"Wait just a minute," Dave Shearon objected in his quiet Tennessee accent. Dave, a lawyer and one of the new students, heads the Tennessee Bar Association's education program. "We lawyers fight all day long. I bet our ratios are way negative, maybe 1:3. That's in the very nature of litigation. Are you saying we should be forced to spend the day sweet-talking?"

"A negative Losada ratio might make an effective lawyer," Barb shot back, "but it may have a huge personal cost. Law is the profession with the highest depression, suicide, and divorce rates. If your colleagues take that office ratio home, they are in trouble. John Gottman computed the same statistic by listening to couples' conversations for entire weekends. A 2.9:1 means you are headed for a divorce. You need a 5:1 ratio to predict a strong and loving marriage—five positive statements for every critical statement you make of your spouse. A habit of 1:3 in a couple is an unmitigated catastrophe."

One of the other students confessed to me later, "Although Barb was talking about work teams, all I could think about was my 'team' at home: my family. I had tears in my eyes as she spoke because I realized in a flash that I was at about 1:1 with my oldest son. We had settled into a dynamic that was all about my focusing on what he hadn't done right instead of what he had done right. While Barb talked, all I could see in my head was a movie reel of having easy, loving relationships that were at least 5:1, juxtaposed with the tense daily exchanges I was having with my sixteen-year-old. I actually wanted to grab my books and drive home right away, because Barb also gave me an idea about how to handle it differently. I envisioned starting conversations with genuine praise and something lighthearted, followed by something about schoolwork, driving too fast, or something else that I was about to criticize. I wanted to go home and try it right away."

I asked this student recently about the outcome. She replied, "He's twenty now, and the relationship is better than ever. The positivity ratio turned it around."

And it is not only the students whose lives change based on the lectures.

"*Daaad!* Can you drive me over to Alexis's house? It's important. Puh-*llllease*?" pleads my daughter Nikki, fourteen. I recounted in *Authentic Happiness* a significant exchange we'd had shortly after her fifth birthday, while she was weeding with me in the garden. At that time, she rebuked me for yelling at her to get to work. She had been a whiner, she explained then, but had successfully resolved on her fifth birthday to change her ways. "That was the hardest thing I've ever done," she said proudly, "and if I can stop whining, you can stop being such a grouch."

Positive psychology emerged from Nikki's rebuke. I saw that I had indeed been a grouch for fifty years, that child rearing for me had been all about correcting weaknesses rather than building strengths, and that the profession of psychology—which I had just been elected to lead—had been almost exclusively about removing the disabling conditions rather than creating the enabling conditions for people to flourish.

Nonetheless, it was eleven-fifteen on a Friday evening, and I had been beating my head all day trying to think through the implications of a new theory that Barbara Fredrickson had just introduced in her MAPP lecture. I couldn't let go of her ideas about a minimally positive ratio to induce flourishing, and I had obsessed about this over dinner with my family.

"Nikki, it's almost midnight. Can't you see I'm working? Go do your homework or get to bed!" I shouted. I saw that look come into Nikki's eyes, the same withering once-over I had seen years before in the garden.

"Daddy, you have a terrible Losada ratio," she said.

So the first ingredient of the magic MAPP is the *content* of positive psychology itself. It is challenging intellectually, like most academic subjects, but unlike most subjects, it is personally informative, even transformative, and it is also fun. Teaching about depression and suicide, which I did for twenty-five years, is a downer. If you take it seriously, teaching about it and learning about it lowers your own mood. You spend a lot of time in a funk. Learning about positive psychology, in contrast, is *fun*—not just the usual joy of learning, but the joy of learning about material that is joyful.

Speaking of fun, MAPP rediscovered the importance of the energy break, classroom activities so physical that they would embarrass my straitlaced deans. The "basic rest and activity cycle," or BRAC, is characteristic of human beings and other diurnal (awake during the day) animals. On average, we are at our most alert in late morning and midevening. We are at the bottom of our cycle—tired, grumpy, inattentive, and pessimistic—at midafternoon and in the wee hours of the morning. So very biological is this cycle that death itself occurs disproportionately at the bottom of BRAC. The bottom of BRAC is exaggerated in MAPP, since classes are held once a month over intense three-day weekends, for nine hours a day, and after a grueling commute from as far away as Kuala Lumpur, London, or Seoul. (One of our students set the Air New Zealand record for miles traveled last year, while the year before, another set the Qantas record.)

So we get ourselves physically active when we are at the bottom of BRAC. Positive psychology was, at its inception, peopled largely by late-middle-aged men with high foreheads. At least half of positive psychology occurs below the neck, however, and it is important that several of the MAPPsters every year are neck-down people: yoga instructors, dance therapists, sports coaches, marathoners, and triathletes. At three o'clock each day, a neck-down cadre leads us in dance, vigorous exercise, meditation, or a brisk walk. At first the high-forehead people ducked out, blushing, but as we witnessed the annihilation of fatigue and the instant return of intellectual energy, we all became avid participants. I can't say enough now for frequent energy breaks in the classroom itself. It's not just kindergarten kids who need them: the older we get, the more they help us to learn and to teach.

PERSONAL AND PROFESSIONAL TRANSFORMATION

The first magic ingredient of MAPP is content that is challenging, personally applicable, and fun. The second ingredient is that MAPP is transformative both personally and professionally.

One way to see this is the effect that positive psychology has on coaches. There are now more than fifty thousand professionals in America making their living as coaches: life coaches, executive coaches, and personal coaches. I fear that coaching has run wild. About 20 percent of the MAPP students are coaches, and one of our aims is to tame and transform coaching.

Coaching and Positive Psychology

Coaching is a practice in search of a backbone. *Two* backbones, actually: a scientific, evidence-based backbone as well as a theoretical backbone. Positive psychology can provide both. Positive psychology can provide coaching with a bounded scope of practice, with interventions and measurements that work, and with adequate credentials to be a coach.

As coaching stands now, I told our graduate students, its scope of practice is without limits: how to arrange your closet, how to paste your memories into a scrapbook, how to ask for a raise, how to be a more assertive leader, how to inspire the volleyball team, how to find more flow at work, how to fight dark thoughts, how to have more purpose in life. It also uses an almost limitless array of techniques: affirmations, visualization, massage, yoga, assertive training, correcting cognitive distortions, aromatherapy, feng shui, meditation, counting your blessings, and on and on. The right to call oneself a coach is unregulated, and this is why scientific and theoretical backbones are urgent.

For this transformation of coaching, you first need the theory; next, the science; and then the applications.

First, the theory: positive psychology is the study of positive emotion, of engagement, of meaning, of positive accomplishment, and of good relationships. It attempts to measure, classify, and build these five aspects of life. Practicing these endeavors will bring order out of chaos by defining your scope of practice and distinguishing it from allied professions such as clinical psychology, psychiatry, social work, and marriage and family counseling.

Second, the science: positive psychology is rooted in scientific evidence that it works. It uses tried-and-true methods of measurement, of experiments, of longitudinal research, and of random-assignment, placebo-controlled outcome studies to evaluate which interventions actually work and which ones are bogus. It discards those that do not pass this gold standard as ineffective, and it hones those that pass. Coaching with these evidence-based interventions and validated measures of well-being will set the boundaries of a responsible coaching practice.

Finally, what we are doing in MAPP will help establish guidelines for training and accreditation. You assuredly do not need to be a licensed psychologist to practice positive psychology or to be a coach. Freud's followers made the momentous error of restricting psychoanalysis to physicians, and positive psychology is not intended as an umbrella for yet another self-protective guild. If you are adequately trained in the techniques of coaching, in the theories of positive psychology, in valid measurement of the positive states and traits, in the interventions that work, and you know when to refer a client to someone who is more appropriately trained, you will be, by my lights, bona fide disseminators of positive psychology.

Transformations

Caroline Adams Miller, perhaps the most striking member of the first MAPP class—six feet tall, muscular, and not easily intimidated—agreed with me. "I'm a professional coach, Marty, and I'm proud of being a coach. One thing I hate, however, is that we get no respect. We are practically laughed out of some professional meetings. I am on a hunt to bring more respectability to coaching, and you have given me just the ammunition I need."

Caroline lived up to her aim. In the years since her MAPP degree she added a major missing piece to the world of coaching. MAPP introduced her to goal-setting theory, which had never been part of any coach-training program that she had heard of. In her capstone project, she linked goal-setting theory to happiness research and to techniques of coaching. She then published *Creating Your Best Life: The Ultimate Life List Guide*, the first book in the self-help section of any bookstore that discusses research-based goal-setting for coaches as well as for the general public. She now speaks to standing-room-only audiences, and her book is used in study groups around the world.

Of her professional transformation, Caroline says, "MAPP turned my job into a calling, and gave me the ability to help others pursue meaningful goals and understand their roles in their own daily happiness. I feel like I'm making a large difference in ways I'd never felt before, and I wake up thinking I'm the luckiest professional on the face of the earth."

David Cooperrider, the co-founder of Appreciative Inquiry, is a perennial favorite teacher in MAPP. His story explains further how positive psychology can be professionally transformative.

"When do we change as individuals? When do organizations change?" David asked the class.

One student rose to the challenge: "We change when we stub our toes, when things go badly wrong. The merciless criticism of others is what goads us into change."

"Exactly what I wanted to hear, Gail," David replied. "This is what almost everyone believes about change: the dark-night-of-the-soul view. It is just for this reason that many corporations use 360, in which all of your coworkers tell nasty stories about you at your worst. This 360-degree view of your failings is then given to you to read, and when you are overwhelmed with all this massive criticism, you are expected to change.

"Appreciative Inquiry, however, tells us just the opposite. Merciless criticism often makes us dig in our heels in defense, or worse, makes us helpless. We don't change. We do change, however, when we discover what is best about ourselves and when we see specific ways to use our strengths more. I go into large organizations and get the whole workforce focused on what it is doing well. They detail the strengths of the corporation and tell stories about their coworkers at their very best. The University of Michigan's Center for Positive Organizational Scholarship has even developed a positive 360.

"Being in touch with what we do well underpins the readiness to change," David continued. "This is related to the Losada ratio. To enable us to hear criticism nondefensively and to act creatively on it, we need to feel secure."

This was a transformative insight for Michelle McQuaid, who had flown in from Melbourne, where she works as the right hand of the CEO of PricewaterhouseCoopers. "Why can't PWC operate on positive psychology and Appreciative Inquiry principles?" she asked the CEO. "Let's act on this." So Michelle and Bobby Dauman, her MAPP classmate and the top Land Rover salesperson in the world for several years and the top Land Rover manager in the world for one year, added a day on to MAPP and hosted a well-attended conference, "What Good Is Positive Business?" Their conference was built around the idea that we have entered an economy of life satisfaction—over and above money—and that for a business to thrive, it must cultivate relationships and create meaning. To this end, they held workshops on creating a better Losada ratio, using gratitude and active-constructive responding, making opportunities for flow, hope and goal-setting, and transforming jobs into callings. Given its enthusiastic reception, they held another conference in Melbourne, sponsored by PWC, in December 2009.

Learning positive psychology is *professionally transforming*. Here's what Aren Cohen wrote me about her *personal transformation*.

When I was a student of positive psychology in 2006–07, I was a single gal. Often I was frustrated when our professors cited the research about the benefits of marriage. Married adults, particularly those in stable marriages, tend to be healthier and live longer than their single counterparts. Marty explained that marriage allows us three kinds of love: a love where we are cared for, a love where we care for someone else, and romantic love.

I didn't need any more convincing—this was what I wanted. But as one of a small minority of single women over thirty sitting in a classroom of happy positive psychologists, I was forced to ask myself . . . how do I get myself married so I can have all of these emotional and physical benefits?

Of course, I wasn't quite as calculating as all that, but I was a seasoned thirty-four-year-old New Yorker who had watched too many episodes of Sex and the City, and I was starting to wonder if I was approaching spinsterhood. There had been many, many dates over the years, and for some reason it still wasn't happening. So, having learned positive interventions in MAPP, I decided to put my knowledge of positive psychology into practice, and amazingly, André, my husband, appeared in my life at exactly the right moment.

How did I change my life to make it "exactly the right moment"? First of all, thanks to what I had learned from the MAPP program, I was becoming a happier person, more attuned to my own spirituality and to reasons to celebrate gratitude. I kept a gratitude journal, and I started using goal-setting for the future and visualizing what I wanted. I wrote my list, starting with phrases ranging from "I will find a man who is . . ." to "My guy will be . . ." thinking that maybe different linguistic expressions would be more friendly to my personal outlook and search. Also, I stopped watching Sex and the City.

I used visualization techniques, including meditation and collaging. My collage had words and images outlining how I wanted my life to be. Finally, I chose my favorite love song, the James Taylor version of "How Sweet It Is (To Be Loved by You)," and every night before bed for the three months before I met my husband, I listened to it religiously, as if to serenade love into my life. The words "How Sweet It Is" were also on my collage, right above the words "Bridal Suite."

So those were the changes I made to get romantic love into my life. Today is our one-year wedding anniversary, and what is the biggest change in my life now? Well, a few things. I compromise more. I get and give a lot more hugs. I smile more. I speak and hear the words "I love you" much more often. I have a new nickname. Most important, I have someone I can trust, whom I love, and who loves me.

And one more thing: I cook more! Nothing brings out positive emotions like preparing a home-cooked meal made with love. Part of the positive psychology we practice together as often as we can is dinner at home. In the tradition of positive psychology, we always say some version of grace to remember we have so much to be grateful for. Particularly each other.

MAPP is *personally and professionally transformative,* in addition to being challenging, applicable, and fun in intellectual *content.* The final ingredient is that MAPPsters are *called* to positive psychology.

Called to Positive Psychology

I did not choose positive psychology. It called me. It was what I wanted from the very first, but experimental psychology and then clinical psychology were the only games in town that were even close to what was calling me. I have no less mystical way to put it. *Vocation*—being called to act rather than choosing to act—is an old word, but it is a real thing. Positive psychology called to me just as the burning bush called to Moses.

Sociologists distinguish among a job, a career, and a calling. You do a job for the money, and when the money stops, you stop working. You pursue a career for the promotions, and when the promotions stop, topped out, you quit or become a time-serving husk. A calling, in contrast, is done for its own sake. You would do it anyway, with no pay and no promotions. "Try to stop me!" is what your heart cries when you are thwarted.

Each month, I hold an optional movie night with popcorn, wine, pizza, and pillows on the floor. I show movies that convey positive psychology better than lectures full of words, but devoid of musical sounds and cinematic sights, can. I have always opened with *Groundhog Day,* and even after having seen it for the fifth time, I am still stunned by how much it presses us, yearning, toward positive personal transformation. I have shown *The Devil Wears Prada,* a movie about integrity—that of Meryl Streep, the boss from hell, and not of

Anne Hathaway, the "fat" one; *The Shawshank Redemption,* and it is not Andy Dufresne (Tim Robbins) the falsely accused banker, who is redeemed, but the narrator, Red (Morgan Freeman); *Chariots of Fire,* with the embodiment of three motives to win: Eric Liddell running for God; Lord Andrew Linley, for beauty; and Harold Abrahams, for self and tribe; and *Sunday in the Park with George,* which even on its twenty-fifth viewing still moves me to tears during the transcendent last scene of the first act in which art, children, Paris, and what abides and what is ephemeral in life are suffused.

Last year I ended the series with *Field of Dreams,* a work of genius, even better than W. P. Kinsella's haunting novel *Shoeless Joe,* on which it is based. I first saw this movie under odd and moving circumstances. One evening in 1989, I was visited by a psychologist from Russia. He was at the university giving a lecture and came over to my home. I had written him some time before to request reprints of his fascinating work on sudden death in animals and he then invited me to speak in Baku, Azerbaijan, in 1979—a trip abrubtly canceled on the advice of the U.S. State Department during a sudden spike in the Cold War.

He told me fragments of his life story in the USSR: he was a Jew and he headed a laboratory. It was the period of Gorbachev's "perestroika," but he was concerned about the rise in anti-Semitism.

I was even more ill at ease than I usually am with strangers, so I took him to the movies. *Field of Dreams* happened to be playing. Enthralled, we watched a baseball field spring forth from an Iowa cornfield, the Chicago Black Sox materialize from the corn, and the scoreboard in Boston's Fenway Park flash "Moonlight Graham." He leaned over toward me as the long-dead father of Ray Kinsella (Kevin Costner) asks him if he'd like to have a catch. In tears, the psychologist whispered, "Thees movie not about bizeboll!"

Not about bizeboll, indeed. This movie is about vocation, about being called, about building something where there was nothing. "If you build it, they will come." Called, that's what I had been. Over the objections of deans, my own department, and trustees, a MAPP program arose on the barren cornfields of Philadelphia. ("Is this heaven?" Shoeless Joe asks. "No, it's Iowa," Ray Kinsella responds.) And who came?

"How many of you were called here?" I ventured timidly. Hands shot up. Everyone's hand.

"I sold my Mercedes to get here."

"I was like a character from *Close Encounters*, sculpting the tower I repeatedly dreamt. Then I saw the ad for MAPP, and here I am at the tower."

"I left my clinical practice and my patients."

"I hate flying, and I get on a goddamn airplane and fly sixty hours from New Zealand and back once a month to be here."

MAPP has been magical, beyond any other teaching experience I have had in forty-five years of teaching. Here are the ingredients in summary:

- Intellectual content: challenging, personally applicable, and fun.
- Transformative: both personally and professionally.
- Calling: students and faculty are called.

These ingredients imply the possibility of a positive education for students of all ages, and it is to this larger vision that I now turn.

Chapter 5

Positive Education: Teaching Well-Being to Young People

First, a quiz:

Question one: in one or two words, what do you most want for your children?

If you are like the thousands of parents I've polled, you responded, "happiness," "confidence," "contentment," "fulfillment," "balance," "good stuff," "kindness," "health," "satisfaction," "love," "being civilized," "meaning," and the like. In short, *well-being* is your topmost priority for your children.

Question two: in one or two words, what do schools teach?

If you are like other parents, you responded, "achievement," "thinking skills," "success," "conformity," "literacy," "math," "work," "test taking," "discipline," and the like. In short, what schools teach is how to succeed in the workplace.

Notice that there is almost no overlap between the two lists.

The schooling of children has, for more than a century, paved the boulevard toward adult work. I am all for success, literacy, perseverance, and discipline, but I want you to imagine that schools could, without compromising either, teach both the skills of well-being and the skills of achievement. I want you to imagine positive education.

Should Well-Being
Be Taught in School?

The prevalence of depression among young people is shockingly high worldwide. By some estimates, depression is about ten times more common now than it was fifty years ago. This is not an artifact of greater awareness of depression as a mental illness, since much of the data arises from door-to-door surveys that ask tens of thousands of people "Did you ever try to kill yourself?," "Did you ever cry every day for two weeks?," and the like without ever mentioning depression. Depression now ravages teenagers: fifty years ago, the average age of first onset was about thirty. Now the first onset is below age fifteen. While there is controversy about whether this rises to the scary appellation *epidemic*, all of us in the field are dismayed by how much depression there is now and how most of it goes untreated.

This is a paradox, particularly if you believe that good well-being comes from a good environment. You have to be blinded by ideology not to see that almost everything is better in every wealthy nation than it was fifty years ago: we now have about three times more actual purchasing power in the United States. The average house has doubled in size from 1,200 square feet to 2,500 square feet. In 1950 there was one car for every two drivers; now there are more cars than licensed drivers. One out of five children went on to post–high school education; now one out of two children does. Clothes—and even people—seem to look more physically attractive. Progress has not been limited to the material: there is more music, more women's rights, less racism, more entertainment, and more books. If you had told my parents, living in a 1,200-square-foot house with me and Beth, my older sister, that all this would obtain in only fifty years, they would have said, "That will be paradise."

Paradise it is not.

There is much more depression affecting those much younger, and average national happiness—which has been measured competently for a half century—has not remotely kept up with how much better the objective world has become. Happiness has gone up only spottily, if at all. The average Dane, Italian, and Mexican is somewhat more satisfied with life than fifty years ago, but the average American, Japanese, and Australian is no more satisfied with life than fifty years ago, and the average Brit and German is less satisfied. The average Russian is much unhappier.

Why this is, no one knows. It is certainly not biological or genetic; our genes and chromosomes have not changed in fifty years. Nor is it ecological; the Old Order Amish of Lancaster County, who live thirty miles down the road from me, have only one-tenth of Philadelphia's rate of depression, even though they breathe the same air (yes, with exhaust fumes), drink the same water (yes, with fluoride), and make much of the food we eat (yes, with preservatives). It has everything to do with modernity and perhaps with what we mistakenly call "prosperity."

Two good reasons that well-being should be taught in schools are the current flood of depression and the nominal increase in happiness over the last two generations. A third good reason is that greater well-being enhances learning, the traditional goal of education. Positive mood produces broader attention, more creative thinking, and more holistic thinking. This is in contrast to negative mood, which produces narrowed attention, more critical thinking, and more analytic thinking. When you're in a bad mood, you're better at "what's wrong here?" When you're in a good mood, you're better at "what's right here?" Even worse: when you are in a bad mood, you fall back defensively on what you already know, and you follow orders well. Both positive and negative ways of thinking are important in the right situation, but all too often schools emphasize critical thinking and following orders rather than creative thinking and learning new stuff. The result is that children rank the appeal of going to school just slightly above going to the dentist. In the modern world, I believe we have finally arrived at an era in which more creative thinking, less rote following of orders—and yes, even more enjoyment—will succeed better.

I conclude that, were it possible, well-being should be taught in school because it would be an antidote to the runaway incidence of depression, a way to increase life satisfaction, and an aid to better learning and more creative thinking.

THE PENN RESILIENCY PROGRAM:
A WAY TO TEACH WELL-BEING IN SCHOOL

My research team, led by Karen Reivich and Jane Gillham, has devoted much of the last twenty years to finding out, using rigorous methods, whether well-being can be taught to schoolchildren. We believe that well-being programs, like any medical intervention, *must be evidence based,* so we have tested two different programs for schools: the Penn Resiliency Program (PRP) and the Strath Haven Positive Psychology Curriculum. Here are our findings.

First, let me tell you about the Penn Resiliency Program. Its major goal is to increase students' ability to handle day-to-day problems that are common during adolescence. PRP promotes optimism by teaching students to think more realistically and flexibly about the problems they encounter. PRP also teaches assertiveness, creative brainstorming, decision making, relaxation, and several other coping skills. PRP is the most widely researched depression-prevention program in the world. During the past two decades, twenty-one studies have evaluated PRP in comparison to control groups. Many of these studies used randomized controlled designs. Together these studies include more than three thousand children and adolescents between the ages of eight and twenty-two. Outcome studies of PRP include:

• Diverse samples. Penn Resiliency Program studies include adolescents from a variety of racial and ethnic backgrounds, community settings (urban, suburban, and rural; white, black, and Hispanic; rich and poor) and countries (for example, the United States, the United Kingdom, Australia, China, and Portugal).

• Variety of group leaders. Group leaders include schoolteachers, counselors, psychologists, social workers, army sergeants, and graduate students in education and psychology.

• Independent evaluations of Penn Resiliency Program. We conducted many of the PRP evaluations; however, several independent research teams have also evaluated PRP, including a massive trial by the UK government, involving one hundred teachers and three thousand students.

Here are the basic findings:

• Penn Resiliency Program reduces and prevents symptoms of depression. A "meta-analysis" averages over all the methodologically sound studies of a topic in the entire scientific literature and a meta-analysis of all the studies reveals significant benefits of PRP at all follow-up assessments (immediately postintervention as well as six and twelve months following the program) compared to controls. Effects endure for at least two years.

• Penn Resiliency Program reduces hopelessness. The meta-analysis found that PRP significantly reduced hopelessness, increased optimism, and increased well-being.

• Penn Resiliency Program prevents clinical levels of depression and anxiety. In several studies, PRP prevented moderate to severe levels of depressive symptoms. For example, in the first PRP study, the program halved the rate of moderate to severe depressive symptoms through two years of follow-up. In a medical setting, PRP prevented depression and anxiety disorders among adolescents with high levels of depressive symptoms at the outset.

• Penn Resiliency Program reduces and prevents anxiety. There is less research on PRP's effects on anxiety symptoms, but most studies find significant and long-lasting effects.

• Penn Resiliency Program reduces conduct problems. There is even less research on PRP's effects on adolescents' conduct problems (such as aggression, delinquency), but most studies find significant effects. For example, a recent large-scale program found significant benefits on parents' reports of adolescents' conduct problems three years after their youngsters completed the program.

• Penn Resiliency Program works equally well for children of different racial/ethnic backgrounds.

• Penn Resiliency Program improves health-related behaviors, with young adults who complete the program having fewer symptoms of physical illness, fewer illness doctor visits, better diet, and more exercise.

• Training and supervision of group leaders is critical. PRP's effectiveness varies considerably across studies. This is related, at least in part, to how much training and supervision the teachers receive. Effects are strong when teachers are members of the PRP team, or are trained and then closely supervised by the PRP team. Effects are less robust and consistent when teachers have minimal training and minimal supervision.

• The fidelity of curriculum delivery is critical. For example, a study of Penn Resiliency Program in a primary care setting revealed significant reductions in depression symptoms in groups with high adherence to the program. In contrast, PRP did not reduce depressive symptoms in groups of patients with low program adherence. Thus, we recommend that teachers of PRP need intensive training and lots of supervision.

So the Penn Resiliency Program reliably prevents depression, anxiety, and conduct problems in young people. Resilience, however, is only one aspect of positive psychology—the emotional aspect. We designed a more comprehensive curriculum that builds character strengths, relationships, and meaning, as well as raises positive emotion and reduces negative emotion. With a $2.8 million grant from the U.S. Department of Education, we carried out a large randomized, controlled evaluation of this high school positive psychology curriculum. At Strath Haven High School, outside of Philadelphia, we randomly assigned 347 ninth-grade students (fourteen- to fifteen-year-olds) to language arts classes. Half the classes incorporated the positive psychology curriculum; the other half did not. Students, their parents, and their teachers completed standard questionnaires before the program, after the program, and over two years of follow-up. We tested students' strengths (for instance, love of learning, kindness), social skills, behavioral problems, and how much they enjoyed school. In addition, we looked at their grades.

The major goals of this global program are (1) to help students identify their signature character strengths and (2) to increase their use of these strengths in their daily lives. In addition to these goals, the intervention strives to promote resilience, positive emotion, meaning and purpose, and positive social relationships. The curriculum consists of more than twenty eighty-minute sessions delivered over the ninth-grade year. These involve discussing character strengths and the other positive psychology concepts and skills, a weekly in-class activity, real-world homework in which students apply these skills in their own lives, and journal reflections.

Here are two examples of the exercises we use in the curriculum:

Three-Good-Things Exercise

We instruct the students to write down daily three good things that happened each day for a week. The three things can be small in importance ("I answered a really hard question right in language arts today") or big ("The guy I've liked for months asked me out!!!"). Next to each positive event, they write about one of the following: "Why did this good thing happen?" "What does this mean to you?" "How can you have more of this good thing in the future?"

Using Signature Strengths
in New Ways

Honesty. Loyalty. Perseverance. Creativity. Kindness. Wisdom. Courage. Fairness. These and sixteen other character strengths are valued in every culture in the world. We believe that you can get more satisfaction out of life if you identify which of these character strengths you have in abundance and then use them as much as possible in school, in hobbies, and with friends and family.

Students take the Values in Action Signature Strengths test (www .authentichappiness.org) and use their highest strength in a new way at school in the next week. Several sessions in the curriculum focus on identifying character strengths in themselves, their friends, and the literary figures they read about, and using those strengths to overcome challenges.

Here are the basic findings of the positive psychology program at Strath Haven:

Engagement in learning, enjoyment of school, and achievement

The positive psychology program improved the strengths of curiosity, love of learning, and creativity, by the reports of teachers who did not know whether the students were in the positive psychology group or the control group. (That's what is called a "blind" study because the raters do not know the status of the students they are rating.) The program also increased students' enjoyment and engagement in school. This was particularly strong for regular (nonhonors) classes, in which positive psychology increased students' language arts grades and writing skills through eleventh grade. In the honors classes, grade inflation prevails and almost all students get As, so there is too little room for improvement. Importantly, increasing well-being did not undermine the traditional goals of classroom learning; rather it enhanced them.

Social skills and conduct problems

The positive psychology program improved social skills (empathy, cooperation, assertiveness, self-control), according to both mothers' and "blind" teachers' reports. The program reduced bad conduct, according to mothers' reports.

So I conclude that well-being should be taught and that it can be taught in individual classrooms. In fact, is it possible that an *entire school* can be imbued with positive psychology?

The Geelong Grammar School Project

I was on a speaking tour in Australia in January 2005 when I had a phone call from a voice I had never heard before. "G'day, mate," it said. "This is your student, Dr. Trent Barry."

"My student?" I queried, not recognizing his name.

"Yeah, you know that live six-month telephone course—I woke up at four in the morning every week to listen to your lectures from the outskirts of Melbourne, where I live. It was fantastic, and I was fanatic, but I never spoke up.

"We want to helicopter you to the Geelong Grammar School. I'm on the school council, and we are in the middle of a fund-raising campaign for a well-being center. We want you to talk to the alumni and help us raise money for the campaign."

"What is the Geelong Grammar School?" I inquired.

"First, it's pronounced *Geee*-long, not *G'long,* Marty. It's one of the oldest boarding schools in Australia, founded more than one hundred fifty years ago. It has four campuses, including Timbertop—up in the mountains where all the year-nine students go for the entire year. If they want a hot shower at Timbertop, they cut their own firewood. Prince Charles went to Timbertop—the only schooling he has fond memories of. The main campus, Corio, is fifty miles south of Melbourne. There are twelve hundred students, and two hundred teachers in all. Unfathomably wealthy.

"The school needs a new gym," he went on, "but the council said we want well-being for the kids as well as a building. I told them about Seligman—they had never heard of you—and they want you to come and convince the rich alums that well-being can actually be taught and that a curriculum can be mounted to give the new building called a well-being center real meaning. We've raised fourteen million dollars in just six months, and we need two million dollars more."

So my family and I boarded a helicopter on a rickety platform in the middle of Melbourne's Yarra River, and six minutes later we landed on the front lawn of Trent's palatial home. My wife, Mandy, whispered to me as we landed, "I have this uncanny feeling that we are going to spend our sabbatical here."

I spoke that afternoon to a rather frowny gathering of about eighty teachers. I noticed particularly that one of the most reserved people was the new headmaster, Stephen Meek. Tall, handsome, exceedingly well dressed, very British, a mellifluous speaker with a voice as much of a basso as mine, he was the stiffest person present. Then that evening, introduced by Stephen, I spoke about positive psychology to about fifty just as spiffily dressed alumni, and I watched enough checks being written right there to meet the $16 million goal. I was told that Helen Handbury, Rupert Murdoch's sister, had given quite a lot of the $16 million. On her deathbed shortly thereafter, she said, "Not another gym; I want well-being for young people."

A week after I returned to Philadelphia, Stephen Meek called. "Marty, I'd like to send a delegation to Philadelphia to meet with you about teaching well-being to the entire school," he said. A few weeks later, a trio of opinion makers from the senior faculty arrived for a week of well-being shopping at Penn: Debbie Cling, the head of curriculum, John Hendry, the dean of students, and Charlie Scudamore, the principal of Corio (the main campus).

"What would you do," they asked Karen Reivich and me, "to imbue an entire school with positive psychology if you had carte blanche and unlimited resources?"

"First and foremost," Karen replied, "I would train the entire faculty for two whole weeks in the principles and exercises of positive psychology. We've been doing this with large numbers of British teachers. The teachers first learn to use these techniques in their own lives and then how to teach them to students."

"Okay," Charlie said. "Then what?"

"Then," Karen went on, "I would leave one or two of America's leading high school teachers of positive psychology in residence at the school to correct the trajectory of the faculty as they teach well-being across all the grade levels."

"Okay. Anything else?"

"Indeed," I chimed in, now asking for the moon, "bring in the stars of positive psychology—Barb Fredrickson, Stephen Post, Roy Baumeister, Diane Tice, George Vaillant, Kate Hays, Frank Mosca, Ray Fowler—one each month, creating a speaker series for the faculty, students, and the community. Then have each of them live on campus for a couple of weeks, teach students and teachers, and advise on the curriculum."

"Okay."

"And if Geelong Grammar can afford all that, I'm coming on sabbatical with my family to live at the school and direct the project. Try and stop me!"

It all happened just that way. In January 2008, Karen and I and fifteen of our Penn trainers (mostly MAPP graduates) flew to Australia to teach one hundred members of the Geelong Grammar faculty. In a nine-day course, we first taught the teachers to use the skills in their own lives—personally and professionally—and then we gave examples and detailed curricula of how to teach them to children. The principles and skills were taught in plenary sessions, and reinforced through exercises and applications in groups of thirty, as well as in pairs and small groups. Aside from the sky-high teaching ratings we got from the teachers (4.8 out of 5.0) *and* the fact that the teachers had given up two weeks of their summer vacation without pay, the transformation of Stephen Meek was emblematic.

The headmaster opened the first day with a broomstick-stiff, chilly welcoming speech, candidly laying out his skepticism about the whole project. Stephen, a vicar's son, is nothing if not completely honest. I didn't yet know this about him, however, and I thought about packing up and going home straightaway during his "welcome." Immediately throwing himself into everything, however, by the second day, Stephen was, by his own account, warming to the project. By the end of the nine days, he was glowing and hugging my faculty. (They are eminently huggable, but not typically by British headmasters.) He wanted more and told his teachers that this was the fourth great event in the school's history: first, the move from the city of Geelong to the country Corio campus in 1910; second, the founding of Timbertop in 1955; third, coeducation in 1978; and now what he dubbed "positive education."

Following the training, several of us were in residence for the entire year, and about a dozen visiting scholars came, each for a week or more, to instruct faculty in their positive psychology specialties. Here's what we devised, which essentially divides into "Teaching it," "Embedding it," and "Living it."

TEACHING POSITIVE EDUCATION
(THE STAND-ALONE COURSES)

Stand-alone courses and course units are now taught in several grades to teach the elements of positive psychology: resilience, gratitude, strengths, meaning, flow, positive relationships, and positive emotion. The two hundred tenth-grade students on the Corio campus (the upper school) each attended a positive education class taught twice weekly by the heads of each of the ten boardinghouses. Students heard several lectures by the visiting scholars, but the backbone of the course was discovering and using their own signature strengths.

During the first lesson, prior to taking the VIA Signature Strengths test, students wrote stories about when they were at their very best. Once they got back their own VIA results, students reread their stories, looking for examples of their signature strengths. Nearly every student found two, and most found three.

Other signature strengths lessons included interviewing family members to develop a "family tree" of strengths, learning how to use strengths to overcome challenges, and developing a strength that was not among an individual's top five. For the final strengths lesson, students nominated campus leaders whom they considered paragons of each of the strengths. Teachers and students now have a new common language of strengths for discussing their lives.

After Signature Strengths, the next series of lessons for the tenth grade focused on how to build more positive emotion. Students wrote gratitude letters to their parents, learned how to savor good memories, how to overcome negativity bias, and how gratifying kindness is to the giver. The blessings journal, in which students kept track nightly of what went well (WWW) that day, is now a staple at the school across all grades.

At the Timbertop campus, built on a mountain near Mansfield, Victoria, all 220 ninth-grade students live a rugged outdoor life for an entire year, which culminates in everyone running a marathon through the mountains. The stand-alone positive education course at Timbertop emphasizes resilience. First, students learn the ABC model: how beliefs (B) about an adversity (A)—and not the adversity itself—

cause the consequent (C) feelings. This is a point of major insight for students: emotions don't follow inexorably from external events but from what you *think* about those events, and you can actually change what you think. Then students learn how to slow down this ABC process through more flexible and more accurate thinking. Finally, students learn "real-time resilience" in order to deal with the "heat-of-the-moment" adversities that ninth graders so often face at Timbertop.

After resilience, the next Timbertop lessons address active-constructive responding (ACR) with a friend and the importance of a 3:1 Losada positive-to-negative ratio. Both the first and second units are taught by the health and physical education teachers, a natural fit given the rugged goals of Timbertop.

While these stand-alone courses teach content and skills, there is much more to positive education than just the stand-alone courses.

EMBEDDING POSITIVE EDUCATION

Geelong Grammar teachers embed positive education into academic courses, on the sports field, in pastoral counseling, in music, and in the chapel. First some classroom examples:

English teachers use signature strengths and resiliency to discuss novels. Even though Shakespeare's *King Lear* is a pretty depressing read (I slogged through it again recently), students identify the strengths of the main characters, and how these strengths have both a good side and a shadow side. English teachers use resiliency to demonstrate catastrophic thinking by characters in Arthur Miller's *Death of a Salesman* and Franz Kafka's *Metamorphosis*.

Teachers of rhetoric have changed their speaking assignments from "Give a speech about a time you made a fool out of yourself" to "Give a speech about when you were of value to others." Student preparation for these speeches takes less time, they speak more enthusiastically, and listening students do not fidget as much during the positive speeches.

Religion teachers ask students about the relationship between ethics and pleasure. Students consider the philosophers Aristotle, Jeremy Bentham, and John Stuart Mill in light of the most current brain research on pleasure and altruism, which suggests that altruism and compassion have underlying brain circuitry that has been favored by natural selection. Students examine perspectives (including their own) about what gives life purpose. Students and their parents engage in a "meaning dialogue," in which they write a series of emails about what makes life meaningful, prompted by a packet of sixty famous quotations on meaning.

Geography teachers usually measure the dismal variables: poverty, drought, malaria, but Geelong Grammar geography teachers also have students measure the well-being of entire nations, and how criteria for well-being differ among Australia, Iran, and Indonesia. They also research how the physical geography of a place (for instance, green space) might contribute to well-being. Instructors in languages other than English have students examine character strengths in Japanese, Chinese, and French folklore and culture.

Elementary teachers start each day with "What went well?" and the students nominate the classmates who displayed the "strength of the week." Music teachers use resilience skills to build optimism from performances that did not go well. Art teachers at all levels teach savoring of beauty.

Athletic coaches teach the skill of "letting go of grudges" against teammates who perform poorly. Some coaches use refocusing skills to remind team members of the good things they did, and these coaches report better play among those students who overcome negativity bias.

One coach developed a character strengths exercise to debrief his team following each game. During the debriefing session, students review the game's successes and challenges through the lens of character strengths. Team members identify—in themselves, in their teammates, and in their coaches—examples when specific strengths were called upon during the game. In addition, students identify "missed opportunities" for using certain strengths, the idea being that identifying these missed opportunities will increase awareness of future opportunities to use strengths.

Chapel is another locus of positive education. Scriptural passages on courage, forgiveness, persistence, and nearly every other strength are referenced during the daily services, reinforcing current classroom discussions. For example, when gratitude was the tenth-grade classroom's topic, Hugh Kempster's sermon in chapel and biblical readings were about gratitude.

In addition to stand-alone courses and embedding positive education into the school day, students and teachers find themselves living it in ways they had not anticipated.

LIVING POSITIVE EDUCATION

Like all Geelong Grammar six-year-olds, Kevin starts his day in a semicircle with his uniformed first-grade classmates. Facing his teacher, Kevin shoots his hand up when the class is asked, "Children, what went well last night?" Eager to answer, several first graders share brief anecdotes such as "We had my favorite last night: spaghetti" and "I played checkers with my older brother, and I won."

Kevin says, "My sister and I cleaned the patio after dinner, and Mum hugged us after we finished."

The teacher follows up with Kevin. "Why is it important to share what went well?"

He doesn't hesitate: "It makes me feel good."

"Anything more, Kevin?"

"Oh, yes, my mum asks me what went well when I get home every day, and it makes her happy when I tell her. And when Mum's happy, everybody's happy."

Elise has just returned from a nursing home where she and her fifth-grade classmates completed their "breadology" project, in which Jon Ashton, a television celebrity chef and one of our visiting scholars, taught the whole fourth grade how to make his granny's bread. Then they all visited a nursing home and gave away the bread to the residents. Elise explains the project:

"First we learned about good nutrition," she said. "Then we learned how to cook a healthy meal, but instead of eating it, we gave the food to other people."

"Did it bother you to not eat the food you'd spent so much time preparing? It smelled really good."

"No, just the opposite," she declares, smiling broadly. "At first I was scared of the old people, but then it felt like a little light went on inside me. I want to do it again."

Elise's best friend quickly chimes in, "Doing something for others feels better than any video game."

Kevin and Elise are two of the threads sewn into the tapestry of "living it" at the Geelong Grammar School. Kevin starts his schoolday with "What went well?" but when Kevin goes home, he lives positive education. No courses are displaced by WWW, but with this enhancement, the days get off to a better start. Even the faculty meetings get off to a better start.

Positive education at Geelong Grammar School is a work in progress and is not a controlled experiment. Melbourne Grammar School up the road did not volunteer to be a control group. So I cannot do better than relate before-and-after stories. But the change is palpable, and it transcends statistics. The school is not frowny anymore. I was back again for a month in 2009, and I have never been in a school with such high morale. I hated to leave and return to my own frowny university. Not one of the two hundred faculty members left Geelong Grammar at the end of the school year. Admissions, applications, and donations are way up.

Positive education alone is a slow and incremental way of spreading well-being across the globe. It is limited by the number of trained teachers and the number of schools willing to take on positive education. Positive computing might be the rabbit out of the hat.

Positive Computing

"We have five hundred million users, and half of them log on at least once a day," said Mark Slee, the strikingly handsome head of research for Facebook. "One hundred million of them are mobile users."

Our jaws dropped. The jaws belonged to leading researchers from

Microsoft, the Massachusetts Institute of Technology media lab, the Stanford Persuasion lab, a couple of video game designers, and a half dozen positive psychologists. The venue was the Penn Positive Psychology Center, for a meeting on positive computing in early May 2010. Our topic was how to go beyond the slow progress in positive education to disseminate flourishing massively. The new and future computing technologies might hold the key.

The organizer was Tomas Sanders, a visionary privacy researcher from Hewlett-Packard. He set the tone for the meeting. "A necessary condition for large-scale flourishing, particularly among young people, is that positive psychology develop a delivery model for its well-being-enhancing interventions that scales up globally. Information technology is uniquely positioned for assisting individuals with their flourishing in a way that is effective, scalable, and ethically responsible," he declared. Tomas then defined positive computing: the study and development of information and communication technology that is consciously designed to support people's psychological flourishing in a way that honors individuals' and communities' different ideas about the good life.

We spent a lot of our time discussing how concretely to adapt existing technology to individual flourishing. Rosalind Picard, the leading researcher in affective computing, which promotes the use of computers to build a better emotional life, presented the idea of a "personal flourishing assistant" (PFA). The PFA is a mobile phone application that maps where you are, who you are with, and what your emotional arousal level is. It then gives you relevant information and exercises; for example, "The last time you were right here at this time, your happiness was maximal. Take a photo of the sunset and transmit it to Becky and Lucius." The PFA will tag your experiences, and it can be searched later—"Show me the four peak moments from last week"—building up a "positive portfolio."

By chance, Major General Chuck Anderson happened over from our comprehensive soldier fitness training (see Chapters 7 and 8) just down the block as this discussion was in progress. "It's amazing," he said. "The first thing my soldiers in Afghanistan ask me when they come out of combat is not for a hamburger, but for Wi-Fi. General [George]

Casey has decided to make psychological fitness just as important for the army as physical fitness. But my soldiers are reminded every day—by push-ups and jogging—of the importance of physical fitness. I have been mulling over how to make psychological fitness just as salient to them just as frequently as physical fitness. I thought I might make every Thursday morning psychological fitness morning and have my brigades do positive psychology exercises. My soldiers are all wired; all of them have a cell phone, and most of them have BlackBerrys or iPhones. Listening to you all, I think the army can do better; we can create the right 'resilience apps,' or maybe you could even create the right games to teach strengths, social skills, and resilience."

Whereupon Jane McGonigal took the floor. "I create serious games, games that build the positives in life," she said. (Go to www.avantgame.com to play one.) In Jane's games, for example, Gaming to Save the World, players solve real-world problems such as food shortages and world peace. "We can teach strengths through gaming," she told us. "Schoolchildren could identify their signature strengths and then in the games tackle problems that will build these strengths."

Along with creative developments in gaming, Facebook seems like a natural for measuring flourishing. Facebook has the audience, the capacity, and is building apps (applications) that speak to the development and measurement of well-being worldwide. Can well-being be monitored on a daily basis all over the world? Here's a beginning: Mark Slee counted the occurrences of the term *laid off* in Facebook every day and graphed the count against the number of layoffs worldwide. Sure enough, they moved in lockstep. Not thrilling, you might think.

But now consider the five elements of well-being: positive emotion, engagement, meaning, positive relationships, and accomplishment. Each element has a lexicon; an extensive vocabulary. For example, the English language has only about eighty words to describe positive emotion. (You can determine this by going to a thesaurus for a word such as *joy* and then looking up all the related words, and then counting the synonyms of all those related words, eventually circling back to the core of eighty.) The hypermassive Facebook database could be accessed daily for a count of positive emotion words—words that signal meaning, positive relationships, and accomplishment—as a first approximation to well-being in a given nation or as a function of some major event.

It is not only measuring well-being that Facebook and its cousins can do, but increasing well-being as well. "We have a new application: goals.com," Mark continued. "In this app, people record their goals and their progress toward their goals."

I commented on Facebook's possibilities for instilling well-being: "As it stands now, Facebook may actually be building four of the elements of well-being: positive emotion, engagement (sharing all those photos of good events), positive relationships (the heart of what 'friends' are all about), and now accomplishment. All to the good. The fifth element of well-being, however, needs work, and in the narcissistic environment of Facebook, this work is urgent, and that is belonging to and serving something that you believe is bigger than the self—the element of meaning. Facebook could indeed help to build meaning in the lives of the five hundred million users. Think about it, Mark."

A New Measure of Prosperity

What is all our wealth for, anyway? Surely it is not, as most economists advocate, just to produce more wealth. Gross domestic product (GDP) was, during the industrial revolution, a decent first approximation to how well a nation was doing. Now, however, every time we build a prison, every time there is a divorce, a motor accident, or a suicide, the GDP—just a measure of how many goods and services are used—goes up. The aim of wealth should not be to blindly produce a higher GDP but to produce more well-being. General well-being—positive emotion, engagement at work, positive relationships, and a life full of meaning—is now quantifiable, and it complements GDP. Public policy can be aimed at increasing general well-being, and the successes or failures of policy can be held accountable against this standard.

Prosperity-as-usual has been equated with wealth. Based on this formulation, it is commonly said in the rich nations that this may be the last generation to do better than its parents. That may be true of money, but is it more money that every parent wants his children to have? I don't believe so. I believe that what parents want for their children is more well-being than they themselves had. By this measure, there is every hope that our children will do better than their parents.

The time has come for a new prosperity, one that takes flourishing seriously as the goal of education and of parenting. Learning to value and to attain flourishing must start early—in the formative years of schooling—and it is this new prosperity, kindled by positive education, that the world can now choose. One of the four components of flourishing is positive accomplishment. The next chapter explores the underlying ingredients of achievement, and it presents a new theory of success and intelligence.

PART 2

The Ways to Flourish

Chapter 6

———

GRIT, Character, and Achievement: A New Theory of Intelligence

The University of Pennsylvania's Psychology Department has an exceedingly competitive PhD program. Every year, we get several hundred applicants, and we take only ten or so. Positive psychology receives around thirty applicants a year and accepts only one. The model admittee is an undergraduate psychology major with a grade point average close to perfect from a major American or European university, with GRE exam scores all well over 700, and with three letters of recommendation—each of which checks the box that says this candidate is "truly exceptional, the best in years." The admissions committee is traditional, but it is constipated (I have never served on it), and it has turned down some amazingly fine candidates.

One that comes to mind was one of the first women to win a major championship in poker. In her essay she said that she saved up lots of money, took a plane to Las Vegas, and entered the world championship, and that she won the tournament. Both the president of the university, Sheldon Hackney, and I argued that she should be admitted for having demonstrated not mere potential but actual world-class performance—but to no avail. Her GREs, we were told, were not high enough. I am still grateful to her, however, for spending part of her interview correcting my poker errors, thus saving me thousands of dollars over the next decade. "Courage," she said, "is the key to high-stakes poker. You must treat the white chip as simply a white chip, whether it is worth just one nickel or one thousand dollars."

Success and Intelligence

Applications are due by January 1, and, after a grueling series of personal interviews, acceptances go out in late February. This has been the operating procedure for the forty-five years that I have been in this department. As far as I know, there has only been a single exception in all this time: Angela Lee Duckworth.

In June 2002, we received a belated application for the class entering in September 2002. It would have been thrown out summarily but for the intercession of the director of graduate training, John Sabini. John, may he rest in peace—he died suddenly at age fifty-nine in 2005—had always been a maverick. He worked on such unconventional topics as gossip, claiming that it is a legitimate form of moral sanction but at a less punitive level than legal sanction. In whatever he did, he rowed upstream against academic social psychology. I had always been the other department maverick, usually loyal to the unpopular argument, the argument that needed hearers. John and I could smell another maverick a mile away.

"I know it's intolerably late, but you must read this admissions essay, Marty," John emailed me. It was written by Angela Lee Duckworth. Here is the content, in part:

> By graduation, I had spent at least as many hours volunteering in the classrooms of the Cambridge Public Schools as I did in Harvard's lecture halls and laboratories. Witnessing in person the reality of failing urban students in failing urban public schools, I chose conscience over curiosity. I made a commitment to pursue public education reform after graduation. During my senior year, I founded a nonprofit summer school for low-income middle school students . . . Summerbridge Cambridge developed into a model for other public schools across the country, was featured on NPR and in many newspapers, was written up as a case study for the Kennedy School of Government, and won the Better Government Competition for the state of Massachusetts.

I spent the next two years at Oxford University on a Marshall fellowship. My research focused on the magnocellular and parvocellular pathways of visual information in dyslexia . . . I chose not to pursue a PhD at that point in my career . . . I spent the next six years as a public school teacher, nonprofit leader, charter school consultant, and education policy writer.

After years of working with students at both ends of the achievement spectrum, I now have a distinctly different view of school reform. The problem, I think, is not only the schools but also the students themselves. Here's why: learning is hard. True, learning is fun, exhilarating, and gratifying—but it is also often daunting, exhausting, and sometimes discouraging. By and large, students who no longer want to learn, who don't think they can learn, and who don't see any point in learning simply won't—no matter how wonderful the school or teacher . . .

To help chronically low-performing but intelligent students, educators and parents must first recognize that character is at least as important as intellect.

I have chosen not to exhume my essay for admission to Penn graduate school in 1964 and compare it to this one.

Conventional wisdom and political correctness have for almost a century blamed the teachers, the schools, the classroom size, the textbooks, the funding, the politicians, and the parents for the failure of the students—putting the blame on anything or anyone but the students themselves. What? Blame the victim? Blame the character of the students? What nerve! Character had long since gone out of fashion in social science.

Positive Character

In the nineteenth century, politics, morality, and psychology were all about character. Lincoln's first inaugural address, appealing to the "better angels of our nature," was emblematic of how Americans explained good behavior and bad behavior. The Haymarket Square riot in 1886 in Chicago was a turning point. There was a general strike, and some-one, unknown to this day, threw a pipe bomb; the police opened fire, and in a five-minute melee, eight policemen and an unknown number of civilians were killed. German immigrants were blamed, and the press condemned them as "bloody brutes," "monsters," and "fiends." The deaths were caused, in popular sentiment, by the bad moral character of the immigrants, and they were labeled anarchists. Four of them were hanged; a fifth committed suicide before his execution.

There was an enormous reaction against the hangings from the left. Riding on the coattails of this protest was a very big idea: an alternative explanation of bad character. All of the condemned came from the lowest class of workers. They were illiterate in English, desperate, on starvation wages, and overcrowded, with whole families living in one small tenement room. The big idea claimed that it was not bad character but a malignant environment that produced crime. Theologians and philosophers took up this cry, and the end result was "social science": a science that would demonstrate that environment, rather than character or heredity, is a better explanation of what people do. Almost the entire history of twentieth-century psychology and her sister disciplines of sociology, anthropology, and political science have acted out this premise.

DRAWN BY THE FUTURE, NOT DRIVEN BY THE PAST

Notice the cascade of changes that follow from giving up character as an explanation of human misbehavior in favor of the environment. First, individuals are no longer responsible for their actions, since the causes lie not in the person but in the situation. This means the interventions must change: if you want to make a better world, you should alleviate the circumstances that produce bad actions rather than waste your time trying to change character or punishing bad behavior and rewarding good behavior. Second, progressive science must isolate the situations that shape crime, ignorance, prejudice, failure, and all the other ills that befall human beings, so that these situations can be corrected. Using money to correct social problems becomes the primary intervention. Third, the focus of inquiry must be bad events, not good events. In social science, it makes sense to excuse Sammy's failure at school because she was hungry, or abused, or came from a home in which learning was not valued. In contrast, we don't take the credit away from people who do good things, because it makes little sense to "excuse" good behavior by invoking the circumstances that led up to it. It is odd to say that Sammy gave such a good speech because she went to good schools, had loving parents, and is well fed. Finally, and so basic as to be almost invisible, the situation view propounds the premise that *we are driven by the past rather than drawn by the future.*

Psychology-as-usual—the psychology of victims and negative emotions and alienation and pathology and tragedy—is the stepchild of Haymarket Square. Positive psychology's take on all of this is very different from psychology-as-usual: sometimes people are indeed victims (I am writing this on the day after the horrific Haitian earthquake, with hundreds of thousands of genuine victims now suffering or dead), but often people are responsible for their actions, and their untoward choices stem from their character. Responsibility and free will are necessary processes within positive psychology. If the circumstances are to be blamed, the individual's responsibility and will are minimized, if not eliminated. If, in contrast, the action emanates from character and choice, individual responsibility and free will are, at least in part, causes.

This has direct implications for how to intervene: in positive psychology, the world can be bettered not only by undoing malignant circumstances (I do not remotely advocate giving up on reform) but also by identifying and then shaping character, both bad and good. Reward and punishment shape character, not just behavior. Good events, high achievement, and positive emotions are just as legitimate objects of science for positive psychology as are awful events, failure, tragedy, and negative emotion. Once we take positive events seriously as objects of science, we notice that we do not excuse or take credit away from Sammy's brilliant performance because she was well fed, or had good teachers, or had parents who cared about learning. We care about Sammy's character, her talents, and her strengths. Finally, human beings are often, perhaps more often, drawn by the future than they are driven by the past, and so a science that measures and builds expectations, planning, and conscious choice will be more potent than a science of habits, drives, and circumstances. That we are drawn by the future rather than just driven by the past is extremely important and directly contrary to the heritage of social science and the history of psychology. It is, nevertheless, a basic and implicit premise of positive psychology.

Angela's proposal that school failure might stem in part from the character of the failing students, and not just from the system that victimizes them, appealed to the positive psychologist in me and to the nurturing of mavericks that was the cornerstone of John Sabini's pedagogy. Here was just the right sort of maverick: someone with very high intellectual credentials and a sterling education but not housebroken enough by politics to prevent her doing serious research on the character strengths of students who succeed and the character deficits of students who fail.

What Intelligence Is

SPEED

We interviewed Angela forthwith. My first impression of her triggered a memory I have to recount. In the 1970s, I was one of two professors at Penn to found a college house system; Alan Kors, a professor of modern European intellectual history, believed that a university education was truly about the life of the mind. But when we taught our undergraduates, we saw the chasm that separated the classroom from what they considered their real lives: they could simulate intellectual passion in the classroom in order to get good grades, but once released, it was party, party, party. Alan and I had experienced this animal life firsthand in the dorms of Princeton in the early 1960s, but we were vouchsafed a safe haven, one that changed both our lives: Wilson Lodge, an eating facility at Princeton in the 1960s. To this day, after a lifetime of intellectual feasts, it remains the best intellectual experience of my entire life. The president of the senior class, Darwin

Labarthe, whom you will hear more of in the next chapter, inspired by university president Robert Goheen, led a walkout against Princeton's entrenched, anti-intellectual, anti-Semitic club system. Together they created Wilson Lodge, open to any student or faculty member, and more than a hundred of the most intensely intellectual students joined, along with forty of the most devoted faculty.

Alan and I believed that a system in which such devoted faculty lived in the dorms with the undergraduates would provide the same antidote to the animal life in Penn's dorms. So we founded Penn's College Houses in 1976. Van Pelt College House was the first one, and Alan, a bachelor—no faculty we could drum up were devoted enough to give up their family life to live with 180 undergraduates—agreed to become the first housemaster. After my divorce, I succeeded him in 1980. I cannot pretend that this was an easy job; in fact, it was the only job I've ever held that I count as a failure. My own inadequacies in dealing in loco parentis twenty-four hours a day with late adolescents, trying to settle the endless squabbles among roommates, the suicide attempts, the date rapes, the meanness of the pranks, the absence of privacy, and, worst of all, an unsympathetic administration that treated the resident faculty not as professors but as hourly employees, made the master's life an endless hassle.

But the intellectual life we created was an improvement, and it survives to this day. And the parties were great. The students called the parties "master blasters." The centerpiece of these parties was a student named Lisa, who was an astonishingly graceful dancer. The music was rock, usually with a heavy, very fast beat. Lisa somehow took two steps for every one beat, dancing twice as fast as anyone else, from the opening and late into the night.

This brings me back to my first impression of Angela Lee Duckworth: she was the verbal equivalent of Lisa—talking twice as fast as anyone else I knew, indefatigably, and still making good sense.

Speed is something that both attracts and repels in academic life, and it plays a central role in what I think intelligence really is. Intellectual speed was highly prized by my parents and my teachers: the prototypes to be emulated were Dickie Freeman and Joel Kupperman, two of the prodigies who starred in *Quiz Kids*, a weekly radio show in the early 1950s. They rattled off the answers to factual questions more quickly than the other contestants, questions such as "What state ends in *ut*?" I know because I competed in the local radio version of this in fourth grade, getting that one right, and guessing correctly that there were five Little Peppers (an old book series). But I came in second to Rocco Giacomino, and therefore failed to make it to the national show when I was stumped by "Who wrote 'Flow Gently Sweet Afton'?"

My parents' and teachers' bias toward speed was not an accidental social convention. It turns out that speed and IQ have a surprisingly strong relationship. In the experimental procedure called "choice-reaction time," subjects are seated in front of a panel with a light and two buttons. They are told to press the left button when the light is green and to press the right button when the light is red, and to do this as fast as they can. IQ correlates almost as high as +.50 with how fast people can do this. Being fast at choice-reaction time is not simple athleticism, however, since its correlation with "simple reaction time" ("When I say, 'Go,' press the button as fast as you can") is negligible.

Why should intelligence be so closely related to mental speed? My father, Adrian Seligman, was deputy state reporter of the Court of Appeals of New York State. His job was to take the unwieldy and ungrammatical opinions of the seven high court judges and translate them into a readable legalese that resembled English. He was blazingly fast. According to my mother, Irene, who as a legal stenographer was a keen observer, Adrian could do in one hour what it took other lawyers the entire working day to do. This gave him seven hours to check and refine his work, rewrite and rewrite, so that the finished product was much better than what other reporters could produce.

Any complex mental task—rewriting legal opinions, multiplying three-digit numbers, mentally counting the windows in your childhood house, deciding which blood vessel to suture first or whether the next hilltop is a likely ambush site—has fast automatic components and slower voluntary components that take much more effort. You are an experienced staff sergeant urgently approaching a hilltop in Afghanistan. You scan the approach, and from your previous encounters, you know instantaneously that the freshly disturbed soil, the silence, and the absence of animal sounds are danger signs. The more components of a task you have on automatic, the more time you have left over to do the heavy lifting. You now have two minutes to radio the base and ask for the latest report on the presence of foreign fighters. You are told that people in the nearest village spotted three strangers this morning. All this spells ambush or an improvised explosive device, and so you take the long route around the hill. The two extra minutes left over save lives.

The staff sergeant's mental speed is a surrogate for what proportion of the task he already had on automatic. I see this in serious bridge every time I play (which averages about three hours a day on the Internet). I have played more than 250,000 hands in my lifetime, and all four-way combinations of thirteen (in bridge, each player holds thirteen cards made up of four suits) are now automatic for me. So if I find out that an opponent has six spades and five hearts, I know—instantaneously—that she either has two diamonds and no clubs, two clubs and no diamonds, or one of each. Less experienced players have to calculate that remainder, and some even have to say it to themselves. I actually had to say "two diamonds and no clubs, or two clubs and no diamonds, or one club and one diamond" silently to myself until about my 100,000th hand. A bridge hand, like most of life's trials, is a timed event. You get only seven minutes for each hand in a duplicate bridge match, and so the more combinations you have on automatic, the more time you have to do the heavy lifting and figure out if the most likely winning play is the simple finesse or the squeeze or the end play.

What distinguishes a great bridge player or a great surgeon or a great pilot from the rest of us mortals is how much they have on automatic. When the bulk of what an expert does is on automatic, people say she has "great intuitions." Therefore, I take speed very seriously.

Angela (whose theory makes up this chapter) puts it like this:

> *Most of us recall from high school physics class that the motion of objects is described in the following terms: distance = speed × time. This equation specifies that the effects of speed*

and time are interdependent and multiplicative rather than independent and additive. If time is zero, whatever the speed, distance will be zero . . .

Distance seemed to me an apt metaphor for achievement. What is achievement, after all, but an advance from a starting point to a goal? The farther the goal from the starting point, the greater the achievement. Just as distance is the multiplicative product of speed and time, it seems plausible that, holding opportunity constant, achievement is the multiplicative product of skill and effort. Leaving out coefficients, achievement = skill × effort.

Tremendous effort can compensate for modest skill, just as tremendous skill can compensate for modest effort, but not if either is zero. Further, the returns on additional effort are greater for highly skilled individuals. A master woodworker will get done more in two hours than an amateur will in the same period.

So a major component of skill is how much you have on automatic, which determines how fast you can complete the task's basic steps. As a youth, I became fast, blazingly fast, and I started my academic career with almost the same rate of speech as Angela. I blazed my way through graduate school, not only talking fast but conducting research fast. I earned my PhD after only two years and eight months from my undergraduate degree, and I received an annoyed note from John Corbit, my former professor at Brown University, about my having broken his old record of three years flat.

THE VIRTUE OF SLOWNESS

There is more to intelligence and high achievement, however, than sheer speed. What speed does is give you extra time to carry out the nonautomatic parts of the task. The second component of intelligence and achievement is slowness and *what you do with all that extra time* that being fast affords you.

Mental speed comes at a cost. I found myself missing nuances and taking shortcuts when I should have taken the mental equivalent of a deep breath. I found myself skimming and scanning when I should have been reading every word. I found myself listening poorly to others: I would figure out where they were headed after their first few words and then interrupt. And I was anxious a lot of the time—speed and anxiety go together.

In 1974 we hired Ed Pugh, a perception psychologist who worked on exacting questions such as how many photons of light are needed to fire off a single visual receptor. Ed was slow. He wasn't physically slow (he had been the quarterback of his Louisiana high school team), and it wasn't just the drawl, it was his rate of speech and his reaction time to a question. We called Ed "thoughtful."

Ed was Penn's incarnation of the legendary William K. Estes, the greatest of the mathematical learning theorists, and the slowest psychologist I ever met. Conversations with Bill were agony. I had worked for a couple of years studying dreaming—in particular researching what dreaming accomplished for *Homo sapiens,* given that we lie there physically paralyzed and vulnerable to predators during rapid eye movement sleep for about two hours a night. I encountered Bill at a convention about thirty years ago and asked him, "What do you think the evolutionary function of dreaming is?"

Bill stared without blinking at me for five seconds, ten seconds, thirty seconds (it was so bizarre, I actually counted). After one full minute, he said, "What, Marty, do you think the evolutionary function of waking is?"

I found myself at a party with Ed, and during a long pause that reminded me of the profundities that could issue from Bill after such a pause, I asked Ed, "How did you become so slow?"

"I wasn't always slow, Marty. I used to be fast; almost as fast as you are. I learned to become slow. Before my PhD, I was a Jesuit. My socius [the mentor who socializes the Jesuit student, in contrast to the other mentor who grades the student] told me I was too fast. So every day he would give me one sentence to read, and then he made me sit under a tree for the afternoon and think about that sentence."

"Can you teach me to be slow, Ed?"

Indeed he could. We read Søren Kierkegaard's *Fear and Trembling* together, but at the rate of one page a week, and to top it off, my sister, Beth, taught me transcendental meditation. I practiced TM faithfully, forty minutes a day for twenty years. I cultivated slowness, and I am now even slower than Ed was then.

What does slowness accomplish in the equation achievement = skill × effort?

Executive Function

Adele Diamond, a professor of developmental psychology at the University of British Columbia and one of my favorite neuroscientists, slows down kindergarten children. Impulsive children have long been known to do worse and worse as they age: Walter Mischel's classic marshmallow study demonstrated that children who gobbled up the one marshmallow in front of them, rather than waiting for two marshmallows a few minutes later, did poorly. More than a decade later, they got lower grades in school and lower SAT scores than children who could wait. Adele believes that the failure of children to control their fast emotional and cognitive impulses is the seed crystal around which the cascade of school failure begins. Teachers get annoyed and frustrated with such children, and school becomes less fun for these kids. They have difficulty complying with rules, and they become more anxious and avoidant. The teachers expect less and less from these kids, school becomes more of a misery, and the vicious cycle of failure has begun.

Adele believes it is crucial to interrupt these fast processes and get these children to slow down. Going slow allows executive function to take over. Executive function consists of focusing and ignoring distractions, remembering and using new information, planning action and revising the plan, and inhibiting fast, impulsive thoughts and actions.

Adele uses techniques from Deborah Leong and Elena Bodrova's Tools of the Mind curriculum to slow down impulsive children. One of their techniques is structured play. When a teacher asks a four-year-old to stand still for as long as he can, one minute is the average. In contrast, in the context of a make-believe game in which the child is the guard at a factory, he can stand still for four minutes. Adele has found that Tools of the Mind kids score higher on tests that require executive function.

What other slow processes, in addition to more use of executive function, does having a large amount of the task done quickly and automatically allow? Creativity is surely one. In the equation achievement = skill × effort, achievement is defined not simply by any motion but by motion toward a specific, fixed goal—a vector—as opposed to sheer distance. There are usually several paths to a goal. Some get you there quickly, some slowly, and some paths are dead ends. Deciding which path to take is the slow process we call "planning," and beyond this, the invention of new paths captures much of what is meant by creativity.

Rate of Learning: The First Derivative of Speed

Mental speed for any given task reflects how much material relevant to that task is already on automatic. We call this material "knowledge," how much you already know that is relevant to the task. Speed on a task can change over time, and this parallels "acceleration," the first derivative of speed in mechanics. Is there such a thing as mental acceleration, the increase of mental speed over time, how fast you can acquire new knowledge—the increase in how much of a given task can be put onto automatic over time and experience? We call this the "rate of learning": how much can be learned per unit time.

Angela was fast, about as fast mentally as it is possible for a human being to be, and she blew us away in the interview. In violation of precedent, the admissions committee gave in and accepted her. She began work immediately on her grand project of examining the character of good and bad students, but then something embarrassing happened. To explain this, we need to go deeper into the nature of achievement.

While Angela was fast, she was ignorant of psychology, woefully so, probably because of the fact that almost all of her prior education was outside of psychology. To socialize her in positive psychology, I invited her in August 2002 to an elite event. Each summer I held a weeklong meeting that brought together twenty very advanced graduate students and postdoctoral students from all over the world with several leading senior positive psychologists. The competition for invitations was fierce and the level of sophistication very high. Never reluctant to pipe up, Angela participated in the conversations, but the feedback I got about her was disappointing. "Who is this clunker you imposed on us?" was one comment from a senior figure.

One criterion of the quality of a car is its speed. Mental speed is a very good quality because it is a surrogate for how much old knowledge is on automatic. But acquiring new knowledge that is not yet on automatic can be slow or fast. Acceleration, how much speed increases per unit of time, is the first derivative of speed, and it is an additional criterion of the quality of a car. Mental acceleration, the rate at which new stuff is learned per unit of time devoted to learning, is another part of the package we call "intelligence." It turned out that Angela's mental acceleration was as breathtaking as her speed.

Everyone learns in graduate school, and it is expected that a graduate student will become an expert in his or her small domain pretty quickly. But no student I have known learned at the rate that Angela did; she became the resident master of the huge and methodologically complex literature on intelligence, motivation, and success. Within months, my other students (and I) were going to Angela for advice about the literature and methodology in the psychology of intelligence. She went from clunker to Ferrari (the Enzo model) in about twelve months.

So far then in our theory of achievement, we have explored the following:

• Speed: the faster, the more material on automatic, the more one knows about the task.

• Slowness: the voluntary, heavyweight processes of achievement, such as planning, refining, checking for errors, and creativity. The faster the speed, the more the knowledge, and thus the more time left over for these executive functions to be used.

• Rate of learning: how fast new information can be deposited into the bank account of automatic knowledge, allowing even more time for the slow executive processes.

SELF-CONTROL AND GRIT

The three cognitive processes described above all make up "skill" in our basic equation, achievement = skill × effort. But the big game that Angela was stalking was not the cognitive processes in academic achievement but the role of character and where character enters the equation is as "effort." Effort is the amount of time spent on the task. As she declared in her essay, what she determined to explore was the noncognitive ingredients. The noncognitive ingredients of achievement are summarized by effort, and effort in turn simplifies to "time on task." The giant in the field of effort is a tall, shy, but unyielding Swede, Professor Anders Ericsson of Florida State University.

Ericsson has argued that the cornerstone of all high expertise is not God-given genius but deliberate practice: the amount of time and energy you spend in deliberate practice. Mozart was Mozart not primarily because he had a unique gift for music but because from toddlerhood, he spent all his time using his gift. World-class chess players are not faster of thought, nor do they have unusually good memories for moves. Rather they have so much experience that they are vastly better at recognizing patterns in chess positions than lesser chess players—and this comes from the sheer amount of their experience. World-class piano soloists log 10,000 hours of solo practice by age twenty, in contrast to 5,000 hours for the next level of pianist, and in contrast to 2,000 hours for merely serious amateur pianists. The prototype of deliberate practice is one of Ericsson's graduate students, Chao Lu, who holds the Guinness World Record for the amazing number of digits of pi he memorized: 67,890! The advice that follows is straightforward: if you want to become world class at anything, you must spend 60 hours a week on it for ten years.

What determines how much time and deliberate practice a child is willing to devote to achievement? Nothing less than her character? Self-discipline is the character trait that engenders deliberate practice, and Angela's first plunge into research on self-discipline was with the students of Masterman High School, the great magnet school in the center of Philadelphia. Masterman accepts promising students beginning in the fifth grade, but many of them wash out, and the real competition begins in the ninth grade. Angela wanted to find out how self-discipline compares with IQ in predicting who will succeed.

IQ and academic performance are part of a well-worked-over field with lots of established measures, but self-discipline is not. So Angela created a composite measure that encompassed the different aspects of self-discipline that eighth graders show: the Eysenck Junior Impulsiveness Scale (yes/no questions about doing and saying things impulsively), a parent and teacher self-control rating scale ("compared to the average child [4], this child is maximally impulsive [7] to maximally self-controlled [1]"), and delay of gratification (over a range of dollars and times; for example, "Would you rather I gave you one dollar today or two dollars two weeks from today?"). Watched over the next year, the highly self-disciplined eighth graders

- earned higher grade point averages,
- had higher achievement test scores,
- were more likely to get into a selective high school,
- spent more time on their homework and started it earlier in the day,
- were absent less often,
- watched less television.

How does IQ compare with self-discipline in predicting grades? IQ and self-discipline do not correlate with each other significantly; in other words, there are just about as many low-IQ kids who are highly self-disciplined as there are high-IQ kids who are highly self-disciplined, and conversely. Self-discipline outpredicts IQ for academic success by a factor of about 2.

This project was Angela's first-year thesis, and I encouraged her to submit it for publication—which she did. I am an old hand at publishing journal articles, but this was the first time in my experience that I saw an acceptance by return mail, from a top journal, and with no request for any major revisions. Angela concludes the article with these ringing sentences:

Underachievement among American youth is often blamed on inadequate teachers, boring textbooks, and large class sizes. We suggest another reason for students falling short of their intellectual potential: their failure to exercise self-discipline . . . We believe that many of America's children have trouble making choices that require them to sacrifice short-term pleasure for long-term gain, and that programs that build self-discipline may be the royal road to building academic achievement.

This also solves one of the perennial riddles about the gap in school achievement between girls and boys. Girls get higher classroom grades than boys all the way from elementary school to college in every major subject, even though girls do not have higher IQs, on average, than boys do. In fact, boys often outperform girls by a little bit on intelligence and achievement tests. IQ overpredicts the grades that boys get and underpredicts the grades that girls get. Could self-discipline be the missing piece in this puzzle?

Angela used her battery of self-discipline measures with girls and boys from the beginning of eighth grade to predict algebra grades, attendance, and math achievement test scores at the end of the year. Girls indeed received higher classroom grades than boys, but the math achievement scores did not differ significantly. The achievement test underpredicted the girls' classroom grades, as expected. Importantly, girls were much more self-disciplined than boys on all components of the composite. The question, then, is: Does the girls' superiority in self-discipline account for their superiority in classroom grades? To answer this, a statistical technique called "hierarchical multiple regression" does the trick: this basically asks, When you remove the difference in self-discipline, does the difference in grades vanish? And the answer is yes.

Angela then repeated this study using IQ the next year at Masterman. Girls once again got higher grades in algebra, English, and social studies, and were much more self-disciplined. Boys had significantly higher IQ scores than this group of girls, and once again the classroom grades of the girls were underpredicted by IQ and standardized tests.

Using multiple regression, girls' self-discipline was again the major factor in their superior classroom grades.

While this solves the question of why women get better grades all the way through college, it assuredly does not tell us why men then go on to more professional and graduate degrees and earn higher salaries than women. Women's superior self-control does not wane with maturity, but after college, many are swamped by cultural factors that dampen the female self-discipline edge.

Self-control predicts matters academic, but how does it predict other outcomes? Obesity, for instance, may have its roots in a critical period: weight gain during early puberty. Angela looked at the school nurses' records of the weight of the fifth graders she had measured for self-discipline in 2003 and asked how much weight had they gained by eighth grade. Self-discipline did the same thing for weight gain that it did for grades. The kids with high self-discipline did not put on as much weight as the kids with low self-discipline. IQ had no impact on weight gain.

GRIT VERSUS SELF-DISCIPLINE

If we want to maximize the achievement of children, we need to promote self-discipline. My favorite social psychologist, Roy Baumeister, believes it is the queen of all the virtues, the strength that enables the rest of the strengths. There is, however, an extreme trait of self-discipline: GRIT. Indeed, Angela went on to explore grittiness, the combination of very high persistence and high passion for an objective. A modicum of self-discipline, we have seen, accounts for considerable achievement, but what accounts for truly extraordinary achievement?

Extraordinary achievement is very rare. That probably sounds like it is true by definition, a tautology: "very rare" just means the same thing as "extraordinary," but this is not a tautology, and why it is not exposes the hidden scaffolding behind genius. Most people believe that "genius," a term I will use as a synonym for truly extraordinary achievement, is simply being in the very extreme of the positive tail of a bell-shaped or "normal" distribution of success. The bell curve works well for ordinary stuff, such as charm, beauty, school grades, and height, but it totally fails to describe the distribution of achievement.

High Human Accomplishment

Charles Murray, the eminent sociologist, in his magnum opus, *Human Accomplishment,* starts with sports. How many PGA tournaments does the average professional golfer win in his lifetime? The mean is between zero and one. (The mode, or most frequent value, is zero.) But four professional golfers have won thirty or more, with Arnold Palmer winning sixty-one and Jack Nicklaus winning seventy-one (as has Tiger Woods at this writing). The shape of the distribution of the number of PGA tournaments won by a player is not remotely bell shaped but concave upward and extremely skewed (like a cliff) to the left.

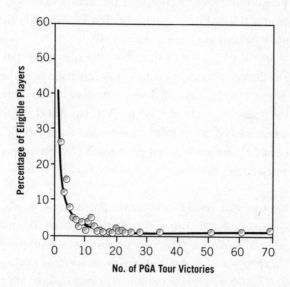

The technical name for this kind of curve is log-normal, which means that the logarithm of the variable is normally distributed. The very same pattern is true of tennis, marathons, chess, and batting championships, and as the accomplishment becomes more demanding, the curve appears more and more clifflike. In each of these domains, there are many fine competitors but only two or three giants. They gobble up all notice and are not on a continuum with the merely fine players. The same is true of wealth in every society: a very few people have vastly more than anyone else. The same is said to be true of business, where it is widely held that 20 percent of the employees are responsible for 80 percent of the profit.

To document this, Murray quantifies the shape of genius in twenty-one intellectual fields, including astronomy, music, mathematics, Eastern and Western philosophy, painting, and literature. In every one of these fields, the citation rate of the leading figures is not remotely bell shaped; rather there are only two or three giants who grab the lion's share of glory and influence. One in Chinese philosophy: Confucius. Two in technology: James Watt and Thomas Edison. Two in Western music: Beethoven and Mozart. One in Western literature: Shakespeare.

Once described, your reaction, like mine, is probably "Of course, I already knew this—at least intuitively." But why should this be, and why should it be universal across endeavors?

The shape of genius—with the top performers outdistancing the average excellent performer by a much greater margin than they would in bell-shaped distributions—follows from multiplying, rather than adding, the underlying causes of genius. William Shockley, the Nobel laureate who invented the transistor, found this pattern in the publication of scientific papers: a very few people published many papers, but most scientists published none or only one. Shockley wrote:

> For example, consider the factors that may be involved in publishing a scientific paper. A partial listing, not in order of importance, might be: (1) ability to think of a good problem, (2) ability to work on it, (3) ability to recognize a worthwhile result, (4) ability to make a decision as to when to stop and write up the results, (5) ability to write adequately, (6) ability to profit constructively from criticism, (7) determination to submit the paper to a journal, (8) persistence in making changes (if necessary as a result of journal action) . . . Now if one man exceeds another by 50 per cent in each of the eight factors, his productivity will be larger by a factor of 25. (p. 286)

This is the underlying rationale for GRIT, the never-yielding form of self-discipline. Very high effort is caused by a personality characteristic of extreme persistence. The more GRIT you have, the more time you spend on the task, and all those hours don't just add to whatever innate skill you have; they multiply your progress to the goal. So Angela developed a test for GRIT. Take the GRIT test now and give it to your kids as well.

Please respond to the following eight items using the following scale:

> 1 = Not like me at all, 2 = Not much like me,
> 3 = Somewhat like me, 4 = Mostly like me,
> 5 = Very much like me

1. New ideas and projects sometimes distract me from old ones.* _____
2. Setbacks don't discourage me. _____
3. I have been obsessed with a certain idea or project for a short time but later lost interest.* _____
4. I am a hard worker. _____
5. I often set a goal but later choose to pursue a different one.*
   _____
6. I have difficulty maintaining my focus on projects that take more than a few months to complete.* _____
7. I finish whatever I begin. _____
8. I am diligent. _____

Asterisked items are reverse scored.

To get your score

1. Add your score on statements 2, 4, 7 and 8.
2. Then add items 1, 3, 5, and 6 and subtract that total from 24.
3. Then add the two steps together and divide by 8.

Here are the norms by sex:

DECILE (TENTHS)	MALE (N = 4,169)	FEMALE (N = 6,972)
1st	2.50	2.50
2nd	2.83	2.88
3rd	3.06	3.13
4th	3.25	3.25
5th	3.38	3.50
6th	3.54	3.63
7th	3.75	3.79
8th	3.92	4.00
9th	4.21	4.25
10th	5.00	5.00
Mean, SD (standard deviation)	3.37, 0.66	3.43, 0.68

What has Angela discovered about GRIT? The more education, the more GRIT. Not surprising, but which comes first? Does more education produce more GRIT, or more likely, do gritty people persevere through many failures and humiliations and so go on to get more education? This is still unknown. More surprising is the fact that, controlling for education, older people have more GRIT than younger people, with those over sixty-five having much more than any other age group.

GRIT'S BENEFITS

Grade Point Average
The GRIT test was taken by 139 of Penn's psychology majors. We knew their SAT scores, which are a good estimate of IQ. Angela followed them through their studies and looked at the grades they went on to

get. High SATs predicted high grades—that is indeed the only proven benefit of having high SATs—and high GRIT also predicted high grades. Importantly, holding SATs constant, higher GRIT continued to predict higher grades. At every level of SAT, the grittier students got better grades than the rest, and students with lower SATs tended to have more GRIT.

West Point

In July 2004, 1,218 plebes entering the U.S. Military Academy took the GRIT test along with a mountain of other tests. The army does numbers and is very serious about trying to predict accomplishment through psychological tests. Interestingly, GRIT seemed like a unique test, since it did not correlate with the "whole candidate score": the sum of SATs, leadership potential ratings, and physical aptitude. GRIT predicted which new arrivals completed the grueling summer training (which used to be called "beast barracks") and which ones dropped out more accurately than any other test and better than all the other tests combined. GRIT also predicted grade point average and military performance scores over the first year, but so did the more traditional tests, and GRIT did not outpredict them. Indeed, a brief self-control scale (a less extreme version of GRIT) outpredicted GRIT for grade point average. Angela replicated this study at West Point in 2006 and then went on to find that GRIT predicted retention in the U.S. Special Forces as well as sales in real estate.

The National Spelling Bee

The Scripps National Spelling Bee involves thousands of kids ages seven to fifteen from all over the world. In 2005, 273 made it to the grueling finals held in Washington, and Angela gave an IQ test and the GRIT test to a large subsample. She also recorded how much time they spent studying the spelling of obscure words. GRIT predicted making it to the final round, while self-control did not. Verbal IQ, the component of IQ about words, also predicted making it to the final round. Finalists who were well above the average GRIT matched for age and IQ had a 21 percent edge in advancing to the final rounds. The statistics showed that gritty finalists outperformed the rest, at least in part because they spent more time studying words. Angela replicated this again the next year and this time found that the additional time practicing accounted for the entire edge GRIT confers.

Building the Elements of Success

Let's review the elements of achievement that have emerged from the theory that achievement = skill × effort:

1. Fast. The sheer speed of thought about a task reflects how much of that task is on automatic; how much skill or knowledge relevant to the task a person has.

2. Slow. Unlike underlying skill or knowledge, the executive functions of planning, checking your work, calling up memories, and creativity are slow processes. The more knowledge and skill you have (acquired earlier by speed and deliberate practice), the more time you have left over to use your slow processes and, hence, the better the outcomes.

3. Rate of learning. The faster your rate of learning—and this is not the same factor as your sheer speed of thought about the task—the more knowledge you can accumulate for each unit of time that you work on the task.

4. Effort = time on task. The sheer time you spend on the task multiplies how much skill you have in achieving your goal. It also enters into the first factor: the more time spent on the task, the more knowledge and skill that accrete, or "stick" with you. The main character determinants of how much time you devote to the task are your self-discipline and your GRIT.

So if your goal is higher achievement for yourself or your child, what should you do?

Not much is known about how to build the first factor: speeding up thought. What speed accomplishes, however, is knowledge; the faster you are, the more knowledge you acquire and put on automatic for each unit of time you spend practicing. Hence, spending more time on the task will build achievement. So even if your child is not innately gifted, deliberate practice will help enormously by building his knowledge base. Practice, practice, practice.

Building slowness allows space for executive function—planning, remembering, inhibiting impulses, and creativity—to grow. As psychiatrist Dr. Ed Hallowell says to children with attention-deficit/hyperactivity disorder, or ADHD, "You have a Ferrari of a mind, and I'm a brake specialist. I am here to help you learn to apply the brakes." Meditation and cultivating deliberation—slow talking, slow reading, slow eating, not interrupting—all work. For young children, Tools of the Mind may work. We need to know much more about how to build patience, an unfashionable but critical virtue.

As far as I know, rate of learning—how much is acquired per unit time—is almost never measured in isolation from the amount of knowledge itself. So nothing is known about how to increase your rate of learning.

The real leverage you have for more achievement is more effort. Effort is no more and no less than how much time you practice the task. Time on task acts in two ways to increase achievement: it multiplies existing skill and knowledge, and it also directly increases skill and knowledge. The best news is that effort is very malleable. How much time you devote to a task comes from the exercise of conscious choice—from free will. Choosing to devote time to an endeavor comes from at least two aspects of positive character: self-control and GRIT.

Higher human accomplishment is one of the four components of flourishing and yet another reason that will and character are indispensible objects of the science of positive psychology. My hope (actually, my prediction) is that this decade will see major discoveries in how to increase GRIT and self-control.

Until recently, I thought of positive education as a worthy ideal, but I wondered if it could ever take hold in the real world. Something big has now happened that is an inflection point for positive education, and that is the story of the next two chapters.

Chapter 7

Army Strong:
Comprehensive Soldier Fitness

"In twenty-five words or fewer," instructed Pete Carroll, the hottest of American college football coaches, fresh from his 2009 Rose Bowl victory with the University of Southern California Trojans, "write down your philosophy of life."

We had two minutes, and along with most of the hundred guests—Special Forces soldiers, intelligence officers, psychologists, a smattering of generals—I sat there dumbfounded. One of the only people actually writing was Brigadier General Rhonda Cornum.

Pete called on Rhonda for her philosophy of life:

"Prioritize.

"A.

"B.

"C.

"Discard C."

Working closely with Rhonda has been one of the great joys of my life. Our collaboration began in August 2008 after a visit to my home from Jill Chambers, the head of a Pentagon program for returning warriors.

A Psychologically Fit Army

Jill, a petite, angular colonel, explained: "We do not want our legacy to be the streets of Washington full of begging veterans, post-traumatic stress disorder, depression, addiction, divorce, and suicide. We have read your books, and we want to know what you suggest for the army."

I had almost forgotten Jill's visit when, in late November 2008, I got invited to lunch at the Pentagon with the chief of staff of the army, the legendary George Casey, former commander of the multinational force in Iraq and former Delta Force hero. General Casey, lithe, short, late fifties, buzz-cut graying hair, walked in, and we all stood to attention. We sat, and I noticed that the three-star general on my left had headed his notes "Seligman Lunch."

"I want to create an army that is just as psychologically fit as it is physically fit," General Casey began. "You are all here to advise me how to go about this cultural transformation."

Cultural transformation indeed, I thought. But right on. My layman's view of the future of warfare was shaped by Major General Bob Scales, the retired head of the U.S. Army War College, a military historian, and the author of the brilliant essay "Clausewitz and World War IV," in the *Armed Forces Journal.* General Scales argued that World War I was a chemical war, World War II was a physics and mathematics war, World War III was a computer war, and that World War IV (which we have entered into already) would be a human war. No sane enemy would confront the United States in the air, on the sea, or with missiles. We are five for five in that kind of warfare. Unfortunately, all the wars that we have fought recently are human wars, and we are zero for seven in these. Vietnam and Iraq are paradigm examples. So it is time for the army to get serious about the human sciences, concludes Scales. An army that was just as psychologically fit as physically fit would be the nose under the tent.

"The key to psychological fitness is resilience," General Casey continued, "and from here on, resilience will be taught and measured throughout the United States Army. Dr. Seligman here is the world's expert on resilience, and he's going to tell us how we are going to do it."

When I had been invited, I'd expected to be told about post-traumatic stress disorder (PTSD) and how the army was treating its veterans. Now, surprised by the turn the meeting had taken, I said a few heartfelt words about what an honor it was to be around a table with this group. Recovering, I repeated what I had told Jill: that focusing on the pathologies of depression, anxiety, suicide, and PTSD was the tail wagging the dog. What the army could do was to move the entire distribution of the reaction to adversity in the direction of resilience and growth. This would not only help prevent PTSD but also increase the number of soldiers who bounce back readily from adversity. Most important, it would increase the number of our soldiers who would grow psychologically from the crucible of combat.

Resilience, at least among young civilians, can be taught. This was the main thrust of positive education, and we had found that depression, anxiety, and conduct problems could be reduced among children and adolescents through resilience training.

"This is compatible with the mission of the army, General Casey," interjected Richard Carmona, the surgeon general of the United States under President George W. Bush. "We spend two trillion dollars every year on health, and seventy-five percent of this goes to treating chronic disease and ministering to old people, like me and Dr. Seligman here. Civilian medicine is perversely incentivized. If we want health, we should concentrate on building resilience—psychologically and physically—particularly among young people. We want a fighting force that can bounce back and cope with the persistent warfare that this next decade promises. Army medicine is incentivized exactly this way. If resilience training works, it will be a model for civilian medicine."

"Let's take this program out of the medical corps, remove the psychiatric stigma, and put resilience into education and training," suggested Lieutenant General Eric Schoomaker, the surgeon general of the army and commander of the medical corps. "If it works, and prevents illness, I know it will cut my budget, since my people are paid by how much illness they treat. But it's the right thing to do."

"That's just what we have started to do," explained the chief of staff. "Dr. Seligman, Comprehensive Soldier Fitness began two months ago. It is under General Cornum's command. The American soldier has rotated between combat and home for more than eight years. The army has incurred a cumulative level of stress that degrades our soldiers' performance and—in many cases—ruins their home-front relationships. I don't know when this era of persistent conflict is going to end, but I am positive that for the foreseeable future American servicemen and women will be in harm's way. It is my responsibility to ensure that our soldiers, their families, and army civilians are prepared both physically and psychologically to continue to serve and support those in combat for years to come. General Cornum, I want you and Marty [Marty!] to put your heads together, put flesh on the skeleton of Comprehensive Soldier Fitness, and report back to me in sixty days."

The next week, Rhonda was at my office at Penn. "Sixty days," she informed me, "is not a lot of time for progress on the three parts of Comprehensive Soldier Fitness that I intend to create. The three components that I want your help in creating are a test of psychological fitness, self-improvement courses to go with the test, and a pilot study of resilience training."

Global Assessment Tool (GAT)

We began by recruiting the people to create the Global Assessment Tool, a self-report questionnaire designed to measure the psychosocial well-being of soldiers of all ranks in four domains: emotional fitness, social fitness, family fitness, and spiritual fitness. The GAT will be used to direct soldiers into different training programs—basic or advanced—as well as a way of evaluating the success of these programs. It will also provide a gauge of the psychosocial fitness of the army as a whole.

Rhonda's tough-minded model for the GAT is work she had done on "financial fitness." It had been common for soldiers to get screwed financially upon leaving the service. Rhonda devised and disseminated a test of financial fitness, tied to a booster course on finance, and she found that it reduced the number of predatory loans among veterans. So our job was to devise a test for these four psychological fitnesses and then find ways of raising each of the four fitnesses parallel to the way the army tests and then trains for high physical fitness.

The army has an outstanding history in the creation of psychological tests that then go on to become standard issue in the civilian world. World War I saw the Army Alpha test for literate soldiers and the Army Beta test for nonliterate soldiers. It was taken by two million soldiers, and its purpose was to separate the mentally "competent" from the "incompetent" and then to select the competent ones for responsible positions. While controversial, group intelligence testing rapidly spread throughout the civilian world, and almost a century later, intelligence testing remains a fixed point in the contemporary world. In World War II, the army developed a variety of tests of more specific abilities. One was the Aviation Psychology Program, which developed new procedures for selecting and classifying flying personnel. It was staffed by a who's who of twentieth-century American psychology. Before World War II, pilots were selected by education, but there were not enough men to fill the slots using just education as the criterion. So a comprehensive battery was developed, including intelligence tests, personality, specific interests, and biographical inventories, along with laboratory tests of alertness, observational acuity, perceptual speed, and coordination. This battery worked: it predicted actual pilot error, although it was not as useful in identifying the most exemplary pilots as it was in identifying the turkeys.

When done well, basic research and applied research are symbiotic, and, perhaps not coincidentally, psychology showed great growth spurts after both wars. Assessment during World War I focused on general ability, and assessment during World War II focused on attitudes and specific ability. Comprehensive Soldier Fitness focuses on assets, and perhaps a similar spurt will happen if this program succeeds in assessing and predicting which soldiers do well. If so, we expect that GAT will become useful to businesses, schools, police and fire departments, and hospitals—any and all settings where doing well—as opposed to the sheer elimination or remediation of doing poorly—is recognized, celebrated, and encouraged.

This was the hope Rhonda and I had in mind for a test of psychological fitness. So we put together a work group of ten expert test makers—half civilian and half military—led by Chris Peterson, a renowned University of Michigan professor and the creator of the VIA Signature Strengths, together with Colonel Carl Castro. They, along with Nansook Park, Chris's colleague at Michigan, worked their butts off over the next few months. They combed through the thousands of relevant items used in prior well-validated tests and created the GAT, which takes only about twenty minutes to complete.

Rhonda's leadership, combining the action orientation of a urological surgeon with the lightning intuition of a general, was very much on display during the creation of the Global Assessment Tool. Soon after it was crafted and then pilot tested on several thousand soldiers, a well-meaning civilian psychologist wrote her querulously, suggesting an improvement in some of the questions. In a terse email to all of us, General Cornum wrote, "The enemy of good is better."

A sampling of Global Assessment Tool items is below. Notice that unlike many psychological tests, the GAT probes for the strengths as well as the weaknesses, the heights as well as the problems, the positives as well as the negatives. It is also entirely confidential: only the soldier sees his or her results. No superior will see the individual results, for two reasons: legal entitlement to privacy, even in the army, and to increase the chances of getting honest answers.

First, the Global Assessment Tool samples *overall satisfaction* (sample items):

All things considered, how satisfied have you been with these parts of your life during the past four weeks?
(Circle one number.)

Very Dissatisfied				Neutral				Very Satisfied	
1	2	3	4	5	6	7	8	9	10

   My life as a whole
   My work
   My friends
   My unit's morale
   My entire family

Think about how you have acted in actual situations described below during the past four weeks. *Please answer only in terms of what you actually did. (You can take a more complete version of the signature strengths part of the Global Assessment Tool in the Appendix.)*

Never									Always
1	2	3	4	5	6	7	8	9	10

— Strengths —

Think of actual situations in which you had the opportunity to do something that was novel or innovative. How often did you use creativity or ingenuity in these situations?

Think of actual situations in which you had a complex and important decision to make. How often did you use critical thinking, open-mindedness, or good judgment in these situations?

Think of actual situations in which you experienced fear, threat, embarrassment, or discomfort. How often did you use bravery or courage in these situations?

Think of actual situations in which you faced a difficult and time-consuming task. How often did you use persistence in these situations?

Think of actual situations in which it was possible for you to lie, cheat, or mislead. How often did you show honesty in these situations?

Think of your everyday life. How often did you feel and show zest or enthusiasm when it was possible to do so?

Think of your everyday life. How often did you express your love or attachment to others (friends, family members) and accept love from others when it was possible to do so?

Think of actual situations in which you needed to understand what other people need or want, and how to respond to them accordingly. How often did you use social skills or social awareness or street smarts in these situations?

Think of actual situations in which you were a member of a group that needed your help and loyalty. How often did you show teamwork in these situations?

Think of actual situations in which you had some power or influence over two or more other people. How often did you use fairness in these situations?

Think of actual situations in which you were a member of a group that needed direction. How often did you use leadership in these situations?

Think of actual situations in which you were tempted to do something that you might later regret. How often did you use prudence or caution in these situations?

Think of actual situations in which you experienced desires, impulses, or emotions that you wished to control. How often did you use self-control in these situations?

— Emotional Fitness (sample items) —
Answer in terms of how you usually think.

Not like me at all
A little like me
Somewhat like me
Mostly like me
Very much like me

When bad things happen to me, I expect more bad things to happen.
I have no control over the things that happen to me.
I respond to stress by making things worse than they are.

These last three items are important to the occurrence of PTSD and depression. They are "catastrophization" items, a cognitive thinking trap that we are specifically concerned to change in resilience training and that I will discuss in the next chapter. If you endorse these items as "very much like me," you are at risk for anxiety, depression, and PTSD.

Some other emotional fitness items:

> *In uncertain times, I usually expect the best.*
> *If something can go wrong for me, it will.*
> *I rarely count on good things happening to me.*
> *Overall, I expect more good things to happen to me than bad.*

These four are optimism items, likely predictors of perseverance under pressure and physical health:

> *My work is one of the most important things in my life.*
> *I would choose my current work again if I had the chance.*
> *I am committed to my job.*
> *How I do in my job influences how I feel.*

These four are engagement items, likely predictors of work performance:

> *I have been obsessed with a certain idea or project for a short time but later lost interest [a GRIT item].*
> *It is difficult for me to adjust to changes.*
> *I usually keep my feelings to myself.*
> *In uncertain times, I usually expect the best.*

— Social Fitness (sample items) —

Please indicate how strongly you agree or disagree with each of the following statements.

> *1 = strongly disagree*
> *2 = disagree*
> *3 = neutral*
> *4 = agree*
> *5 = strongly agree*

My work makes the world a better place.

I trust my fellow soldiers to look out for my welfare and safety.

My closest friends are people in my unit.

Overall, I trust my immediate superior.

— *Spiritual Fitness (sample items)* —

My life has a lasting meaning.

I believe that in some way my life is closely connected to all humanity and all the world.

The job I am doing in the military has lasting meaning.

— *Family Fitness (sample items)* —

I am very close to my family.

I am confident that the army will take care of my family.

The army puts too much of a burden on my family.

The army makes it easy for my family to do well.

Because it is strength-based, the Global Assessment Tool introduces a common vocabulary for describing what is right about soldiers, and as this vocabulary becomes familiar, it will become a way to talk about one's own assets as well as those of other soldiers. Because all soldiers must take the GAT, this may reduce the stigma surrounding mental health services. No soldier will feel singled out, and all soldiers will receive feedback phrased in terms of their strengths. Finally, the GAT will be used to refer soldiers to online courses tailored to their own profile of psychological fitness.

The test was made final in the fall of 2009 when massive testing began. All soldiers will take this test at least once a year throughout their careers. At this writing (September 2010), over 800,000 soldiers have taken it. The initial findings demonstrate validity: as rank and experience go up, so does psychological fitness. As emotional fitness goes up, PTSD symptoms decline. As emotional fitness goes up, health care costs decline. One-fifth of the army is now female, and they are just as psychologically fit as the males. There is only one salient difference: the women score lower on issues of trust than the men.

Since there are 1.1 million soldiers in the army, and many more family members, this will create one of the largest and most complete psychological and physical databases in history. The army will marry the psychological profiles to the performance and medical results over time. This involves the massive job of merging twenty-nine huge databases. It is staggering to imagine the definitive answers we will get to questions that no one has ever been able to answer before, such as:

- What strengths protect against suicide?
- Does a high sense of meaning result in better physical health?
- Do soldiers high in positive emotion heal from wounds faster?
- Does the strength of kindness predict more medals for bravery?
- Does high family fitness predict rapid promotion?
- Does high trust predict more post-traumatic growth?
- Does a good marriage protect against infectious illness?
- Does psychological fitness cause lower health care costs, holding all physical risk factors constant?
- Are there "superhealthy" soldiers, characterized by very high physical and psychological fitness, who rarely get ill, recover rapidly, and perform superbly under stress?
- Is optimism contagious from the commander to the troops?

The Global Assessment Tool is tied to the $1.3 million Soldier Fitness Tracker (SFT), created just for it. The Soldier Fitness Tracker, a massive system of data records, provides an unparalleled information technology platform to support the chief of staff's vision for Comprehensive Soldier Fitness. The SFT provides an agile delivery mechanism for the Global Assessment Tool as well as a powerful data collection and reporting capability. It was built to measure, track, and assess the psychological fitness of all U.S. Army soldiers—not just those on active duty but also those in the National Guard, and Reserve. Online training to improve the soldier's fitness in each domain is also immediately available after completion of the assessment, and I will discuss these training modules shortly. A modified version of the GAT, and these training modules, are available to adult U.S. Army family members and Department of the Army civilian employees. The Soldier Fitness Tracker assesses soldiers beginning when recruits enter the army, with reassessments at appropriate intervals, and it continues through the transition back to civilian life.

Completion of the Global Assessment Tool is a requirement for all soldiers, and to ensure compliance, commanders will be able to "see" who completed the GAT, while still maintaining the confidentiality of the individuals' scores. Commanders can track completion percentages by unit as well as view individual compliance. The Soldier Fitness Tracker will also track the use of online training modules (see below) for the different fitness dimensions. At the Department of the Army level, additional reports can be generated according to rank, sex, and age; average length of time to complete the GAT; and score distribution by location.

Keep this fantastic database and mated technology in mind when we discuss positive health in Chapter 9. This database will allow science to unravel with precision what health assets predict health and illness over and above the usual risk factors.

Online Courses

The army gives college credit for courses on military history, economics, and the like. The second thrust of Comprehensive Soldier Fitness is an online course in each of the four fitnesses, as well as a course in post-traumatic growth for all soldiers. General Cornum invited a leading positive psychologist to head up the development of each course: Barbara Fredrickson for emotional fitness, John Cacioppo for social fitness, John and Julie Gottman for family fitness, Ken Pargament and Pat Sweeney for spiritual fitness, and Rick Tedeschi and Rich McNally for post-traumatic growth. When a soldier takes the Global Assessment Tool, he or she will get back the score and a profile along with recommendations for what courses to take.

Here are the Global Assessment Tool scores for a male lieutenant and how his scores compare to the norms:

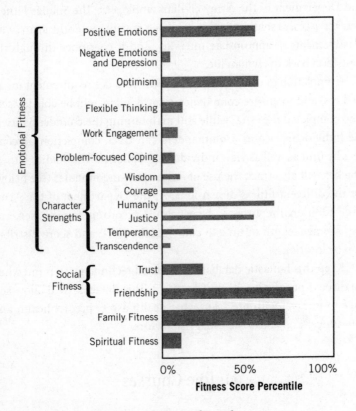

Here is the profile this soldier gets from these scores:

He is a cheerful and optimistic individual, and he is strongly oriented to friends and family. These are his signal assets, but when compared with other soldiers, he is not strongly engaged in his work, and he seems to lack a strong sense of purpose. He is not active in his coping, and he is not a flexible thinker. These characteristics may limit his ability to handle stress and adversity effectively.

So this soldier might benefit from training that encourages flexible thinking and active problem solving as taught in the Penn Resiliency Program for the army as well as the online spiritual fitness training course that helps him see the larger significance of his work. Given his already strong relationships with friends and family, he might further benefit from advanced training in the online family fitness course with an eye to using these assets to enhance his fitness in other domains.

Emotional Fitness Module

Sara Algoe and Barbara Fredrickson take soldiers on a tour of what our emotions do for us and how to use our emotions to better advantage. Negative emotions warn us about a specific threat: when we feel fear, it is almost always preceded by a thought of danger. When we feel sad, there is almost always a thought of loss. When we feel angry, there is almost always a thought of trespass. This leaves us room to pause and identify what is going on when our negative emotional reaction is out of proportion to the reality of the danger, loss, or trespass out there. Then we can modulate our emotional reaction into proportion. This is the essence of cognitive therapy, but in a preventive mode.

What this module teaches soldiers about positive emotion is right at the cutting edge of Fredrickson's research on the Losada ratio. Building a robust Losada ratio (more positive thoughts than negative) by having positive emotions more frequently builds psychological and social capital. This strategy is just as important in a military setting as it is in the boardroom, in a marriage, or in raising teenagers. So this module coaches soldiers on tactics for having more positive emotion as "resource builders." Here are some excerpts from the Algoe and Fredrickson lesson on how to build positive emotion:

— *Take Advantage of Your Emotions* —

Today we are going to discuss how you can take advantage of your positive emotions.

To "take advantage" of positive emotions is not to suggest that you are going to be walking through life only seeing the positive in everything and having a big smile on your face at all times.

The yellow smiley face icon is not the objective. By knowing how they work and what they signal, you will learn to (a) become an active participant in capitalizing on the opportunities that come from positive emotions, (b) find ways to increase the number of instances and the duration of positivity, and (c) be a good citizen of your community.

This training is to give you the tools to become an active participant in your own emotional life . . . In fact, positive emotions are heavy hitters in the emotional system: it is through cultivating the positive that we are able to learn, grow, and flourish. Note that this is not the pursuit of some far-off concept of "happiness." This is just the simple cultivation of moments of different types of positive emotions that can lead you on the path to success.

Positive emotions: the resource builders

The key to taking advantage of positive emotions is to regard them as "resource builders." Please think of a really clear example of a time when you felt one of the positive emotions—pride, gratitude, pleasure, satisfaction, interest, hope—whether it happened today or last week. After you recall some of the details of that event, give it a name (for example, "thinking about the future"), and specify which emotion it was.

Now that you have an example to keep in mind, let's go back to what we know about emotions: the feeling (the emotion) works for us in two ways, by (1) drawing attention and (2) coordinating a response. Positive emotions shine a light on things that are going particularly well for us or that have the potential to do so—that is, situations that are congruent with our goals. These can be thought of as opportunities for resources to be built; for example, if you are interested or inspired, or if you feel that someone has been particularly kind.

Let's take some examples.

- *If you feel admiration toward someone, it means you think they did something to display great skill or talent. As a paragon of success (at least in that domain), if you pay attention this individual, you may pick up on how he or she performs that skill. It would certainly save you a lot of trial-and-error time to do so. Your admiration alerts you to the chance to rapidly learn a culturally valued skill.*

- *If you feel great joy, it means that you have gotten (or are getting) what you desire. Perhaps you received a promotion, had your first child, or are simply enjoying the company of good friends at dinner. Joy represents a satisfied state, which provides the opportunity for growth. In that moment, you are not worried about other things, you are feeling safe and open. Your joy alerts you to opportunities for new experiences.*

- *If you feel pride, it means that you believe you have personally demonstrated some culturally valued skill or talent. Pride gets a bad reputation because, like too much of anything, people can get carried away with their pride, and it becomes self-aggrandizing hubris. However, in appropriate doses, pride alerts you to your own skills and talents, allows you to take credit for them, and sets you up for future successes.*

- *Finally, if you feel gratitude, it means you think that someone has just demonstrated that he or she cares about you as a person and will be there for you in the future. Gratitude marks opportunities to solidify relationships with people who seem to care.*

Having established that positive emotions can be very useful, it is critical to pause and draw attention to the fact that people often do not know that they have such power within them. You have the power within you to figure out what inspires you, what makes you laugh, or what gives you hope, and to cultivate those emotions . . . This can help you optimize your life by setting up moments of genuine positivity for yourself. Do not underestimate the benefits of doing this. These moments can help you to build your own personal and social resources that can be drawn upon in the future. Moreover, the positive effects of your emotions can spread to other people. As you become happier and more satisfied with your life and the things in it, you will have more to give to others.

Family Fitness Module

America is now engaged in the first war in which almost all soldiers have cell phones, Internet access, and webcams. This means that they can contact home at any time. So even in the combat theater, the soldier is virtually in the presence of both the comforts and, unfortunately, the thorns of home life. These thorns are a significant cause of depression, suicide, and PTSD for soldiers. The majority of suicides by our soldiers in Iraq involves a failed relationship with a spouse or partner.

John and Julie Gottman are the preeminent psychologists of marriage in the United States today, and they agreed to create the family fitness module for CSF. Here is what they report:

> *Combat-stress clinics in theater have found that the one major critical incident that precedes suicidal and homicidal ideation in Iraq and Afghanistan is a stressful relationship emotional event. Critical incidents we have collected include such events as phone calls that end in powerful arguments; fights over control and power at home; communications that leave both partners feeling abandoned, lonely, and alienated; an inability of partners to simply be good friends having supportive conversations; not knowing how to relate to their children acting out because they miss their parent terribly; threats to leave the relationship by one or both partners; and major periodic sudden crises in trust and betrayal. Internet pornography for the immediate masturbatory gratification of the soldier and an array of actual sexual opportunities on the Internet for the deployed soldier are a major issue for partners back home. Trust and betrayal are common issues soldiers and partners fight about.*

The Gottmans' module teaches soldiers marriage and relationship skills that they validated in civilian life. It includes skills for "creating and maintaining trust and safety; creating and maintaining friendship and intimacy; increasing trust and honesty; being able to have supportive phone conversations; managing conflict constructively and gently; avoiding conflict escalation leading to violence; cognitive self-soothing; containing and managing physiological and cognitive flooding; soothing one's partner; managing stresses external to the relationship; dealing with and healing from betrayal; converting post-traumatic stress disorder to post-traumatic growth through the relationship; creating and maintaining shared meaning; building and maintaining a positive relationship with each child; practicing effective child discipline; helping each child to learn at home; supporting the child to form healthy peer relationships; skills for breaking up an unhealthy relationship, such as knowing the signs of an unhealthy relationship; reaching out for support from family and friends; reaching out for professional support when needed; buffering the children from the negative effects of a breakup; and making life-affirming new relationship choices for the children and for the self."

Social Fitness Module

> A tribe including many members who, from possessing in a
> high degree the spirit of patriotism, fidelity, obedience, courage, and sympathy, were always ready to aid one another, and
> to sacrifice themselves for the common good, would be victorious over most other tribes; and this would be natural selection.
> —Charles Darwin

John Cacioppo, professor of psychology at the University of Chicago, is one of America's leading social psychologists, a neuroscientist, and the world's foremost expert on the subject of loneliness. It is through his research that the devastating effects of loneliness itself—over and above depression—on mental and physical health have become crystal clear. In a society that overvalues privacy, his work begins to redress the balance between the solitary individual and the flourishing community. John agreed to apply his knowledge to Comprehensive Soldier Fitness by creating the online social fitness module, which he calls Social Resilience.

Social resilience is "the capacity to foster, engage in, and sustain positive social relationships and to endure and recover from stressors and social isolation." It is the glue that holds groups together, provides a purpose larger than the solitary self, and allows entire groups to rise to challenges.

For fifty years, it has been fashionable within evolutionary theory to regard human beings as basically and inexorably selfish. Richard Dawkins's 1976 book *The Selfish Gene* is emblematic of the dogma that natural selection works only through a solitary individual's superior survival and reproductive prowess edging other competing individuals out of the gene pool. Individual selection works well to explain a lot about motivation and behavior, but altruism is an explosive puzzle for selfish-gene theorists. Their way out is to postulate "kinship altruism": the more genes you have in common with the object of your altruism, the more likely you will act altruistically. You may lay down your life for an identical twin, but less readily for a nonidentical sibling (or fraternal twin) or a parent, only remotely for a first cousin, and not at all for an unrelated person.

This convoluted argument flies in the face of ordinary altruism (the fact that nothing makes us feel better than helping another person) and heroic altruism (for example, Christians hiding Jews in their attics in German-occupied European countries during World War II). So common is altruism toward strangers that it led Dacher Keltner to claim in his eye-opening book that we are "Born to be good."

Darwin, quoted above, considered an additional evolutionary pressure, one that I believe fills out the picture: group selection. He postulated that if one group (comprised of genetically unrelated individuals) outsurvives or outreproduces a competing group, the winning group's entire gene pool will multiply. So imagine that cooperation—and hive emotions such as love, gratitude, admiration, and forgiveness, which support cooperation—lead to an edge in survival for that group. A cooperative group will bring down a mastodon more readily than an asocial group. A cooperative group can form the "turtle" in battle: a Roman offensive formation that sacrifices the men on the outer flanks, but easily defeats a group of selfish-only soldiers. A cooperative group can create agriculture, towns, technology, and music (singing, marching, and laughing *tunes* the group). To the extent that cooperation and altruism have a genetic basis, this entire group will pass on its genes more readily than a group that lacks cooperation and altruism. David Sloan Wilson and E. O. Wilson (unrelated genetically), the most forceful advocates of group selection as a supplement to individual selection, ask us to consider the lowly chicken:

How would you select hens to maximize egg production? The selfish gene tells farmers to select the individual hens that produce the most eggs in generation one, breed them, and do the same thing for several generations. By generation six, the farmer should have much better egg production, correct? Wrong! By generation six, using this scheme, there is almost no egg production, and most of the hens have been clawed to death by their hyperaggressive and hyper-egg-laying competitors.

Hens are social, and they live in clutches; so group selection suggests a different way to maximize egg production. Breed the entire clutch that produces the most eggs in each successive generation. Using this method, egg production does indeed become massive. The same logic of natural selection seems to hold for the social insects as well. These enormously successful species (half the biomass of all insects is social) have factories, fortresses, and systems of communication, and their evolution is more compatible with group selection than with individual selection. Human beings, on this account, are ineluctably social, and it is our sociality that is our secret weapon.

In the Social Resilience Module, Cacioppo stresses that "we are not a particularly impressive physical animal. We do not have the benefit of natural weaponry, armor, strength, flight, stealth, or speed relative to many other species. It is our ability to reason, plan, and work together that sets us apart from other animals. Human survival depends on our collective abilities, our ability to join together with others in pursuing a goal, not on our individual might. The cohesiveness and social resilience of the group, therefore, matters. Warriors who understand one another and who communicate well with each other, who are a cohesive group, who like one another and work well together, who take advantage of differences rather than use those differences to avoid one another, and who put themselves at risk for one another are the most likely to survive and emerge victorious."

The Social Resilience Module emphasizes empathy: being able to identify the emotions that another soldier is feeling. First soldiers learn about mirror neurons, and the parallels between the brain activity you undergo when you experience pain yourself and the brain activity of the mirror neurons when you observe that *another* person is in pain. The activity is similar, but not identical, allowing us to empathize but also to tell the difference between our own suffering and that of others. Then soldiers are given photos to practice accurately identifying emotion in others. The module emphasizes racial and cultural diversity; in the U.S. Army, diversity has a long and hallowed tradition, and it is a backbone of army strength, not just a convenient political slogan.

Another core topic of the social fitness module is the important new findings on the contagion of emotion. More than fifty years ago, over five thousand residents of Framingham, Massachusetts, were surveyed for physical health. They were followed across the twentieth century, with cardiovascular disease the main target, and it was this study that gave us the knowledge of the dangers of high blood pressure and cholesterol for heart attacks. Because these residents were followed so intensively, researchers in fields other than heart disease have mined this data set.

In addition to physical data, a few items were psychological (sadness, happiness, loneliness, and the like) and were administered several times; and, of course, the actual location of every house was known. This allowed researchers to draw an emotional "sociogram": a plot of how physical proximity influences emotion into the future. The closer someone lived to someone who was lonely, the lonelier the second individual felt. The same was true for depression, but the blockbuster was about happiness. Happiness was even more contagious than loneliness or depression, and it worked across time. If person A's happiness went up at time 1, person B's—living next door—went up at time 2. And so did person C's, two doors away, by somewhat less. Even person D, three doors away, enjoyed more happiness.

This has significant implications for morale among groups of soldiers and for leadership. On the negative side, it suggests that a few sad or lonely or angry apples can spoil the morale of the entire unit. Commanders have known this forever. But the news is that positive morale is even more powerful and can boost the well-being and the performance of the entire unit. This makes the cultivation of happiness—a badly neglected side of leadership—important, perhaps crucial.

I made just this point to the European Space Agency at a Netherlands meeting of space psychologists planning the European Mars mission scheduled for 2020. Space psychologists are habitually concerned with minimizing negatives in space: suicide, murder, fear, and mutiny. They stand by—on the ground—waiting to give advice when an astronaut gets into emotional trouble. One American astronaut, we were told, almost aborted an entire earth-orbit mission by shutting off communications for several orbits, out of pique that his music player had not yet been repaired in spite of his repeated requests. However, the Mars mission cannot benefit much from psychologists sitting at Mission Control in Noordwijk or Houston: Mars is so far away that there is a ninety-minute communication lag between Earth and a Mars orbiter.

> Astronaut: "That f**ing captain! I am going to shut his oxygen off!"
> [Ninety-minute delay.]
> Psychologist in Houston: "Perhaps you should think critically about how the captain might have trespassed on some right you hold dear."
> Mission control: "Captain. Captain! . . . Come in, Captain!"

Countering negative emotion, perhaps by preloaded modules ("Press one if enraged. Press two if anxious. Press three if despairing"), is important, but to my mind, almost equally important is happiness in space. The entire thrust of this book is that optimal performance is tied to good well-being; the higher the positive morale, the better the performance. This means that fostering happiness in space, particularly over a three-year mission—poker, building flow, strong friendships, a heightened sense of purpose, graded accomplishment—can spell the difference between success and failure. It is particularly scandalous that at present the choice of the six crew members will not be dictated by well-thought-out psychological compatibility but by politics: a correct national, racial, and gender balance.

I blush to tell you that I brought up the topic of gratifying and binding sex in space—three years away from Earth with six high-testosterone women and men. Arranging sexual compatibility seems pretty important. This turns out to be a third-rail issue in Houston—no one dares bring it up—but it was at least discussable in Noordwijk (which is only an hour from Amsterdam). Once they labeled this the "Seligman issue," we then went on to discuss it at length. Antarctic explorations, Himalayan climbing, and Russian space missions, we were told about in detail, have been shattered—utterly destroyed—by sexual conflict. So what to do? What couplings to plan for, what to forbid, what sexualities to select for? Group sex, homosexuality, bisexuality, monogamy, or asexuality? I did not hear any solution to the Seligman issue, which particularly runs afoul of preselecting a politically popular international balance, without regard to what will go on below the neck. But at the least the Europeans are now thinking about it, and well-being in space is now on the training table.

Given the new data on the contagion of positive morale, the right leadership among army units becomes crucial. Twenty years ago, Karen Reivich and I wanted to predict which National Basketball Association teams would come back from defeat and which ones would collapse. To do this, we got all the sports page quotes from every member of the teams over an entire season. We then took each quote and blindly rated it for optimism or pessimism. ("We lost because we suck" got a 7 for pessimism, while "We lost because of that referee's stupid call" got a 7 for optimism.) We then formed an average team profile and tried to predict how each team would do against the point spread after a defeat in the next season. The point spread is the difference between the final scores of the winning and losing teams in a game, as predicted by the expert handicappers in Las Vegas. In the next season, as we forecast, the Boston Celtics (an optimistic team) consistently beat the point spread in the game after a defeat, while the Philadelphia 76ers (a pessimistic team) consistently lost to the point spread after a defeat. Optimistic teams did better than expected after a defeat; pessimistic teams did worse.

This was an enormously laborious study to carry out: extracting and rating every single newspaper quote of every team member for these two teams for a whole season. It was just too much work even for the most dedicated scientist or gambler. After the fact, we decided to look just at the quotes from the coaches. Sure enough, the coaches' optimism predicted resilience just as well as the optimism of the whole team. Maybe we should have known, but now we are convinced that the contagion of happiness and the powerful role of the leader make selecting for positivity and nurturing the well-being of those in command of an army unit especially crucial.

Spiritual Fitness Module

March 16, 1968, was a searing day for America's armed forces. Lieutenant William Calley and his platoons massacred 347 unarmed civilians in the South Vietnamese hamlet of My Lai. Chief Warrant Officer Hugh Thompson was piloting a helicopter over the village while the massacre was taking place. Risking court-martial and the lives of his two-man crew, he put a stop to it by landing and ordering his gunner and crew chief to open fire on the American soldiers if they continued to shoot civilians. An outraged Thompson then reported the horrific incident to his commanding officers and later testified before Congress and at Calley's court-martial. The My Lai tragedy highlights the awful dilemmas that face soldiers both when they are ordered to carry out heinous actions and when they defy regulations to answer to a higher call.

There are two basic rationales for the spiritual fitness module of Comprehensive Soldier Fitness. First, the army has decided that it indeed wants its soldiers to answer to a higher moral order, so that by strengthening soldiers' moral and ethical values, the army's operations—which present knotty moral dilemmas frequently—will be carried out ethically. Second, there is considerable evidence that a higher level of spirituality goes hand in hand with greater well-being, less mental illness, less substance abuse, and more stable marriages, not to mention better military performance—an advantage that is particularly salient when people face major adversity such as combat. Hugh Thompson's spiritual struggle as he prepared to fire on American soldiers in My Lai was likely a fork in the road in his life. His decision was a precondition for growth, and had he let the massacre continue, it likely would have begun a process of personal spiritual decline. We should keep this in mind when we discuss post-traumatic growth in the next chapter.

The First Amendment of the Constitution forbids the government from establishing religion, and so in this module, spiritual fitness is not theological but human. It takes no stand on the validity of religious or secular frameworks. Rather it supports and encourages soldiers to search for truth, self-knowledge, right action, and purpose in life: living by a code that is rooted in belonging to and serving something the soldier believes is larger than the self.

Ken Pargament, professor of psychology at Bowling Green State University, and Colonel Pat Sweeney, professor of behavioral science and leadership at West Point, designed the module. It focuses on the soldier's "spiritual core," consisting of self-awareness, sense of agency, self-regulation, self-motivation, and social awareness.

> *The soldier's spiritual core forms the foundation of the human spirit and is comprised of an individual's most central values and beliefs concerning purpose and meaning in life, truths about the world, and vision for realizing one's full potential and purpose . . .*
>
> *Self-awareness involves reflection and introspection to gain insights into life's pressing questions. These questions pertain to identity, purpose, meaning, truth in the world, being authentic, creating a life worth living, and fulfilling one's potential . . .*
>
> *Sense of agency refers to the individual's assumption of responsibility for the continuous journey to develop one's spirit. This requires people to accept their shortcomings and imperfections and to realize that they are the primary authors of their lives . . .*
>
> *Self-regulation involves the ability to understand and control one's emotions, thoughts, and behavior . . .*
>
> *Self-motivation regarding the human spirit entails the expectancy that the individual's path will lead to the realization of one's deepest aspirations . . .*

Social awareness refers to the realization that relationships play an important role in the development of the human spirit . . . Particularly important is the recognition that other people have the right to hold different values, beliefs, and customs, and that one must, without giving up one's own beliefs, show others due consideration and openness to alternate viewpoints.

The module consists of three tiers of ascending difficulty. The first tier starts with composing a eulogy for a fallen friend and highlights the values and purpose the friend lived by. It is interactive, and the soldier crafts her own parallel eulogy, identifying her strengths and stressing the values at her spiritual core. The second tier is about navigating the moral forks in the road by working through interactive military stories in which the outcome of spiritual struggle leads to growth or decline. Tier three helps soldiers find a deeper connection to the values and beliefs of other people and other cultures. The soldier is introduced to people from diverse backgrounds and works interactively to find common ground with their life experiences and what they hold dear.

These four modules are elective: soldiers will be able to take basic and increasingly advanced versions as they choose. But one module is deemed so essential that it will be required of all soldiers. It is about post-traumatic stress disorder and post-traumatic growth.

Chapter 8

Turning Trauma into Growth

"That is a big idea, Dr. Seligman," said General David Petraeus, "producing more post-traumatic growth rather than just focusing on post-traumatic stress disorder, and approaching training through our soldiers' strengths rather than drilling their weaknesses out of them." I had just briefed the twelve four-star generals led by General Casey about resilience training and the effect it should have on a soldier's reaction to combat.

So let's get literate about post-traumatic stress disorder. This will illuminate one of the basic rationales for Comprehensive Soldier Fitness and will explain what I meant when I told the four-stars that focusing on PTSD was the tail wagging the dog.

Post-Traumatic Stress Disorder

Shell shock and combat fatigue were psychiatric diagnoses from World War I and World War II. But modern thinking about the psychological damage caused by combat begins not in a war but with a flood. In the early morning of February 26, 1972, the dam on Buffalo Creek in the coal region of West Virginia collapsed, and within a few seconds, 132 million gallons of sludge-filled black water roared down upon the residents of the Appalachian mountain hollows below. Kai Erikson, son of the famed psychologist Erik Erikson, wrote a landmark book about this disaster. *Everything in Its Path,* published in 1976, marks the inflection point for thinking about trauma. In it, Erikson articulates what would soon become the criteria for diagnosing PTSD in the third edition of the American Psychiatric Association's *Diagnostic and Statistical Manual,* and was to be liberally (some say "promiscuously") and immediately applied to veterans of the Vietnam War. Listen to the survivors of Buffalo Creek, as chronicled by the younger Erikson.

Wilbur, his wife, Deborah, and their four children managed to survive.

> For some reason, I opened the inside door and looked up the road—and there it came. Just a big black cloud. It looked like twelve or fifteen foot of water . . .
>
> Well, my neighbor's house was coming right up to where we live, coming down the creek . . . It was coming slow, but my wife was still asleep with the baby—she was about seven years old at the time—and the other kids were still asleep upstairs. I screamed for my wife in a bad tone of voice so I could get her attention real quick . . . I don't know how she got the girls downstairs so fast, but she run up there in her sliptail and she got the children out of bed and downstairs . . .
>
> We headed up the road . . . My wife and some of the children went up between the gons [railway gondolas]; me and my baby went under them because we didn't have much time . . . I looked around and our house was done gone. It didn't wash plumb away. It washed down about four or five house lots from where it was setting tore all to pieces.

Two years after the disaster, Wilbur and Deborah describe their psychological scars, the defining symptoms of a post-traumatic stress disorder. First, Wilbur *relives* the trauma repeatedly in his dreams:

> What I went through on Buffalo Creek is the cause of my problem. The whole thing happens over to me even in my dreams, when I retire for the night. In my dreams, I run from water all the time, all the time. The whole thing just happens over and over again in my dreams . . .

Second, Wilbur and Deborah have become *numb* psychologically. Affect is blunted, and they are emotionally anesthetized to the sorrows and joys of the world around them. Wilbur says:

> *I didn't even go to the cemetery when my father died [about a year after the flood]. It didn't dawn on me that he was gone forever. And those people that dies around me now, it don't bother me like it did before the disaster . . . It just didn't bother me that my dad was dead and never would be back. I don't have the feeling I used to have about something like death. It just don't affect me like it used to.*

And Deborah says:

> *I'm neglecting my children. I've just completely quit cooking. I don't do no housework. I just won't do nothing. Can't sleep. Can't eat. I just want to take me a lot of pills and just go to bed and go to sleep and not wake up. I enjoyed my home and my family, but outside of them, to me, everything else in life that I had any interest in is destroyed. I loved to cook. I loved to sew. I loved to keep house. I was all the time working and making improvements on my home. But now I've just got to the point where it don't mean a thing in the world to me. I haven't cooked a hot meal and put it on the table for my children in almost three weeks.*

Third, Wilbur experiences symptoms of *anxiety,* including hyperalertness and phobic reactions to events that remind him of the flood, such as rain and impending bad weather:

> *I listen to the news, and if there is a storm warning out, why, I don't go to bed that night. I sit up. I tell my wife, "Don't undress our little girls; just let them lay down like they are and go to bed and go to sleep and then if I see anything going to happen, I'll wake you in plenty of time to get you out of the house." I don't go to bed. I stay up.*

My nerves is a problem. Every time it rains, every time it storms, I just can't take it. I walk the floor. I get so nervous I break out in a rash. I am taking shots for it now . . .

Wilbur also suffers from survival *guilt*:

At that time, why, I heard somebody holler at me, and I looked around and saw Mrs. Constable . . . She had a little baby in her arms, and she was hollering, "Hey, Wilbur, come and help me; if you can't help me, come get my baby" . . . But I didn't give it a thought to go back and help her. I blame myself a whole lot for that yet. She had her baby in her arms and looked as though she were going to throw it to me. Well, I never thought to go help that lady. I was thinking about my own family. They all six got drowned in that house. She was standing in water up to her waist, and they all got drownded.

These symptoms were officially ratified into a *disorder* in 1980 in the third edition of the *DSM*. Here from the fourth edition are the latest criteria for diagnosing a case of PTSD:

— *309.81 DSM-IV Criteria for Post-traumatic Stress Disorder* —
   A. The person has been exposed to a traumatic event.
   B. The traumatic event is persistently reexperienced.
   C. Persistent avoidance of stimuli associated with the trauma and numbing of general responsiveness.
   D. Persistent symptoms of increased arousal.
   E. Duration of the disturbance (symptoms in Criteria B, C, and D) is more than one month.
   F. The disturbance causes clinically significant distress or impairment in social, occupational, or other important areas of functioning.

An important qualifier, more honored in the breech, is that the symptoms must not be present before the trauma.

PTSD started to make its debut toward the end of the Vietnam

War and was widely applied immediately. Here is a composite case of PTSD from the Iraq War.

Mr. K, a 38-year-old National Guard soldier, was assessed in an outpatient psychiatric clinic several months after he returned home from a 12-month deployment to the Sunni Triangle in Iraq, where he had his first exposure to combat in his 10 years of National Guard duty. Before deployment, he worked successfully as an automobile salesman, was a happily married father with children ages 10 and 12 years, and was socially outgoing with a large circle of friends and was active in civic and church activities. While in Iraq, he had extensive combat exposure. His platoon was heavily shelled and was ambushed on many occasions, often resulting in death or injury to his buddies. He was a passenger on patrols and convoys in which roadside bombs destroyed vehicles and wounded or killed people with whom he had become close. He was aware that he had killed a number of enemy combatants, and he feared that he may also have been responsible for the deaths of civilian bystanders. He blamed himself for being unable to prevent the death of his best friend, who was shot by a sniper. When asked about the worst moment during his deployment, he readily stated that it occurred when he was unable to intercede, but only to watch helplessly, while a small group of Iraqi women and children were killed in the crossfire during a particularly bloody assault.

Since returning home, he has been anxious, irritable, and on edge most of the time. He has become preoccupied with concerns about the personal safety of his family, keeping a loaded 9-mm pistol with him at all times and under his pillow at night. Sleep has been difficult, and when sleep occurs, it has often been interrupted by vivid nightmares during which he thrashes about, kicks his wife, or jumps out of bed to turn on the lights. His children complained that he has become so overprotective that he will not let them out of his sight. His wife reported that he has been emotionally distant since his return. She also believed that driving the car had become dangerous when he is a passenger because he has sometimes reached over suddenly to grab the steering wheel because he thinks he has seen a road-side bomb. His friends have wearied of inviting him to social gatherings because he has consistently turned down all invitations to get together. His employer, who has patiently supported him, has reported that his work has suffered dramatically, that he seems preoccupied with his own thoughts and irritable with customers, that he often makes mistakes, and that he has not functioned effectively at the automobile dealership where he was previously a top salesman. Mr. K acknowledged that he has changed since his deployment. He reported that he sometimes experiences strong surges of fear, panic, guilt, and despair and that at other times he has felt emotionally dead, unable to return the love and warmth of family and friends. Life has become a terrible burden. Although he has not been actively suicidal, he reported that he sometimes thinks everyone would be better off if he had not survived his tour in Iraq.

The diagnosis has been a staple of the U.S. Medical Corps throughout the present Iraq and Afghanistan wars, with as many as 20 percent of the soldiers said to be afflicted, and this is exactly what had brought me the invitation to lunch with the generals.

I told the generals that there is a bell-shaped distribution of the human response to high adversity. At the extremely vulnerable end, the result is pathology: depression, anxiety, substance abuse, suicide, and what had now found its way into the official diagnostic manual as PTSD. Every soldier going to Iraq or Afghanistan has heard of PTSD. But the human species has evolved through millennia of trauma, and far and away the usual response to high adversity is resilience—a relatively brief episode of depression plus anxiety, followed by a return to the previous level of functioning.

At West Point, we found that more than 90 percent of cadets had heard of post-traumatic stress disorder, which in reality is relatively uncommon, but less than 10 percent had heard of post-traumatic growth, which is not uncommon. This is medical illiteracy that matters. If all a soldier knows about is PTSD, and not about resilience and growth, it creates a self-fulfilling downward spiral. Your buddy was killed yesterday in Afghanistan. Today you burst into tears, and you think, *I'm falling apart; I've got PTSD; my life is ruined.* These thoughts increase the symptoms of anxiety and depression—indeed, PTSD is a particularly nasty combination of anxiety and depression—which in turn increases the intensity of the symptoms. Merely knowing that bursting into tears is not a symptom of PTSD but a symptom of normal grief and mourning, usually followed by resilience, helps to put the brakes on the downward spiral.

Post-traumatic stress disorder surely increases in likelihood because of the self-fulfilling nature of the downward spiral that catastrophizing and believing you have PTSD engenders. Individuals who are catastrophizers to begin with are much more susceptible to PTSD. One study followed 5,410 soldiers through their army careers from 2002 to 2006. Over this five-year period, 395 were diagnosed with PTSD. More than half of them were in the bottom 15 percent of mental and physical health to begin with. This is most reliable—and one of the least quoted—facts in the entire PTSD literature: the people who are in bad shape to begin with are at much greater risk for PTSD than more psychologically fit people, and PTSD can often better be seen as an exacerbation of preexisting symptoms of anxiety and depression than as a first case. It is just these findings that underpin one rationale for the resilience training in CSF (below): by strengthening our soldiers psychologically before combat, we can prevent some cases of PTSD.

Here I must assume a curmudgeonly voice. The residents were suing the Pittston Company, the owners of the dam, for more than $1 billion. In my opinion, that kind of money can lead to exaggerated and prolonged symptoms even though the literature suggests that the survivors were not malingering. They won the lawsuit eventually, so we will never know what effect the financial incentive had. A parallel system is at work in military PTSD, unfortunately. A diagnosis of full-blown PTSD will earn a veteran a disability payment of around $3,000 a month for the rest of his life. Becoming gainfully employed or experiencing remission of the symptoms ends the reimbursement. Once veterans get the diagnosis and the disability payments begin, 82 percent do not return for therapy. We do not know what effect this substantial incentive is having on the diagnosis of PTSD from our wars, but the 20 percent rate often reported from Iraq and Afghanistan is way above the rates in previous wars or the rates shown in other armies that do not reimburse PTSD as a disability. British soldiers returning from Iraq and Afghanistan have a PTSD rate of 4 percent. I have combed the Civil War writings and can find almost no PTSD or anything much like it from that horrific epoch.

Skepticism aside, I want to say clearly that I am sure there is a core PTSD. I do not believe that PTSD is malingering. My doubts are about overdiagnosis. I believe that our society owes much more than we now give to our returning veterans by way of gratitude and by way of money. I do not believe, however, that the gratitude should come by way of a disability diagnosis and a system that robs our veterans of their pride.

Post-Traumatic Growth

Never to be forgotten, finally, is post-traumatic growth (PTG). A substantial number of people also show intense depression and anxiety after extreme adversity, often to the level of PTSD, but then they grow. In the long run, they arrive at a higher level of psychological functioning than before. "What does not kill me makes me stronger," said Nietzsche. Those old soldiers who populate Veterans of Foreign Wars posts and tell war stories are not in denial—war was indeed the best time of their lives.

A few years ago, Chris Peterson, Nansook Park, and I added a link to my Authentic Happiness website www.authentichappiness.org. The new questionnaire listed the fifteen worst things that can happen in a person's life: torture, grave illness, death of a child, rape, imprisonment, and so on. In a month, 1,700 people reported at least one of these awful events, and they took our well-being tests as well. To our surprise, individuals who'd experienced one awful event had more intense strengths (and therefore higher well-being) than individuals who had none. Individuals who'd been through two awful events were stronger than individuals who had one, and individuals who had three—raped, tortured, and held captive for example—were stronger than those who had two.

Brigadier General Rhonda Cornum is a poster child for post-traumatic growth. I had read about Rhonda back in 1991 when she was a major and a prisoner of war of Saddam Hussein's army. Cornum—MD urologist, PhD biochemist, flight surgeon, jet pilot, civilian helicopter pilot—was on a rescue mission over the Iraqi desert when her helicopter was hit by enemy fire. As it went down, the tail boom was blown off, and all but three of the eight-person crew were killed.

Rhonda, both arms and a leg broken, was taken prisoner. She was sexually assaulted and brutally treated. Released eight days later, she came back a war hero. She describes the aftereffects of her traumatic experience:

- Relating to patients: "I felt much better prepared to be a military physician and surgeon than previously. The concerns of my patients were no longer academic."
- Personal strength: "I felt far better equipped to be a leader and commander. That is the standard by which other experiences are now based, and so I feel much less anxiety or fear when faced with challenges."
- Appreciation of family: "I became a better, more attentive parent and spouse. I made the effort to remember birthdays, to visit grandparents, and so on. No doubt, coming that close to losing them made me appreciate them more."
- Spiritual change: "An out-of-body experience changed my perceptions; I was now open to at least the possibility of a spiritual life versus a physical life."
- Priorities: "While I had always organized my life into the A, B, and C piles of priority, I became much more rigorous about dispensing with the C pile. (I always go to my daughter's soccer games!)"

After she was freed, a colonel said to her, "It's too bad you are a woman, Major, otherwise you could be a general." I have since seen the legend personally: when she walked into a cavernous auditorium where we were both speaking in August 2009, 1,200 majors and colonels rose to their feet and applauded. As the general in charge of CSF, Rhonda takes more than a detached professional interest in the PTG module.

Post-Traumatic Growth Course

She recruited two professors of psychology to oversee the PTG module: Richard Tedeschi, the academic leader of the PTG field, from the University of North Carolina at Charlotte, and Harvard's Richard McNally. The module begins with the ancient wisdom that personal transformation is characterized by renewed appreciation of being alive, enhanced personal strength, acting on new possibilities, improved relationships, and spiritual deepening, all of which often follow tragedy. Data support this: in just one example, 61.1 percent of imprisoned airmen tortured for years by the North Vietnamese said that they had benefited psychologically from their ordeal. What's more, the more severe their treatment, the greater the post-traumatic growth. This is not remotely to suggest that we celebrate trauma itself; rather we should make the most of the fact that trauma often sets the stage for growth, and we must teach our soldiers about the conditions under which such growth is most likely to happen.

Post-Traumatic Growth Inventory

Dr. Tedeschi uses the Post-Traumatic Growth Inventory (PTGI) to measure the phenomenon. Here are some sample items:

> *0 = I did not experience this change as a result of my crisis.*
> *1 = I experienced this change to a very small degree as a result of my crisis.*
> *2 = I experienced this change to a small degree as a result of my crisis.*

3 = I experienced this change to a moderate degree as a result of my crisis.

4 = I experienced this change to a great degree as a result of my crisis.

5 = I experienced this change to a very great degree as a result of my crisis.

I have a greater appreciation for the value of my own life.

I have a better understanding of spiritual matters.

I established a new path for my life.

I have a greater sense of closeness with others.

New opportunities are available which wouldn't have been otherwise.

I put more effort into my relationships.

I discovered that I'm stronger than I thought I was.

The module teaches soldiers interactively about five elements that are known to contribute to post-traumatic growth. The first element is to *understand the response to trauma* itself: shattered beliefs about the self, others, and the future. This is, I want to emphasize, the normal response to trauma; it is not a symptom of post-traumatic stress disorder, nor does it indicate a defect of character. The second element is *anxiety reduction,* which consists of techniques for controlling intrusive thoughts and images. The third element is *constructive self-disclosure.* Bottling up trauma likely leads to a worsening of physical and psychological symptoms, so soldiers are encouraged to tell the story of the trauma. This leads to the fourth element: *creating a trauma narrative.* The narrative is guided, with the trauma seen as a fork in the road that enhances the appreciation of paradox. Loss and gain both happen. Grief and gratitude both happen. Vulnerability and strength both happen. The narrative then details what personal strengths were called upon, how some relationships improved, how spiritual life strengthened how life itself was better appreciated, and what new doors opened. Finally, overarching *life principles and stances that are more robust to challenge* are articulated. These include new ways to be altruistic, accepting growth without survivor guilt, crafting a new identity as a trauma survivor or a newly compassionate person, and taking seriously the Greek ideal of the hero who returns from Hades to tell the world an important truth about how to live.

Master Resilience Training

The first two components of CSF are the Global Assessment Tool and the five online fitness courses. The real challenge is training, however. Can the army train soldiers to become more psychologically fit, just as the army trains for physical fitness? At the November 2008 meeting, General Casey ordered us to come back in sixty days and report. Sixty days later, we were back at lunch at the Pentagon.

"We have developed a test to measure psychological fitness, sir," General Cornum said to General Casey. "It takes only twenty minutes, and it has been constructed by a group of the leading civilian and military test experts. We are piloting it now with several thousand soldiers."

"Fast work, General. What do you and Marty want to do next?"

"We want to do a pilot study on resilience training." Rhonda and I had planned our response to this question at length. "Marty has shown in his work on positive education that ordinary schoolteachers can be taught to deliver resilience training effectively to adolescents. The students then have less depression and anxiety. Who are the schoolteachers in the army? The sergeants, of course. [The drill sergeants, my God!] So here is what we want to do: a proof-of-concept study in which we take one hundred sergeants at random and give them master trainer resiliency classes for ten days at Penn—teaching the teachers. These sergeants will then train the soldiers under their command in resilience. We can then compare these two thousand soldiers to a control group."

"Hold on," General Casey thundered. "I don't want a pilot study. We've studied Marty's work. They've published more than a dozen replications. We are satisfied with it, and we are ready to bet it will prevent depression, anxiety, and PTSD. This is not an academic exercise, and I don't want another study. This is war. General, I want you to roll this out to the whole army."

"But, sir," Rhonda began gently to demur. As she started to enu-
merate all the bureaucratic and budgetary steps a whole-army rollout
entails, my mind wandered back to a memorable conversation on the
streets of Glasgow, Scotland, three years before with Richard Layard.

Richard is a world-class economist from the London School of
Economics. In medieval monasteries, the post of abbot bridged the
worlds of the secular and the sacred. This is the role that Richard plays
in British politics, bridging academic research and the real political
scrum. He is also the author of *Happiness,* a radical view of government in which he argues that government policy should be measured
not by increases in gross domestic product but by increases in global
well-being. He and his wife, Molly Meacher, are one of only two couples in the House of Lords. Merit lords, not hereditary lords.

Richard and I were strolling through a seedy section of Glasgow in
between sessions of the inaugural event of Scotland's Centre for Confidence and Well-Being, a quasi-governmental institution intended to
counter the "c'nnot do" attitude said to be endemic to Scottish education and commerce. We were the keynote speakers.

"Marty," Richard said in his mellifluous Etonian accent, "I've read
your work on positive education, and I want to take it to the schools of
the United Kingdom."

"Thanks, Richard," I said, appreciative that our work was being
considered in high Labor Party circles. "I think I am just about ready
to try a pilot study in a Liverpool school."

"You don't get it, do you, Marty?" said Richard, a mildly scathing
tone in his voice. "You, like most academic types, have a superstition
about the relation of public policy to evidence. You probably think that
Parliament adopts a program when the scientific evidence mounts and
mounts, up to a point that it is compelling, irresistible. In my whole
political life, I have never seen a single example of this. Science makes
it into public policy when the evidence is sufficient and the political
will is present. I'm telling you that your positive education evidence is
sufficient—'satisficing,' as we economists call it—and the political will
is now present in Whitehall. So I'm going to take positive education to
the schools of the United Kingdom."

This was the single most sensible statement of the mysterious relationship between the micro and the macro that I have ever heard. It was a conversion experience for me. I emphasize it above for that reason, and if you are an academic and you remember nothing else from this book, remember what Lord Layard told me in Glasgow. The most frustrating experience of my professional life had been to see fine scientific ideas, backed by ample laboratory evidence, die again and again on some boardroom floor or just gather dust in the library. I wondered—and this is at the very heart of this book—why positive psychology is so popular now with the general public and in the press. It is certainly not that the evidence is irresistible. The science is quite new, and the evidence, if not scanty, is far from irresistible. Why had I worn out my knees begging granting agencies—often in vain—for so many years about learned helplessness, about explanatory style and depression, about cardiovascular disease and pessimism, when, now, generous individuals, unasked, would just write large checks upon hearing me lecture once about positive psychology?

As I tuned back in to the generals from this musing, General Cornum was reminding General Casey of all the budgetary and bureaucratic steps that she would have to go through and how long they took. "Battlemind, our current psychological program, sir, has been through only six of the ten steps, and it's been around for more than a year."

"General Cornum," said General Casey, ending the meeting, "you are to make resilience training happen for the whole army. Move out."

Talk about strength of will.

So the question that Rhonda and I confronted in February 2009 was how to disseminate resilience training rapidly and widely. We also had to figure out how to do it responsibly, allowing us to make trajectory corrections in the training materials as well as track its effectiveness, so that in the worst case, we could pull the plug on the program if it was not working.

The positive education teacher training course we had developed was written for civilian schoolteachers. Our first step now was to rewrite all the training material for sergeants and for their troops.

Dr. Karen Reivich, Penn's number one master trainer and the Oprah Winfrey of positive psychology, was in charge of "militarizing" the material. Over the next eight months, Karen and her staff met with more than a hundred Iraq and Afghanistan veterans and went over our training materials with them word by word.

Our first big surprise emerged from these conversations. We thought that our civilian examples—being dumped by a girlfriend or failing a test—would be irrelevant to warriors. How wrong we were.

"This is the first war that you have a cell phone and can call your wife from the front line," observed General Cornum's executive officer, Colonel Darryl Williams. A six-foot-three-inch West Point football star and Iraq veteran, he'd been the carrier of the "football" with the nuclear war codes for President Bill Clinton. "Watching out for improvised explosive devices is trouble enough, but squabbling about the dishwasher and the kids' grades makes it worse," he continued. "Much of the depression and anxiety our soldiers have is about what is going on at home. So your civilian examples fit well as they are. Just add some good military ones."

We reworked the examples and began the full-blown Master Resilience Training (MRT) in December 2009. Now, every month, 150 sergeants come to Penn for eight days, and we simulcast the training to forts, where our Penn-trained facilitators were stationed. We spend the first five days providing the sergeants firsthand experience practicing the skills for use in their own lives as soldiers, leaders, and family members. They attend full-group sessions in which lead trainer Dr. Karen Reivich presents core content, demonstrates the use of the skills, and leads discussions. Following the plenary sessions, the sergeants go to thirty-person breakout sessions in which they practice what they learned using role playing, work sheets, and small-group discussion. Each breakout session is led by a trainer (trained by Karen) and four facilitators: two civilian (most of them master of applied positive psychology graduates) and two army (also trained by Karen). We have found that the ratio of five training-team members for thirty participants works well.

Following the first five days, the sergeants get a second set of materials (MRT trainer manual, MRT soldier guide, PowerPoint presentations) that they will use when they teach Master Resilience Training to their soldiers. Three full days are then devoted to preparing the sergeants with the depth of knowledge and teaching skills to deliver the program with fidelity. They work through a series of activities: role plays in which one sergeant assumes the role of teacher and five others assume the roles of soldiers; five-person teams of sergeants crafting challenging questions that must be answered by another five-person team; identifying delivery mistakes and content confusions during mock sessions led by the MRT trainer; and identifying the appropriate skills to use with actual soldier problem situations.

We divide the content of the training into three parts: building mental toughness, building strengths, and building strong relationships. All of these parts are patterned after the well-validated program we use to teach civilian teachers.

Building Mental Toughness

The theme of this part is learning the skills of resilience. We start with Albert Ellis's ABCDE model: C (the emotional consequences) do not stem directly from A (the adversity) but from B (your beliefs about the adversity). This simple fact comes as a surprise to many of the sergeants, dispelling the common belief that adversity sets off emotion directly. The sergeants work through a series of professional A's (You fall out of a three-mile run) and personal A's (You return from deployment, and your son does not want to play basketball with you), with the goal of being able to separate the adversity (A) from what he says to himself in the heat of the moment (B) and from the emotions or actions his thoughts generate (C). By the end of this skill session, the sergeants can identify specific thoughts that drive particular emotions: for instance, thoughts about trespass drive anger; thoughts about loss drive sadness; thoughts about danger drive anxiety.

We then focus on thinking traps. I'll give you an example. To illustrate the thinking trap of overgeneralizing (judging a person's worth or ability based on a single action), we present the following: "A soldier in your unit struggles to keep up during physical training and is dragging the rest of the day. His uniform looks sloppy, and he makes a couple of mistakes during artillery practice. You think to yourself, *He's soup sandwich! He doesn't have the stuff of a soldier.*" Following this case, the sergeants describe the thinking trap and discuss its effects on the soldier he is leading and on the sergeant himself.

One sergeant commented, "I hate to admit it, but I think that way a lot. I write people off if they screw up. I guess I'm not big on second chances because I think you can judge a person's character through their actions. If that guy had a strong character, he wouldn't be dragging and his uniform wouldn't be in disarray." The sergeants then ask, "What *specific* behaviors explain the situation?" learning to focus on behaviors, as opposed to the soldier's general worth.

We then turn to "icebergs," deeply held beliefs that often lead to out-of-kilter emotional reactions (such as, "Asking for help is a sign of weakness"), and they learn a technique for identifying when an iceberg drives an out-of-proportion emotion. Once the iceberg is identified, they ask themselves a series of questions to determine: (1) if the iceberg continues to be meaningful to them; (2) if the iceberg is accurate in the given situation; (3) if the iceberg is overly rigid; (4) if the iceberg is useful. The iceberg "Asking for help shows weakness" is frequent and poignant, because it undermines the willingness to seek help and rely on others. This iceberg requires sergeants to do a lot of work to change because historically soldiers felt stigmatized if they sought out help and were often ridiculed for not being strong enough to handle their own problems.

Many sergeants commented that they believe the culture around help seeking is now shifting in the army. One sergeant commented, "There was a time when I would have called a soldier a [expletive] for seeing a counselor or going to a chaplain. And if I didn't say it to his face, I sure would have thought it. I don't see it that way anymore. Multiple deployments have taught me that we're all going to need help from time to time, and it's the strong ones that are willing to ask for it."

Following icebergs, we deal with how to *minimize catastrophic thinking.* We are bad-weather animals, naturally attracted to the most catastrophic interpretation of adversity, since we are the descendants of people who survived the Ice Age. Those of our ancestors who thought, *It's a nice day in New York today; I bet it will be nice tomorrow,* got crushed by the ice. Those who thought, *It only looks like a nice day; here comes the ice, the flood, the famine, the invaders, oy! Better store some food!* survived and passed down their brains to us. Sometimes thinking and planning for the very worst is useful; more often, however, it is paralyzing and unrealistic, so learning to calibrate the catastrophic realistically is a crucial battlefield and home-front skill.

Here the sergeants watch a video clip of a soldier unable to contact his wife via email. He thinks, *She's left me,* and this produces depression, paralysis, and fatigue. Now we introduce a three-step model, "Putting It in Perspective," for disputing catastrophic thinking: worst case, best case, most likely case.

You've called home several times and haven't been able to reach your wife. You think to yourself, *She's running around on me.*

That's the worst case.

Now let's put it in perspective. What's the best possible case?

"Her patience and strength never waver even for a second."

Okay, now what's the most likely case?

"She's out with a friend, and she'll email me later tonight or tomorrow. My wife will rely on others instead of me while I'm deployed. I will be envious and angry when my wife relies on others; she will feel lonely and scared while I'm away."

After the most likely outcome is identified, they develop a plan for coping with the situation, and then practice this skill with both professional examples (a soldier has not returned from a land navigation drill; you received a negative review from a superior) and personal examples (your child is doing poorly at school, and you are not home to help; your spouse is having a hard time managing the finances while you are deployed).

The Hot Seat: Fighting Catastrophic Thoughts in Real Time

These skills are used when there is a task that requires immediate attention, and performance will be compromised if the soldier is distracted by "mental chatter." Examples include: going in front of a promotion board, leaving the forward operating base to check for improvised explosive devices, demonstrating your combat skills, or pulling into your driveway after a stressful day on post.

There are three strategies for challenging the catastrophic beliefs in real time: gathering evidence, using optimism, and putting it in perspective. Sergeants learn how to use these skills and how to correct unrealistic errors midstream (one time/one thing, owning the situation, and taking appropriate responsibility). This skill is not about replacing every negative thought with a positive one. It is designed to be a stopgap so that the soldier is able to focus right now and does not put himself (or others) at greater risk because of paralyzing, unrealistic thoughts. There is a time and place to focus on persistent negative thoughts because often there is something that can be learned from them.

For example, one sergeant said that he was constantly barraged by negative thoughts about whether his wife truly loved him and that these thoughts often interfered with his ability to stay focused. He believed the theme of his thoughts came from the iceberg "I'm not the kind of guy women love." It is important to fight off these thoughts at certain times, such as when trying to get much-needed sleep or when engaging in high-risk maneuvers. It is also important to pay attention to these beliefs and thoughtfully evaluate them during the more appropriate breathing spells.

It is important that these mental-toughness skills perfectly capture the skills of learned optimism, the skills that resist learned helplessness. Recall that the aim of Comprehensive Soldier Fitness is to move the entire distribution of trauma responses toward more resilience and post-traumatic growth. But this should also have a preventive effect on post-traumatic stress disorder (the tail of the distribution). PTSD is a nasty combination of anxiety and depressive symptoms, and resilience (optimism) training has a clear preventive effect on both. It is, moreover, the soldiers in the bottom 15 percent in mental fitness and physical fitness who are particularly vulnerable to PTSD, so arming them in advance with antianxiety and antidepression skills should be preventive. Finally, in a 2009 review of 103 studies of post-traumatic growth, Italian researchers Gabriele Prati and Luca Pietrantoni found that optimism was a major contributor to growth. So the theory suggests that building mental toughness should both move soldiers toward growth as well as prevent PTSD. We won't rest on theory, however, since the army will be measuring all of this very carefully. Stay tuned.

Hunt the Good Stuff

Throughout the program, the sergeants keep a gratitude journal (also called a three-blessings journal). The purpose of "Hunt the Good Stuff" is to enhance positive emotions; our rationale is that people who habitually acknowledge and express gratitude see benefits in their health, sleep, and relationships, *and* they perform better. Each morning of the MRT course, several of the sergeants share something that they had "hunted" from the day before, as well as their reflection on what the positive event meant to them. These range from "I had a great conversation with my wife last night; I used what we learned in class, and she said it was one of the best conversations we've ever had," to "I stopped and talked to a homeless guy, and I learned a lot from him," to "The owner of the restaurant didn't charge us for our dinner as a way to say thank you to the army."

As the week unfolds, the blessings become more personal. The morning of the final day, one sergeant said, "I talked to my eight-year-old son last night. He told me about an award he won at school, and usually I'd just say something like 'That's nice.' But I used the skill we learned yesterday, and I asked a bunch of questions about it: Who was there when he got the award? How did he feel receiving it? Where's he going to hang the award?

"About halfway through the conversation, my son interrupted me and said, 'Dad, is this really you?!' I knew what he meant by that. That was the longest we ever talked, and I think we were both surprised by it. It was great."

Character Strengths

After the mental-toughness skills, we turn to identifying character strengths. The *Army Field Manual* describes the core character strengths of a leader: loyalty, duty, respect, selfless service, honor, integrity, and personal courage. We review these and then have the sergeants complete the online Values in Action Signature Strengths survey and bring to class a printout of their twenty-four strengths, ranked in order. We define "signature strength," and the sergeants post their names around the room on large flip charts, each labeled with one of the strengths. Flip charts that are very full of Post-it notes reveal what the most common sergeant strengths are. The sergeants look for patterns within the group and discuss what the group strength profile reflects about them as leaders. Following this activity, small groups discuss: "What did you learn about yourself from the strengths survey? Which strengths have you developed through your service in the military? How do your strengths contribute to your completing a mission and reaching your goals? How are you using your strengths to build strong relationships? What are the shadow sides of your strengths, and how can you minimize these?"

We then shift the focus to using strengths to overcome challenges. Colonel Jeff Short of the Comprehensive Soldier Fitness team presents a case study that describes how he led his unit, the 115th, out of Fort Polk, Louisiana, to set up a combat support hospital at Abu Ghraib prison to provide all detainee health care, including inpatient and outpatient care. As Jeff describes the challenges of setting up the field hospital and caring for the detainees, the sergeants keep track of each instance of an individual or the team pulling on a character strength and the specific actions it enabled. For example, the field hospital needed a "wound vacuum," but none was available. A nurse demonstrated the strength of creativity when she came up with a way to create one out of an old vacuum cleaner.

Next the sergeants break into small groups and tackle a mission that they need to complete as a unit. We instruct them to use their team's character strengths to complete the mission, with the team using the strengths available. Finally, the sergeants write their own "Strengths in Challenges" stories. One sergeant described how he used his strengths of love, wisdom, and gratitude to help an undisciplined soldier who was acting out and stirring up conflicts. The sergeant used his strength of love to engage the soldier, whereas most others avoided the troublemaker because he was so hostile. The sergeant discovered that the soldier felt consumed by anger at his wife, and his anger spilled over to the soldiers in his unit. Then, operating from his strength of wisdom, the sergeant helped the soldier to understand the wife's perspective and worked with him to write a letter in which the soldier described the gratitude he feels because his wife has to handle so much on her own during his three deployments.

Building Strong Relationships

Our final module focuses on how to strengthen relationships with other soldiers and at home. Our goal is to provide practical tools that build relationships and to challenge beliefs that interfere with positive communication. The work of Dr. Shelly Gable shows that when an individual responds actively and constructively (as opposed to passively and destructively) to someone sharing a positive experience, love and friendship increase. So we teach the four styles of responding: active constructive (authentic, enthusiastic support), passive constructive (understated support), passive destructive (ignoring the event), and active destructive (pointing out negative aspects of the event). We demonstrate each through a series of role plays. The first role play focuses on two privates who are close friends:

> Private Johnson tells Private Gonzales "Hey, my wife called and told me she got a great job on post."
>
> Active constructive: "That's great. What's the new job? When does she start? What did she say about how she got it and why she deserved it?"
>
> Passive constructive: "That's nice."
>
> Passive destructive: "I got a funny email from my son. Listen to this . . ."
>
> Active destructive: "So who's going to be looking after your son? I wouldn't trust a babysitter. There are so many horror stories you hear about babysitters abusing kids."

After each role play, the sergeants complete a worksheet about their own typical ways of responding and identify what makes it hard for them to respond actively and constructively (such as being tired or being overly focused on themselves), as well as how they can use their signature strengths to stay active and constructive: for example, using the strength of curiosity to ask questions, using the strength of zest to respond enthusiastically, or using the strength of wisdom to point out valuable lessons to be learned from the situation.

We then teach Dr. Carol Dweck's work on effective praise. What do you say when praise is warranted? For example: "I aced my PT test." "We cleared the building without sustaining any casualties." "I was promoted to master sergeant." We teach the sergeants to praise the specific skills as opposed to a vague "Way to go!" or "Good job!" Praising the details demonstrates to their soldier (a) that the leader was really watching, (b) that the leader took the time to see exactly what the soldier did, and (c) that the praise is authentic, as opposed to a perfunctory "Good job."

Finally, we teach assertive communication, describing the differences among passive, aggressive, and assertive styles. What is the language, voice tone, body language, and pace of each style? What messages does each style convey? For example, the passive style sends the message "I don't believe you'll listen to me anyway." We found in our positive education work that a critical aspect is to explore the icebergs that lead to one style of communicating over another. Someone who has the belief "People will take advantage of any sign of weakness" tends toward an aggressive style. A person who believes "It's wrong to complain" will have a passive style, and the belief "People can be trusted" brings about an assertive style.

So we teach a five-step model of assertive communication:

1. Identify and work to understand the situation.
2. Describe the situation objectively and accurately.
3. Express concerns.
4. Ask the other person for his/her perspective and work toward an acceptable change.
5. List the benefits that will follow when the change is implemented.

The sergeants practice this with military scenarios: your battle buddy has started drinking too much and has been seen drinking and driving; your husband is spending money on things you don't consider essential; a fellow soldier continues to take your belongings without asking permission. Following these role plays, the sergeants identify a thorny situation that they are currently confronting and practice using assertive communication. One poignant area is exploring how they talk to their own families. Many sergeants tell us they communicate too aggressively with spouses and too forcefully with their children because it is difficult to change from the fast-paced, command-oriented world of their job to the more democratic focus that works so much better at home.

One sergeant stopped me in the hallway after this session and thanked me, saying, "If I had learned this stuff three years ago, I wouldn't be divorced."

In spite of the intention to help our soldiers and others through my work with the army, as I've discussed in these two chapters, some journalists have chosen to look at it through a glass darkly and persist in searching for some nefarious intent on my part to use science to harm. Some critics have claimed that this program "brainwashes" soldiers with positive thinking: "Moreover, wouldn't soldiers like their officers to consider worst-case scenarios before ordering them into combat? . . . The healthy option to negative thinking is not positive thinking but critical thinking." We do not teach mindless positive "thinking." What we teach *is* critical thinking: the thinking skills to distinguish between irrational worst-case scenarios that paralyze action and the more likely scenarios. This is a thinking skill that enables planning and action.

Other critics have even implied that I supported the use of my work in learned helplessness for the purposes of psychological intimidation and the torture of detainees and supposed terrorists by some parts of the military during the George W. Bush administration's so-called war on terror.

This could not be further from the truth. I have never and would never provide assistance in torture. I strongly disapprove of torture. I condemn it.

Here is what I know about the torture controversy: the military's Joint Personnel Recovery Agency invited me to give a three-hour lecture at the San Diego Naval Base in mid-May 2002. I was invited to speak about how American troops and American personnel could use what is known about learned helplessness to *resist* torture and evade successful interrogation by *their* captors. This is what I spoke about.

I was told then that because I was (and am) a civilian with no security clearance, they could not detail American methods of interrogation with me. I was also told then that their methods did not use violence or brutality.

Yet a report dated August 31, 2009, by the Physicians for Human Rights states: "In fact, on at least two occasions, Seligman presented his learned helplessness research to CIA contract interrogators referred to in the Inspector General's report." This is false. The "interrogators" were presumably James Mitchell and Bruce Jessen, two psychologists who have been reported to have worked with the CIA to help develop "enhanced" interrogation methods. They were in the audience of between fifty and one hundred when I presented my research on learned helplessness. I did not present it "to them." I presented it to the Joint Personnel Recovery Agency, and, again, I spoke about how American troops and American personnel could use what is known about learned helplessness to *evade* successful interrogation by *their* captors. There was no other occasion on which I presented my research to Mitchell and Jessen or to anyone else associated with this controversy.

I have not had contact with Joint Personnel Recovery Agency since that meeting. Nor have I had professional contact with Jessen and Mitchell since then. I have never worked under government contract (or any other contract) on any aspect of torture, nor would I ever be willing to do work on torture.

I have never worked on interrogation; I have never *seen* an interrogation, and I have only a passing knowledge of the literature on it. With that qualification, my opinion is that the point of interrogation is to get at the truth, not to get at what the interrogator wants to hear. I think learned helplessness would make someone more passive, less defiant, and more compliant, but I know of no evidence that it leads reliably to more truth telling. I am grieved and horrified that good science that has helped so many people overcome depression may have been used for such dubious purposes.

The Rollout

We were, frankly, nervous that these hard-boiled drill sergeants of legend would find resilience training "girly" or "touchy-feely" or "psychobabble." They did not, and more important, they loved (there is no more apt word for it) the course. To our amazement, the training received a rating of 4.9 out of 5.0 overall, with Karen Reivich receiving 5.0 out of 5.0 in their anonymous evaluations. Their comments brought tears to our eyes.

> *The most enjoyable, but more importantly, insightful training I have received since being in the army.*

> *I am amazed at how simple but greatly effective this course was for me. I can only imagine the impact it will have on my soldiers, family, and the army as a whole.*

> *This will save lives, marriages, and prevent suicides and other things like alcohol dependency and drug use post deployment. It needs to get to soldiers downrange now.*

> *We need every soldier, army civilian, and family member to receive this training.*

> *I've already started using my newfound techniques in my family life.*

And this is truly a representative sample of the evaluations from the allegedly grizzled drill sergeants.

Here is the rollout plan: for 2010, 150 sergeants will come to Penn each month for eight days of training to become the trainers. Another large group of sergeants will receive a simulcast of the training at their home forts. We will select the best of the sergeants to become master trainers and to be cofacilitators with our Penn trainers, so that by the end of 2010, we will have trained about 2,000 sergeants and will have selected and trained up to 100 of them to become the master trainers. These sergeants will devote one hour per week to resilience training. In 2011 we will continue to train at Penn as well as migrate the training into the forts. In the not too distant future, resilience training will be taught to all incoming soldiers, and the army will fully staff the training.

When General Casey, General Cornum, and I briefed the two- and three-star generals, their first question was "What about our wives and kids? The resilience of a soldier directly reflects the resilience of his family." General Casey thereupon ordered that the entire army family would have access to resilience training and that this would be an addition to Rhonda's portfolio. So we are creating mobile units, consisting of a lead trainer and a staff of master trainers to deploy and teach resilience to distant outposts such as Germany and Korea, as well as to spouses and kids.

In the meantime, we have been getting letters from the "front." Here's what Staff Sergeant Keith Allen wrote us:

Being an infantry soldier, I'm used to getting concrete details about any mission given me. When I was told I'd be attending Master Resilience Training, I naturally asked what I could expect . . . I was told to keep an open mind. Being a soldier, I translated this as "This will probably be worthless, but we've been ordered to support it."

I came to the training fully expecting to encounter teams of psychologists who would talk over my head, or would have nothing relevant to offer, or both. On the first day of class, I (along with the two NCOs from my unit) came to the classroom thirty minutes early, hoping to select a seat in the back row. To our chagrin, all the other participants had the same plan . . . The only seats remaining were in the front row.

We occupied the seats. I, admittedly, sat in the classic non-believer pose (slumped back in my chair, with my arms folded across my chest). By the second day, I found myself sitting upright, engaged in the class. By the time we were into Avoiding Thinking Traps, I was leaning forward in my chair, fully sur-

prised and somewhat disappointed when it was time to break for meals.

I recognized some of the skills as things I may have done instinctively or as a result of finding success with the methods through experience. I recognized the lack of some of the skills in some of the leaders/peers/soldiers I have encountered throughout my career.

When the discussion turned to our Values in Action Character Strengths results, I eagerly anticipated discussion. Some things were right where I thought they should be; others, to my surprise, were not as high on my list of strengths as I would have thought. After honest reflection (self-awareness), and communication with my wife, I realized my strengths were in a pretty accurate order. Knowing which strengths were lower than I would have thought showed me where to direct some of my efforts in the future.

I have used these skills since returning to my unit with success. Equally as important, if not more so, I have found success with my family. Some of our decisions in my unit are collaborative in nature; when I offer my input, I now have firm language to use to describe how I arrive at some of my decisions. My commander and senior leaders have since pulled me aside and asked more about Master Resilience Training. Two of them will be in the next training. Two of my children (fifteen and twelve years old, respectively) have taken the VIA, and it has helped our interaction. I have used active-constructive responding and taken my twelve-year-old through problem solving, and we both found unexpected success.

Staff Sergeant Edward Cummings wrote:

I went through Master Resilience Training last November, and since the course, it has done nothing but help me, not only in my professional life but more importantly in my personal life. My philosophy with the army is that if you are happy and successful at home, it will only help you at work . . . From the beginning of the course, I began to learn how to interject this into my everyday life. It has opened new doors for me to be able to talk to my wife and more importantly to listen. I have caught myself so many times doing the passive constructive, which, after taking a step back and knowing what I was doing, I didn't realize I was actually harming my marriage. By just listening to my wife about something I used to consider mundane, I found that her days got better, and as we all know, "If the wife ain't happy, nobody is happy!"

I have found myself able to handle struggles at work a lot easier as well. I used to get very upset when things weren't going as I thought they should and usually overreacted. Now I take that step back . . . try to get all of the information before making a rash decision. It has helped me calm down and approach those types of situations differently. I have found many icebergs and now can actually do something about them . . .

I used to wonder if I would be like my parents and have a marriage that would last thirty-six-plus years; now I am more confident that I will. I used to worry about my career and dwell on so many different choices I have made in my career and wonder if I did the right thing and if I would be a success. Now I know that no matter what happens in the future, I will be able to better take on the challenges. With this knowledge, I will be able to better take care of soldiers as well. I believe that if you cannot take care of yourself, how can you take care of soldiers? There are a lot of new soldiers who have a very hard time adjusting to the army life and time away from loved ones. I used to be one. If I had this information back then, I know I would have been a lot better off and able to handle the challenges better. With this knowledge, I know when the soldiers come to me with an issue, I can use some of the different techniques such as the ABCs, problem solving, or be able to identify their icebergs and be able to help them and do my job as their leader . . .

Overall the course was a great success . . . I have told my family about it and many friends who are going through tough times. The use of positive psychology is awesome!

The army and Penn will not rest easy with testimonials only. The outcome of our training will be evaluated rigorously in a massive study under the command of Colonel Sharon McBride and Captain Paul Lester. Since Master Resilience Training rolls out gradually, we will be able to evaluate the performance of the soldiers who have had resilience training in contrast to those who have not yet had it. This is called a "wait-list control" design. At least 7,500 soldiers who have been taught the materials of the Penn Resiliency Program by their sergeants will be followed for the next two years. They will be compared to soldiers who have not had the training. McBride and Lester will be able to ask if resilience training produces better military performance, less PTSD, better physical health, and ultimately a better family life and civilian life when they come back home.

This chapter would not be complete unless I confessed my deepest feelings about working with the army. I view the United States as the country that gave my grandparents, persecuted unto death in Europe, a safe haven where their children and grandchildren would flourish. I view the U.S. Army as the force that stood between me and the Nazi gas chambers, and thus I count my days with the sergeants and the generals as the most fulfilling and gratitude laden of my life. All my work with Comprehensive Soldier Fitness is pro bono. As I sit with these heroes, this verse from Isaiah 6:8 comes back to me:

> *"Whom shall I send? And who will go for us?"*
> *And I said, "Here am I. Send me!"*

Chapter 9

Positive Physical Health:
The Biology of Optimism

*Health is a state of complete physical, mental, and social well-being
and not merely the absence of disease or infirmity.*

—Preamble to the Constitution of the
World Health Organization, 1946

Turning Medicine on Its Head

I have been a psychotherapist for thirty-five years. I am not a very
good one—I confess that I'm better at talking than at listening—but
once in a while I have done pretty good work and helped my patient get
rid of almost all of her sadness, almost all of her anxiety, and almost
all of her anger. I thought that my work was done, and I would have a
happy patient.

Did I get a happy patient? No. As I said in Chapter 3, I got an empty
patient. That is because the skills of enjoying positive emotion, being
engaged with the people you care about, having meaning in life, achieving your work goals, and maintaining good relationships are entirely
different from the skills of not being depressed, not being anxious, and
not being angry. These dysphorias get in the way of well-being, but
they do not make well-being impossible; nor does the absence of sadness, anxiety, and anger remotely guarantee happiness. The takeaway

lesson from positive psychology is that positive mental health is not just the absence of mental illness.

It is all too commonplace not to be mentally ill but to be stuck and languishing in life. Positive mental health is a presence: the presence of positive emotion, the presence of engagement, the presence of meaning, the presence of good relationships, and the presence of accomplishment. Being in a state of mental health is not merely being disorder free; rather it is the presence of flourishing.

This is directly contrary to the wisdom that Sigmund Freud handed down from Mount Sinai: that mental health is just the absence of mental illness. Freud was a follower of the philosopher Arthur Schopenhauer (1788–1860). Both believed that happiness was an illusion and the best we could ever hope for was to keep our misery and suffering to a minimum. Let there be no doubt about this: traditional psychotherapy is not designed to produce well-being, it is designed just to curtail misery—which is itself no small task.

Physical health has accepted the same "wisdom": that physical health is merely the absence of physical illness. Disclaimers such as the World Health Organization's (above), and the very name of the National Institutes of *Health* notwithstanding (misleading because more than 95 percent of its budget goes to curtail illness), a scientific discipline of health barely exists. It was with all of this in their minds that Robin Mockenhaupt and Paul Tarini, officials from the huge Robert Wood Johnson Foundation (RWJF), asked to come speak with me about positive psychology.

"We would like you to turn medicine on its head," said Paul, director of the Pioneer branch. The Pioneer branch is just what it sounds like. Most of RWJF's medical funding goes to gold bond ideas such as reducing obesity, so the Pioneer branch is the foundation's way to balance its research portfolio by investing in innovative ideas well outside the mainstream of medical research—ideas that just might have a major payoff for health and health care in America.

"We've been following what you have done in mental health—to show that it is something real, something over and above the absence of mental illness—and we would like you to try the same thing for physical health," he continued. "Are there positive properties—health assets—that constitute an actual state of physical health? Is there a state that increases longevity, which decreases morbidity, which results in a better prognosis when illness finally strikes, and which decreases lifetime health care costs? Is health a real thing, or is all that medicine needs to be after is the absence of illness?"

That was enough to set my heart pumping. I had been working on just one piece of this grand puzzle: discovering one psychological state—optimism—that predicts and might cause less physical illness, and a tantalizing panorama of findings has emerged. This started forty years before my chat with Paul and Robin.

Origins of
Learned Helplessness Theory

I was part of a threesome—Steve Maier and Bruce Overmier were my partners—who discovered "learned helplessness" in the mid-1960s. We found that animals—dogs, rats, mice, and even cockroaches—later become passive and gave up in the face of adversity once they had first experienced noxious events that they could do nothing about. After that first experience with helplessness, thereafter they merely lay down in mildly painful shock and took it, just waiting it out, with no attempt to escape. Animals that first had exactly the same physical shock—but the shock was escapable—did not become helpless later on. They were immunized against learned helplessness.

Human animals do just what nonhuman animals do: in the paradigm human experiment, carried out by Donald Hiroto and replicated many times since, subjects are randomly divided into three groups. This is called the "triadic design." One group (escapable) is exposed to a noxious but nondamaging event, such as loud noise. When they push a button in front of them, the noise stops, so that their own action escapes the noise. A second group (inescapable) is *yoked* to the first group. The subjects receive *exactly* the same noise, but it goes off and on regardless of what they do. The second group is helpless by definition, since the probability of the noise going off given that they make any response is identical to the probability of the noise going off given that they do *not* make that response. Operationally, learned helplessness is defined by the fact that nothing you do alters the event. Importantly the escapable and inescapable groups have exactly the same objective stressor. A third group (control) receives nothing at all. That is part one of the triadic experiment.

Go back over this paragraph, and be sure that you understand the triadic design, since the rest of this chapter will little sense otherwise.

Part one induces learned helplessness, and part two displays the dramatic aftereffects. Part two takes place later and in a different place. Commonly in part two, all three groups encounter a "shuttle box." The person puts his hand in one side of the box and the loud noise goes on. If he moves his hand a few inches to the other side, noise goes off. People from the escapable group and from the control group readily learn to move their hands to escape noise. The people from the inescapable group typically do not move. They just sit there taking the noise until it goes off by itself. In part one, they had learned that nothing they did mattered, and so in part two, expecting that nothing they do will matter, they do not try to escape.

I was aware of a legion of anecdotes about people taking sick and even dying when helpless, so I began to wonder if learned helplessness somehow could reach inside the body and undermine health and vitality themselves. I also wondered about the inverse: Paul Tarini's question. Could the psychological state of mastery—the opposite of helplessness—somehow reach inside and strengthen the body?

Here is the rationale for the triadic design—three groups: escapable, inescapable, and normal control—that is the hallmark of all well-executed experiments on learned helplessness. The presence of a normal control group, which has no prior experience with the stressor, allows bidirectional inferences. Does helplessness damage the person, along with does mastery enhance the person? The answer to "Does helplessness damage?" (the "pathological" question) lies in the part two comparison of the people who received inescapable noise in part one to the normal control that got no noise at all in part one. If the inescapable group does worse than the normal control group in part two, helplessness has damaged the person.

The bipolar question is "Does mastery strengthen the person?" The answer to that question (the "positive psychology question") lies in the part two comparison of the people who learned in part one to escape the noise to those in the normal control group. If they do better than the normal control group in part two, mastery has strengthened them. Notice that the poor performance of the helpless group relative to the mastery group is of less scientific interest than the comparison of both these groups to the control group—since the helpless group would do worse than the mastery group if helplessness weakens people, or if mastery strengthens people, or if both were true.

This is the insight underlying Paul Tarini's question, an insight so obvious that it is easy to miss altogether. Psychology and medicine, following Freud and the medical model, view the world through the lens of pathology and look only at the toxic effects of malign events. Psychology and medicine get turned on their heads when we ask about the opposite of pathology: about the strengthening effects of benevolent events. Indeed, any endeavor—nutrition, the immune system, welfare, politics, education, or ethics—that is fixated on the remedial misses this insight and does just half the job: correcting deficits while failing to build strength.

Psychology of Illness

It was through learned helplessness that I got involved in the psychology of physical illness. Our best attempt to ask about physical health in the triadic design used rats and cancer. Madelon Visintainer and Joe Volpicelli—both my graduate students at the time—implanted a tumor that had a 50 percent lethality rate (LD 50) on the flanks of rats. We then randomly assigned the rats to one of the three psychological conditions: one session of sixty-four mildly painful escapable shocks (mastery), or one session of the identical shocks but inescapable shocks (helplessness), or no shock (the control group). That was part one.

In part two, we just waited to see which rats got cancer and died and which rats rejected the tumor. As expected, 50 percent of the control group, which had no experience with shock, died. Three-quarters of the rats in the inescapable group died, showing that helplessness weakened the body. One-quarter of the rats in the escapable group died, demonstrating that mastery strengthened the body.

I should mention that this experiment—published in *Science* in 1982—was the last time that I have been involved in an animal experiment, and I want to tell you why: on the ethical side, I am an animal lover—my life has continually been enriched by our dogs at home. So I found it very difficult to inflict suffering on animals for any purpose at all, even a humanitarian purpose. But the scientific argument is more telling for me: there are usually more direct ways of answering the questions that most interest me with human participants rather than animal subjects. All animal experiments that try to make inferences to humans must tangle with the problem of external validity.

This is a crucial, neglected, and really hairy issue. What attracted me to experimental psychology in the very first place was its rigor, what is called internal validity. Performing a controlled experiment is the gold standard of internal validity because it discovers what causes what. Does the fire cause the water to boil? Turn on the fire, and the water boils. Without the fire (the control group), the water does not boil. Do uncontrollable bad events spur tumor growth? Give one group of rats inescapable shock, give another group identical escapable shock, and compare them to a group that receives no shock. Rats that get inescapable shock grow the tumor at a greater rate; hence, inescapable shock causes tumor growth in rats. But what does this tell us about the causes of cancer in human beings, and about how being helpless influences cancer in people? This is the problem of external validity.

When laypeople complain about psychological experimentation with the gibe "white rats and college sophomores," it is external validity that is the issue. Far from being a philistine complaint that psychologists have conveniently chosen to ignore, it is a profound one. *Homo sapiens* is different in so many ways from the white laboratory version of *Rattus norvegicus*. Inescapable shock is different in many ways from finding out that your child drowned in a boating accident. The tumor that we implanted on *Rattus norvegicus* is different in many ways from the naturally occurring tumors that afflict *Homo sapiens*. So even if the internal validity is perfect—rigorous experimental design, the control group exactly right, the numbers large enough to ensure randomization, and the statistics impeccable—we still cannot infer with confidence that this illuminates the effect uncontrollable bad events exert on the progression of illness in people.

If it is not worth doing, it is not worth doing well.

I have come to think that establishing external validity is an even more important but much more nettlesome scientific inference than establishing internal validity. Academic psychology requires entire courses on internal validity—"methodology" courses—of all serious psychology graduates. These courses are entirely about internal validity and almost never even touch on external validity, which is often passed off as mere ignorance about science on the part of laymen. Hundreds of professors of psychology make their living teaching about internal validity; no one makes a living teaching about external validity. Unfortunately, public doubts about the applicability of basic, rigorous science are often warranted, and this is because the rules of external validity are not clear.

The choice of experimental subjects, for example, has been overwhelmingly a matter of academic convenience as opposed to a matter of deliberation about what inferences would be warranted if the experiment works. White rats never would have been used in psychology if video games had been around in 1910. College sophomores never would have become the subjects of choice in psychology if the World Wide Web had been around in 1930. The bottom line for me, scientifically, is to avoid problems of external validity as much as possible by working with human beings on real-world mastery and real-world helplessness under repeatable conditions. There are, to be sure, instances in which I believe animal experimentation is justifiable, but they are limited to domains in which the problems of external validity are small, the ethical problems of doing the experiment with humans are insuperable, and the human benefits are large. I believe that all the issues that this book addresses can be better illuminated by research with humans, and I now turn back to these issues.

To my description of learned helplessness above, I have to add one important fact: when we gave inescapable noise to people or inescapable shock to animals, not all of them became helpless. With regularity, about one-third of people (and one-third of rats and one-third of dogs) never became helpless. With regularity, about one-tenth of people (and one-tenth of rats and one-tenth of dogs) were helpless to begin with, and they required no laboratory events to induce passivity. It was that observation that led to the field called learned optimism.

We wanted to find out who never became helpless, so we looked systematically at the way that the people whom we could not make helpless interpreted bad events. We found that people who believe that the causes of setbacks in their lives are temporary, changeable, and local do not become helpless readily in the laboratory. When assailed with inescapable noise in the laboratory or with rejection in love, they think, *It's going away quickly, I can do something about it, and it's just this one situation.* They bounce back quickly from setbacks, and they do not take a setback at work home. We call them optimists. Conversely, people who habitually think, *It's going to last forever, it's going to undermine everything, and there's nothing I can do about it,* become helpless readily in the laboratory. They do not bounce back from defeat, and they take their marital problems into their jobs. We call them pessimists.

So we devised questionnaires to measure optimism as well as content analytic techniques for blindly rating the optimism of every "because" statement in speeches, newspaper quotes, and diaries for measuring people—presidents, sports heroes, and the dead—who won't take questionnaires. We found that pessimists get depressed much more readily than optimists, that they underachieve in their jobs, in the classroom, and on the sports field, and their relationships are rockier.

Do pessimism and optimism, the great amplifiers of learned helplessness and mastery, respectively, influence illness? And by what mechanisms? How do other positive psychological variables, such as joy, zest, and cheer, influence illness? I will discuss this illness by illness, in the following order: cardiovascular disease, infectious illness, cancer, and all-cause mortality.

Cardiovascular Disease (CVD)

In the mid-1980s, 120 men from San Francisco had their first heart attacks, and they served as the untreated control group in the massive Multiple Risk Factor Intervention Trial (MR FIT) study. This study disappointed many psychologists and cardiologists by ultimately finding no effect on CVD by training to change these men's personalities from type A (aggressive, time urgent, and hostile) to type B (easygoing). The 120 untreated controls, however, were of great interest to Gregory Buchanan, then a graduate student at Penn, and to me because so much was known about their first heart attacks: extent of damage to the heart, blood pressure, cholesterol, body mass, and lifestyle—all the traditional risk factors for cardiovascular disease. In addition, the men were all interviewed about their lives: family, job, and hobbies. We took every single "because" statement from each of their videotaped interviews and coded them for optimism and pessimism.

Within eight and a half years, half the men had died of a second heart attack, and we opened the sealed envelope. Could we predict who would have a second heart attack? None of the usual risk factors predicted death: not blood pressure, not cholesterol, not even how extensive the damage from the first heart attack. Only optimism, eight and a half years earlier, predicted a second heart attack: of the sixteen most pessimistic men, fifteen died. Of the sixteen most optimistic men, only five died.

This finding has been repeatedly confirmed in larger studies of cardiovascular disease, using varied measures of optimism.

Veterans Affairs Normative Aging Study
In 1986, 1,306 veterans took the Minnesota Multiphasic Personality Inventory (MMPI) and were tracked for ten years. During that time, 162 cases of cardiovascular disease occurred. The MMPI has an optimism-pessimism scale that reliably predicts mortality in other studies. Smoking, alcohol use, blood pressure, cholesterol, body mass, family history of CVD, and education were measured, as was anxiety, depression, and hostility, and all of these were controlled for

statistically. Men with the most optimistic style (one standard deviation above average) had 25 percent less CVD than average, and men with the least optimism (one standard deviation below the mean) had 25 percent more CVD than average. This trend was strong and continuous, indicating that greater optimism protected the men, whereas less optimism weakened them.

European Prospective Investigation

More than 20,000 healthy British adults were followed from 1996 to 2002, during which 994 of them died, 365 of them from CVD. Many physical and psychological variables were measured at the outset of the study: smoking, social class, hostility, and neuroticism, for example. Sense of mastery was also measured by seven questions:

1. I have little control over the things that happen to me.
2. There is really no way I can solve some of the problems I have.
3. There is little I can do to change many of the important things in my life.
4. I often feel helpless in dealing with the problems of life.
5. Sometimes I feel that I am being pushed around in life.
6. What happens to me in the future mostly depends on me.
7. I can do just about anything I really set my mind to do.

These questions capture the continuum from helplessness to mastery. Death from cardiovascular disease was strongly influenced by a sense of mastery, holding smoking, social class, and the other psychological variables constant. People high (one standard deviation above the mean) in mastery had 20 percent fewer CVD deaths than those with an average sense of mastery, and people high in a sense of helplessness (one standard deviation below the mean in a sense of mastery) had 20 percent more CVD deaths than average. This was also true of deaths due to all causes and—to a lesser extent but still significant statistically—of deaths from cancer.

Dutch Men and Women

Beginning in 1991, 999 sixty-five- to eighty-five-year-olds were followed for nine years in the Netherlands. In that time, 397 of them died. At the outset, researchers measured health, education, smoking, alcohol, history of cardiovascular disease, marriage, body mass, blood pressure, and cholesterol, along with optimism, which was measured by four items answered on a 1-to-3 scale of agreement:

1. I still expect much from life.
2. I do not look forward to what lies ahead for me in the years to come.
3. I am still full of plans.
4. I often feel that life is full of promises.

Pessimism was very strongly associated with mortality, particularly when holding all the other risk factors constant. Optimists had only 23 percent the rate of CVD deaths of the pessimists, and only 55 percent the overall death rate compared to the pessimists. Interestingly this protection was specific to optimism, a future-oriented cognition, and present-oriented mood items such as "Happy laughter often occurs" (this must read better in Dutch) and the items such as "Most of the time, I am in good spirits," did not predict mortality.

In contrast, in the 1995 Nova Scotia Health Survey, a team of nurses rated the positive emotion (joy, happiness, excitement, enthusiasm, contentment) of 1,739 healthy adults. Over the next ten years, participants with high positive emotion experienced less heart disease, with 22 percent less heart disease for each point on a five-point scale of positive emotion. Optimism was not measured, so we cannot determine if positive emotion worked through optimism.

The influence of Dutch optimism was a continuous trend, with more optimism associated with fewer deaths along the entire dimension. These findings show that the effect is bipolar: high optimists die at a lower rate than average, and high pessimists die at a higher rate than average. Recall here the thrust of Paul Tarini's question: Are there health assets that protect, and not just risk factors that weaken, the body? Optimism, in this study, strengthened people against cardiovascular disease when compared to the average person, just as pessimism weakened them compared to average.

Is depression the real culprit? Pessimism, in general, correlates pretty highly with depression, and depression, in many studies, also correlates with cardiovascular disease. So you might wonder if the lethal effect of pessimism works by increasing depression. The answer seems to be no, since optimism and pessimism exerted their effects even when depression was held constant statistically.

Women's Health Initiative

In the largest study of the relationship between optimism and cardiovascular disease to date, 97,000 women, healthy at the outset of the study in 1994, were followed for eight years. As usual in careful epidemiological studies, age, race, education, religious attendance, health, body mass, alcohol, smoking, blood pressure, and cholesterol were recorded at the start. Epidemiological studies investigate patterns of health in large populations. Optimism was measured in yet another way by the well-validated Life Orientation Test (LOT), which poses ten statements such as: "In unclear times, I usually expect the best," and "If something can go wrong for me, it will." Importantly, depressive symptoms were also measured and their impact assessed separately. The optimists (the top quarter) had 30 percent fewer coronary deaths than the pessimists (bottom quarter). The trend of fewer deaths, both cardiac and deaths from all causes, held across the entire distribution of optimism, indicating again that optimism protected women and pessimism hurt them relative to the average. This was true holding constant all the other risk factors—including depressive symptoms.

Something Worth Living For

There is one trait similar to optimism that seems to protect against cardiovascular disease: *ikigai*. This Japanese concept means having something worth living for, and *ikigai* is intimately related to the meaning element of flourishing (M in PERMA) as well as to optimism. There are three prospective Japanese studies of *ikigai*, and all point to high levels of *ikigai* reducing the risk of death from cardiovascular disease, even when controlling for traditional risk factors and perceived stress. In one study, the mortality rate from CVD among men and women without *ikigai* was 160 percent higher than that of men and women with *ikigai*. In a second study, men with *ikigai* had only 86 percent of the risk of mortality from CVD compared to men without *ikigai*; this was also true of women, but less robustly so. And in a third study, men with high *ikigai* had only 28 percent of the risk for death from stroke relative to their low-*ikigai* counterparts, but there was no association with heart disease.

SUMMARY OF
CARDIOVASCULAR DISEASE

All studies of optimism and CVD converge on the conclusion that optimism is strongly related to protection from cardiovascular disease. This holds even correcting for all the traditional risk factors such as obesity, smoking, excessive alcohol use, high cholesterol, and hypertension. It even holds correcting for depression, correcting for perceived stress, and correcting for momentary positive emotions. It holds over different ways of measuring optimism. Most important, the effect is bipolar, with high optimism protecting people compared to the average level of optimism and pessimism, and pessimism hurting people compared to the average.

Infectious Illness

How long do your colds last? For some people, colds last only seven days, but for many others, they last two or three weeks. Some people ward off colds, even when everyone else is in bed; others get a half dozen colds a year. Your reflexive demurrer is probably "This must be due to immune system differences," but I need to caution you about rampant immunomythology. I wish that science had established that people with "stronger" immune systems ward off infectious illness better, but this is far from having been nailed down. Surprisingly, however, the influence of psychological states on susceptibility to colds has been nailed down better. The unraveling of the influence of emotion on infectious illness is one of the most elegant stories in all of psychology. The protagonist is a shy and soft-spoken professor of psychology at Carnegie Mellon University, Sheldon Cohen, one of those rare scientists whose research successfully bridges biology and psychology.

It is commonplace that happy people do not complain much: they report fewer symptoms of pain and illness, and they report better health generally. In contrast, sad people complain more about pain, and they report worse health. It is plausible that both actually have the same physical symptoms, but sadness and happiness change only how they perceive their bodily symptoms. Alternatively, this could merely reflect a bias in reporting symptoms, with sad people obsessed with negative symptoms, and happy people focused on what is going well. (Notice that this bias does not explain the optimism-CVD findings, since the outcome here is not the reporting of coronary symptoms but death itself.) So it is parsimonious to pass off the many observations that depressed people have more pain and more colds, and happy people less pain and fewer colds, as uninteresting artifacts of reporting. That is exactly where medical science stood until Sheldon Cohen came along.

Sheldon had the courage to actually infect volunteers with known doses of rhinovirus, the virus that brings you the common cold. I use the word *courage* because the harrowing story of his getting approval from Carnegie Mellon's institutional review boards (IRB, explained below) to allow these studies remains untold. But as we shall see, we can be grateful that these studies passed ethical muster.

Ethics and Institutional Review Boards

My admiration of Sheldon's courage and my gratitude that he was allowed to do the experiments I will shortly describe is based in a deep worry about the shackling of science in the United States today. Beginning in the 1970s, all scientists were required to submit their proposed research to an arm's-length committee for ethical approval. The group is called an institutional review board, or IRB, and this demand for ethical review came in the wake of scandals in which patients and research subjects were not fully informed about the potentially dangerous procedures they were to undergo. IRBs help prevent universities from getting sued, and they speak well to the ethic of a fully open society. On the downside, IRBs are very costly; I would guess that Penn (just one of thousands of American research institutions) spends a lot more than $10 million per year running IRBs. Institutional review boards mire scientists in a mountain of red tape—my guess is that my laboratory spends five hundred hours per year filling out IRB forms.

The review boards started out to warn people fully about being in a scientific study that might subject them to serious harm, but they have now developed mission creep of the first magnitude: every time a scientist wants to even pilot an innocuous questionnaire on happiness, her first task is to provide hours' worth of documentation to her institution's IRB. As far as I know, IRBs have not—in forty years and at the cost of many billions of dollars—saved even a single life. But most important, they have a chilling effect on attempts to conduct potentially lifesaving science. Here's an example of the most lifesaving study I know in the history of psychology—perhaps in the history of medicine—and this exposes just what is wrong with institutional review boards.

The worst epidemic of madness in recorded history began a few years after Christopher Columbus discovered the New World, and it continued with mounting ferocity until the early twentieth century. We have come to call this disorder general paresis. It begins with a weakness in the arms and legs, proceeds to symptoms of eccentricity followed by downright delusions of grandeur, then finally progresses to massive paralysis, stupor, and death. Its cause was unknown, but there was some suspicion that it was caused by syphilis. Reports of cases in which paretics were known to have had syphilis were clearly not sufficient, since these were contradicted by the many paretics who adamantly denied ever having syphilis and who showed no evidence of the sexually transmitted virus. Some 65 percent of paretics had a demonstrable history of syphilis, compared to only 10 percent of nonparetics. That evidence, of course, was merely suggestive: it did not demonstrate cause, since it did not show that 100 percent of paretics had prior histories of syphilis.

The overt symptoms of syphilis—the sores on the genitals—disappear in a few weeks, but the disease does not. Like measles, if you contract syphilis once, you can't get it again. More bluntly, if someone who has already become syphilitic (a paretic) comes in contact with another syphilitic germ, he will not develop sores on his genitals.

There was one means, but a risky one, of finding out by way of an experiment if all paretics had previously had syphilis. If you injected paretics with the syphilis germ, one startling result would come about. The paretics would not contract the disease, since you cannot get syphilis twice. Betting on this outcome, the German neurologist Richard von Krafft-Ebing (1840–1902) performed this critical experiment. In 1897 he inoculated with material from syphilitic sores nine paretics, all of whom had denied ever having had syphilis. None developed sores, leading to the conclusion that they must have already been infected.

So successful was Krafft-Ebing's work that the most common mental illness of the nineteenth century was soon eradicated with antisyphilitic medication and hundreds of thousands of lives were saved.

The moral of this story is that this experiment could not be carried out today. No institutional review board would approve it. But much worse, no scientist—not even the most courageous one—would even submit such a proposal to an IRB—no matter how many lives she believed would be saved.

Sheldon Cohen's studies, like Krafft-Ebing's, deserve the appellation *courageous* because they have the potential to save many lives. Cohen pioneered the causal influence of positive emotion on infectious illness within a bold experimental design. In all of Cohen's studies, large numbers of healthy volunteers are first interviewed nightly for seven nights. They are well paid and fully informed of the risks. Yet many IRBs would not allow even this study to go forward because to them "well paid" equals "coercion."

From these interviews and tests, the average mood—positive emotion and negative emotion—is rated. Positive emotion consists of the observer ratings "full of pep," "energetic," "happy," "at ease," "calm," and "cheerful." Negative emotion consists of "sad," "depressed," "unhappy," "nervous," "hostile," and "resentful." Notice that these are not ratings of the future-oriented traits of optimism and pessimism (for instance, "I expect many bad things to recur"), as in the medical literature concerning the association between mood and cardiovascular disease, but rather ratings of momentary emotional states. Possible confounds, or lurking extraneous factors, are also measured: age, sex, race, health, body mass, education, sleep, diet, exercise, antibody levels, and optimism.

Then all of the volunteers get rhinovirus squirted into their noses (shades of Krafft-Ebing) and are kept under observation and in quarantine for six days to let the cold develop. The cold is measured not only by self-report of symptoms (which could be biased by how much different individuals complain), but more directly by mucus production (the snotty tissues are weighed) and congestion (the amount of time it takes a dye injected into the nose to reach the back of the throat). The results are remarkable and conclusive:

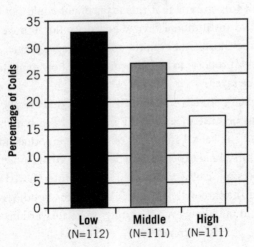

Positive Emotional Style
(by Interviews)

People with high positive emotion before the rhinovirus develop fewer colds than people with average positive emotion. And *they*, in turn, get fewer colds than people with low positive emotion. The effect is bidirectional, with high positive emotion strengthening volunteers compared to average, and low positive emotion weakening volunteers compared to average:

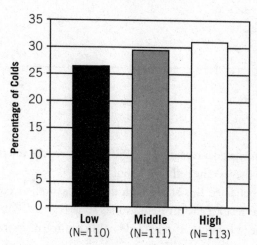

Negative Emotional Style
(by Interviews)

There is a smaller effect of negative emotion, with people low in negative emotion having fewer colds than the others. Importantly, positive emotion, not negative emotion, is clearly the driving force.

By what biological mechanism does positive emotion reduce colds? Since the volunteers are kept in quarantine and closely observed, differences in sleep, diet, cortisol, zinc, and exercise are ruled out. The key difference is interleukin-6, a protein that causes inflammation.

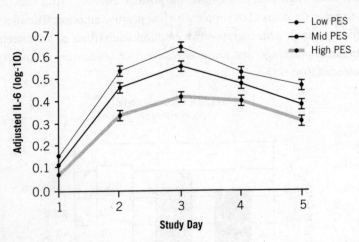

**Daily Adjusted IL-6 by PES Levels
(Infected Ss Only)**

The higher the positive emotion (PES), the lower the interleukin-6 (IL-6), and so the less the inflammation.

Sheldon replicated this study with flu virus as well as cold virus, with the same results: positive emotional style is the driving factor. In addition, he ruled out self-reported health, optimism, extraversion, depression, and self-esteem differences.

Cancer and
All-Cause Mortality

Are positive states a panacea? In my very first speculations about helplessness and illness in the 1970s, I cautioned about the limits that psychological influences such as optimism might have on physical disease. In particular, I was concerned with the severity of illness, and I guessed that lethal and terminal illness could not be influenced by the psychological state of the victim. I wrote hyperbolically that "if a crane falls on you, optimism is not of much use."

Barbara ("I Hate Hope") Ehrenreich

I have been reminded of this in recent years by an Australian study showing that hope and optimism have no measurable effect on prolonging life in patients with inoperable cancer. Barbara Ehrenreich recently published *Bright-Sided: How the Relentless Promotion of Positive Thinking Has Undermined America,* in which she describes her personal experience with well-meaning health care workers telling her that her breast cancer could be relieved if only she were a more positive person. She then goes on to dismiss positive psychology. Ehrenreich is resentful of the happiness police insisting that she adopt a cheerful posture in order to conquer her breast cancer. There is no reason at all to believe that faking positive emotion in order to live longer will work, and I know of no one who advocates urging patients to fake well-being. In spite of this, Ehrenreich titled the British edition of her book *Smile or Die.*

I had a revealing exchange with Ehrenreich right after *Smile or Die* was published in England. I sent her a hot-off-the-press article about baseball players' longevity: the intensity of smiling in the 1952 *Baseball Register* photos predicted how long players would live, with those showing a genuine (Duchenne) smile living seven years longer than those not smiling.

"I guess I'm doomed," she quipped in her return email.

"As wrongheaded and evidence-ignoring as I believe your analysis is," I responded, and here is the point that Ehrenreich misses, "cardiovascular disease, all-cause mortality, and quite possibly cancer are not a function of fake smiling but rather of PERMA, some configuration of positive emotion, plus meaning, plus positive relationships, plus positive accomplishment. You may be low on the first (as am I), but you have many of the others, I gather, and your book—as uncongenial as I find it—is surely a meaningful and positive accomplishment. So—ironically—taking on the positive as you do is itself a major positive (when "positive" is appropriately understood to be broader than enforced smiling) in your life.

"So you are not doomed."

In her book, Ehrenreich failed to address the full range of the scientific literature, but her book triggered some glowing reviews, in which the reviewers took Ehrenreich's conclusions at face value. The most egregious review came from Michael Shermer, founding editor of *Skeptic* magazine. "Ehrenreich systematically deconstructs—and then demolishes—what little science there is behind the positive psychology movement and the allegedly salubrious effects of positive thinking. Evidence is thin. Statistical significance levels are narrow. What few robust findings there are often prove to be either nonreplicable or contradicted by later research." As the reader can see from this chapter, the evidence is robust, significance levels are high, and the findings replicate over and over.

So, Ehrenreich's and Shermer's rants aside, what is the actual state of the evidence about positivity and cancer? The most complete review, "Optimism and Physical Health: A Meta-Analytic Review," was published in *Annals of Behavioral Medicine* in 2009. It meta-analyzes eighty-three separate studies of optimism and physical health. A "meta-analysis" averages over all the methodologically sound studies of a topic in the entire scientific literature. Conflicting findings are the rule for the effect of psychological well-being on survival per se and for almost every other finding in the social-science literature. (This is indeed how science progresses.)

To what extent, the authors ask, does optimism predict mortality from all causes, cardiovascular disease, immune function, and cancer? Eighteen of these eighty-three studies, involving a total of 2,858 patients, concern cancer. Taken together, they find that more optimistic people have better cancer outcomes, at a robust level of significance The largest and most recent study involved 97,253 women from the Women's Health Initiative study above, and measured the relationship of optimism and of "cynical hostility" to the prediction of cardiovascular disease, all-cause mortality, and cancer. Pessimism was a major predictor of CVD mortality, as mentioned above. Importantly, pessimism and cynical hostility were both significant predictors of cancer, particularly among African-American women, although the effect was smaller than for CVD.

Ehrenreich asked me for help preparing her book. We had two face-to-face meetings largely about the research literature on health. I then sent her an extensive bibliography and articles. Rather than present the full range of studies, however, Ehrenreich cherry-picks her way though some of the research, highlighting the minority of null evidence and failing to review the well-done studies that find that optimism significantly predicts better cardiovascular, all-cause mortality, and cancer outcomes. Cherry-picking is in the abstract one of the minor forms of intellectual dishonesty, but in matters of life and death, cherry-picking to dismiss the value of optimism and hope for women with cancer is, in my opinion, dangerous journalistic malpractice.

Of course, there are no experimental studies in which people are randomly assigned to "getting optimism" and "getting cancer," so it is possible to doubt whether pessimism *causes* cancer and death. But these studies control for the other risk factors for cancer and still find that optimistic patients fare better. The evidence is sufficient to warrant a random-assignment, placebo-controlled experiment in which pessimistic women with cancer are randomly assigned to Penn Resiliency Training or to a health information control group, and followed for morbidity, mortality, quality of life, and health care expenditure.

So my overview of the cancer literature is that it leans quite heavily in the direction of pessimism as a risk factor for developing cancer. But because a noticeable minority of the cancer studies do *not* find significant effects (although not a single one shows that pessimism benefits cancer patients), I conclude that pessimism is a likely but a weaker risk factor for cancer than it is for cardiovascular disease and all-cause mortality.

Therefore, I would hazard from the entirety of the cancer literature that hope, optimism, and happiness may well have beneficial effects for cancer patients when the disease is not extremely severe. But caution is in order before dismissing positivity altogether even there. A letter in response to my crane-falling article on the limits of optimism began: "Dear Dr. Seligman: A crane fell on me, and I am alive today only because of my optimism."

Studies that look at mortality from all causes are relevant to whether psychological well-being can actually help you if a crane falls on you. Yoichi Chida and Andrew Steptoe, psychologists from the

University of London, recently published an exemplary comprehensive meta-analysis. Chida and Steptoe averaged seventy studies together, thirty-five of which began with healthy participants and thirty-five of which began with diseased participants.

Their meta-analysis finds that over all seventy studies, psychological well-being protects. The effect is quite strong if you are presently healthy. People who have high well-being are 18 percent less likely to die of any cause than those with low well-being. Among the studies that start out with sick people, those with high well-being show a smaller but significant effect, dying at the rate of 2 percent less than those with lower well-being. As for cause of death, a sense of well-being protects people against death from CVD, renal failure, and HIV, but not significantly for cancer.

Is Well-Being Causal, and How Might It Protect?

I conclude that optimism is robustly associated with cardiovascular health, and pessimism with cardiovascular risk. I conclude that positive mood is associated with protection from colds and flu, and negative mood with greater risk for colds and flu. I conclude that highly optimistic people *may* have a lower risk for developing cancer. I conclude that healthy people who have good psychological well-being are at less risk for death from all causes.

Why?

The first step in answering why is to ask if these are really causal relations or just correlations. This is a crucial scientific question, since some third variable, such as a loving mother or an excess of serotonin might be the real cause, with a loving mother or high serotonin causing both good health *and* psychological well-being. No observational study can eliminate all possible third variables, but most of the studies above eliminate the likely possibilities by statistically equating people for exercise, blood pressure, cholesterol, smoking, and a host of other plausible confounds.

The gold standard for eliminating all third variables is a random-assignment placebo-controlled experiment, and there exists only one in the optimism-health literature. Fifteen years ago, when Penn's freshman class was admitted, I sent the entire class the Attributional Style Questionnaire, and everyone took it. (Students are very cooperative upon admission.) Gregory Buchanan and I then wrote the most pessimistic quarter of freshmen, at risk for depression on the basis of their very pessimistic explanatory style scores, and randomly invited them into one of two groups: an eight-week "stress management seminar" consisting of the Penn Resiliency Program (Learned Optimism), as discussed in the "Positive Education" and "Army Strong" chapters, or a no-intervention control group. We found that the seminar raised optimism markedly and lowered depression and anxiety over the next thirty months, as we'd predicted. We also assessed the students' physical health over that period. Participants in the seminar group had better physical health than did the controls, with fewer self-reported symptoms of physical illness, fewer doctor visits overall, and fewer illness-related visits to the student health center. The seminar group was more likely to visit doctors for preventive checkups, and its members had healthier diets and exercise regimens.

This lone experiment suggests that it is the change in optimism itself that improved health, since random assignment to intervention versus control eliminates the unknown third variables. We do not know if this causal path is true of optimism in the cardiovascular disease literature, since no one has yet conducted a random-assignment study, teaching patients optimism to prevent heart attacks. One cheer, so far, for causality.

Why Optimists Are Less Vulnerable to Disease

How might optimism work to make people less vulnerable and pessimism to make people more vulnerable to cardiovascular disease? The possibilities divide into three large categories:

1. Optimists take action and have healthier lifestyles. Optimists believe that their actions matter, whereas pessimists believe they are helpless and nothing they do will matter. Optimists try, while pessimists lapse into passive helplessness.

Optimists therefore act on medical advice readily, as George Vaillant found when the surgeon general's report on smoking and health came out in 1964; it was the optimists who gave up smoking, not the pessimists. Optimists may take better care of themselves.

Even more generally, people with high life satisfaction (which correlates highly with optimism) are much more likely to diet, not to smoke, and to exercise regularly than people with lower life satisfaction. According to one study, happy people also sleep better than unhappy people.

Optimists not only follow medical advice readily, they also take action to avoid bad events, whereas pessimists are passive: optimists are more likely to seek safety in tornado shelters when there is a tornado warning than pessimists, who may believe the tornado is God's will. The more bad events that befall you, the more illness.

2. Social support. The more friends and the more love in your life, the less illness. George Vaillant found that people who have one person whom they would be comfortable calling at three in the morning to tell their troubles were healthier. John Cacioppo found that lonely people are markedly less healthy than sociable people. In an experiment, participants read a script over the phone to strangers—reading in either a depressed voice or a cheerful voice. The strangers hang up on the pessimist sooner than on the optimist. Happy people have richer social networks than unhappy people, and social connectedness contributes to a lack of disability as we age. Misery may love company, but company does not love misery, and the ensuing loneliness of pessimists may be a path to illness.

3. Biological mechanisms. There are a variety of plausible biological paths. One is the *immune system*. Judy Rodin (whom I mentioned in the opening of the book), Leslie Kamen,

Charles Dwyer, and I collaborated together in 1991 and took blood from elderly optimists and pessimists and tested the immune response. The blood of optimists had a feistier response to threat—more infection-fighting white blood cells called T lymphocytes produced—than the pessimists. We ruled out depression and health as confounds.

Another possibility is *common genetics*: optimistic and happy people might have genes that ward off cardiovascular disease or cancer.

Another potential biological path is a pathological circulatory response to *repeated stress*. Pessimists give up and suffer more stress, whereas optimists cope better with stress. Repeated episodes of stress, particularly when one is helpless, likely mobilize the stress hormone cortisol and other circulatory responses that induce or exacerbate damage to the walls of blood vessels and promote atherosclerosis. Sheldon Cohen, you will recall, found that sad people secrete more of the inflammatory substance interleukin-6, and that this results in more colds. Repeated episodes of stress and helplessness might set off a cascade of processes involving higher cortisol and lower levels of the neurotransmitters known as catecholamines, leading to long-lasting inflammation. Greater inflammation is implicated in atherosclerosis, and women who score low in feelings of mastery and high in depression have been shown to have worse calcification of the major artery, the trunk-like aorta. Helpless rats, in the triadic design, develop atherosclerosis at a faster rate than rats that demonstrate mastery.

Excessive production by the liver of *fibrinogen,* a substance used in clotting the blood, is another possible mechanism. More fibrinogen leads to more blood clots in the circulatory system by making the blood sludgy. People with high positive emotion show less of a fibrinogen response to stress than those with low positive emotion.

Heart rate variability (HRV), surprisingly, is another candidate for protection against cardiovascular disease. HRV is the short-term variation in beat-to-beat intervals, which is partly controlled by the parasympathetic (vagal) system of the central nervous system. This is the system that produces relaxation and relief. Accumulating evidence suggests that people with high heart rate variability are healthier, have less CVD, less depression, and better cognitive abilities.

The mechanisms proposed above have not been well tested. They are simply reasonable hypotheses, but each can be bidirectional, with optimism adding to protection compared to the average, and pessimism weakening people compared to the average. The gold standard for finding out if optimism is causal and how it works is the optimism intervention experiment. There is an obvious and expensive experiment very much worth doing: we take a large group of people vulnerable to CVD, randomly assign half to optimism training and half to a placebo, monitor their action, social, and biological variables, and see if optimism training is lifesaving. And this takes me back to the Robert Wood Johnson Foundation.

All of this—learned helplessness, optimism, CVD, and how to pin down the mechanism—raced through my mind when Paul Tarini visited me. "We want to invite you to send us two proposals," Paul concluded after a long discussion, "one exploring the very concept of positive health, and the second proposing an optimism intervention to prevent CVD deaths."

Positive Health

In due course, I submitted both proposals. The intervention proposal mobilized the Cardiology Department at Penn and we proposed the random-assignment Penn Resiliency Program intervention given to large numbers of people after their first heart attack. The other proposed exploring the concept of positive health, and it was this one that the foundation funded in the belief that a well-defined concept of positive health came first. The positive health group has now been at work for a year and a half, and it has four main thrusts:

- Defining positive health
- Reanalysis of existing longitudinal studies
- Cardiovascular health assets
- Exercise as a health asset

DEFINING
POSITIVE HEALTH

Is health more than the absence of illness, and can it be defined by the presence of positive health assets? We don't yet know what the health assets actually are, but we have strong clues about what some of them may be, such as optimism, exercise, love, and friendship. So we start with three entire classes of potential positive independent variables. First, subjective assets: optimism, hope, a sense of good health, zest, vitality, and life satisfaction, for example. Second, biological assets: the upper range of heart rate variability, the hormone oxytocin, low levels of fibrinogen and interleukin-6, and longer repetitive strands of DNA called telomeres, for example. Third, functional assets: excellent marriage, walking briskly up three flights of steps at age seventy without breathlessness, rich friendships, engaging pastimes, and a flourishing work life, for example.

The definition of positive health is empirical, and we are investigating the extent to which these three classes of assets actually improve the following *health and illness targets*:

- Does positive health extend life span?
- Does positive health lower morbidity?
- Is health care expenditure lower for people with positive health?
- Is there better mental health and less mental illness?
- Do people in positive health not only live longer but have more years in good health?

- Do people in positive health have a better prognosis when illness finally strikes?

So the definition of positive health is the group of subjective, biological, and functional assets that actually increase health and illness targets.

Longitudinal Analysis of Existing Data Sets

The definition of positive health will thus emerge empirically, and we have started by reanalyzing six large long-term studies of predictors of illness—studies that originally focused on risk factors, not on health assets. Under the leadership of Chris Peterson, the leading scholar of strengths, and Laura Kubzansky, a young Harvard professor who reanalyzes cardiovascular disease risk for its psychological underpinnings, we are asking if these studies, reanalyzed for assets, predict the health targets above. While the existing data sets concentrate on the negative, these six contain more than a few snippets of the positive, which until now have been largely ignored. So, for example, some of the tests ask about levels of happiness, exemplary blood pressure, and marital satisfaction. We will see what configuration of positive subjective, biological, and functional measures emerge as health assets.

Chris Peterson is hunting down character strengths as health assets. The ongoing Normative Aging Study, begun in 1999, includes two thousand men who were healthy at the outset and are assessed every three to five years for cardiovascular disease. They also undergo a battery of psychological tests each time. One of these is the Minnesota Multiphasic Personality Inventory-2, from which a "self-control" measure has been derived. Chris reports that, holding the usual risk factors constant (and even controlling for optimism), self-control is a major health asset: men with the highest self-control have a 56 percent reduced risk for CVD.

This is an example of how we are comparing health assets to risk factors. We can also make quantitative comparisons of the potency of health assets to risk factors; for example, we estimate that being in the upper quartile of optimism seems to have a beneficial effect on cardiovascular risk roughly equivalent to not smoking two packs of cigarettes daily. (But don't hold me to the number *two* just yet.) Furthermore, does any specific configuration of these health assets optimally predict the targets? Such an optimal configuration of health assets, if it exists, defines empirically the latent variable of positive health with respect to any given disease. That configuration of health assets that is general across a range of diseases defines general positive health.

Once a single positive independent variable is convincingly shown to be a health asset, positive health suggests intervening to build this variable. So, for example, if the risk of cardiovascular death is lower with optimism, or exercise, or a harmonious marriage, or being in the upper quarter of heart rate variability, these become tempting (and inexpensive) targets of intervention. In addition to the practical value of discovering a lifesaving intervention in random-assignment, controlled designs, such intervention studies isolate cause. Positive health then seeks to quantify the cost-effectiveness of such positive interventions and to compare their cost-effectiveness to traditional interventions, such as lowering blood pressure, as well as to combine positive health interventions with traditional interventions and to investigate their joint cost-effectiveness.

Army Database: A National Treasure

Our collaboration with the army will, we expect, become the mother of all future longitudinal studies. Roughly 1.1 million soldiers are taking the Global Assessment Tool, measuring all the positive dimensions and health assets together with the usual risk factors over their entire careers. We expect to join their performance records and their lifetime medical records to the GAT. There are data sets in the army containing information on:

- Health care utilization
- Diagnoses of illness
- Medication
- Body mass index
- Blood pressure
- Cholesterol
- Accidents and mishaps

- Combat and noncombat injuries
- Physical shape
- DNA (needed to identify corpses)
- Job performance

So we can test in a very large sample the extent to which subjective, functional, and biological health assets (taken together and taken separately) predict the following:

- Specific illnesses
- Medication
- Health care utilization
- Mortality

This means that we will be able to answer definitively questions such as:

- Do emotionally fit soldiers suffer fewer infectious illnesses (as measured by antibiotic medication) and better prognosis (as measured by briefer courses of medication) when infection occurs, holding other health variables constant?
- Do soldiers satisfied with their marriage incur lower health care costs?
- Do soldiers who function well socially recover faster from childbirth, a broken leg, or heatstroke?
- Are there identifiable "superhealthy" soldiers (high in subjective, functional, and physical indicators) who need minimal health care, rarely get ill, and recover rapidly when they do?
- Are psychologically fit soldiers less likely to have accidents and to be wounded in combat?
- Are psychologically fit soldiers less likely to be evacuated for nonbattle injuries, disease, and psychological health issues during a deployment?
- Is the physical health of the leader contagious to the health of subordinates? And if so, is it in both directions (good and bad health contagion)?

- Do particular strengths as measured by the Signature Strengths test predict better health and lower costs?
- Does Penn Resilience Training save lives, both on the battlefield, and from naturally occurring illness?

We are under way, as I write, in reanalyzing the six promising data sets and marrying our Robert Wood Johnson efforts to the U.S. Army's Comprehensive Soldier Fitness initiative. Stay tuned.

Cardiovascular Health Assets

I am just back from my fiftieth high school reunion. What amazed me was how healthy my classmates are. Fifty years ago, sixty-seven-year-old men were packing it in, sitting in rocking chairs on porches and waiting to die. Now they run marathons. I gave a brief speech about our expected mortality.

> *A healthy man at age sixty-seven today has a life expectancy of around twenty years. So, unlike our fathers and grandfathers, who were near the end of life at sixty-seven, we are just entering the last quarter of our lives. There are two things we can do to maximize the chances that we will attend our seventieth reunion. The first is to be future oriented: to be drawn into the future, as opposed to dwelling in the past. Work not just for your personal future but the future of your family, this school (the Albany Academies), your nation, and your dearest ideals.*
> *Second, exercise!*

This was my summary of the present state of the science of cardiovascular health as we conceive it. Is there a set of subjective, biological, and functional assets that will boost your resistance to cardiovascular disease beyond average? Is there a set of subjective, biological, and functional assets that will improve your prognosis beyond average if you should have a heart attack? This vital question is largely ignored in CVD research, which focuses on the toxic weaknesses that decrease resistance or undermine prognosis once a first heart attack occurs. The beneficial effect of optimism as a health asset on CVD is a good start, and the aim of our Cardiovascular Health Committee is to broaden our knowledge of health assets.

The committee, at work as I write, is headed by Dr. Darwin Labarthe, director of cardiovascular epidemiology at the U.S. Centers for Disease Control (CDC). This, I must mention, completes a circle in life for me. Darwin was my idol during my college years: he was president of the senior class at Princeton when I entered as a freshman in 1960, and he gave the unforgettable first speech—about honor and acting in the nation's service—on my very first day. Darwin went on to found Wilson Lodge, the nonselective anticlub organization, which was the home and haven for many of the seriously intellectual and activist Princeton undergraduates. While I followed in his footsteps in the leadership of Wilson Lodge, I only admired him from afar as a student, and it has been a matter of immense personal gratification to work with him fifty years later in the service of human flourishing.

Exercise as a Health Asset

"Who should head the exercise committee?" I asked Ray Fowler.

Few of us are lucky enough to acquire mentors after age fifty. Ray became mine when I became president of the American Psychological Association in 1996. He had been president ten years before and had served as CEO (the real seat of power) ever since. In my first couple of months, as an innocent academic, I bumbled my way around the politics of psychotherapy, getting a bloody nose trying to convince the leading private practitioners to get behind evidence-based therapy. Pretty soon I was in "deep shit" with the practitioners.

I reported all this to Ray, and in his soft Alabama accent, he gave me the best political advice I ever heard. "These committee people have great sitting power. APA is a political minefield, and they have been mining it for two decades. You can't begin to deal with them using transactional leadership—they are the grand masters of process. You shine at transformational leadership. Your job is to transform psychology. Use your creativity and come up with a new idea to lead APA."

That, along with my five-year-old daughter telling me I should stop being a grouch and Atlantic Philanthropies, was the start of positive psychology. Since then, I have leaned on Ray repeatedly for advice.

Ray is a seventy-nine-year-old marathoner and a man of legendary willpower. Thirty years ago as a depressed, overweight couch potato, he decided he would transform himself and never having run before, he would run the Boston Marathon the following year. And he did. He is now about 120 pounds and all muscle. There is an annual ten-mile run at the APA convention every summer, and Ray always wins his division. (He says that the only reason he wins is that the competition in his age group is thinning out.) It is now called the Ray Fowler Race.

Ray was one of the visiting scholars who stayed with me at the Geelong Grammar School in Australia in January 2008. One extremely hot evening, he lectured to the faculty about physical exercise and cardiovascular disease, presenting the data that people who walk ten thousand steps every day markedly lower their risk for heart attack. We applauded politely at the end of the lecture, but in real tribute, we all went out and bought pedometers the next day. As Nietzsche tells us, good philosophy always says, "Change your life!"

In response to my question about who should head the exercise committee, Ray advised, "The leading person in exercise, Marty, bar none, is Steve Blair. Everything I know about exercise I learned from Steve. Try to get him to head the committee."

I asked Steve, and he said yes. Like Ray, Steve is all muscle, but unlike Ray, who is shaped like a string bean, Steve is shaped like an eggplant: a five-foot-three-inch, 190-pound eggplant. Like Ray, Steve is a runner and a walker. If you looked at a silhouette of Steve, you would call him obese, and his work is at the center of the obesity-exercise controversy.

Fitness Versus Fatness

The United States has a great deal of obesity, enough so that many call it an epidemic, and huge resources are expended by the government and by private foundations, Robert Wood Johnson included, to curtail this epidemic. Obesity is undeniably a cause of diabetes, and on that ground alone, measures to make Americans less fat are warranted. Steve believes, however, that the real epidemic, the worst killer, is the epidemic of inactivity, and his argument is not lightweight. Here is the argument:

Poor physical fitness correlates strongly with all-cause mortality, and particularly with cardiovascular disease.

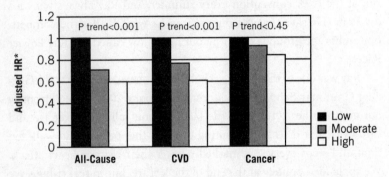

Adjusted Hazard Ratio for All-Cause, CVD, and Cancer Mortality in 4,060 Adults 60+, 989 Deaths

*Adjusted for age, sex, exam year, BMI, smoking, abnormal exercise ECG responses, MI, stroke, HTN, DM, cancer, or hypercholesterolemia, family history of CVD or cancer, and percent maximal heart rate achieved during exercise.

X. Sui et al., *JAGS* 2007

These data (and many others) show clearly that highly fit men and women over sixty have a lower death rate from cardiovascular disease and all causes than the moderately fit, who in turn have a lower death rate than the unfit. This may or may not be true of death from cancer. Lack of exercise and obesity go hand in hand. Fat people don't move around much, whereas thin people are usually on the go.

So which of these two—obesity or inactivity—is the real killer?

There is a huge literature that shows that fat people die of cardiovascular disease more than thin people, and this literature is careful, adjusting for smoking, alcohol, blood pressure, cholesterol, and the like. Very little of it, unfortunately, adjusts for exercise. But Steve's many studies do. Here is a representative one:

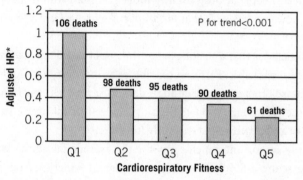

Multivariate + % Body Fat Adjusted HR of All-Cause Mortality by Fitness Groups, ACLS, 2,603 Adults 60+

*Adjusted for age, exam year, smoking, abnormal exercise ECG, baseline health conditions, and percent body fat.

X. Sui et al., *JAMA* 2007; 398; 2507–16

This is the all-cause rate of death for five categories of fitness, holding constant body fat, age, smoking, and the like. The better the fitness, the lower the death rate. This means that two individuals—one in the top fifth of fitness and the other in the bottom fifth of fitness—who weigh exactly the same, have very different risks of death. The fit, but fat, individual has almost half the risk of death of the unfit, fat individual.

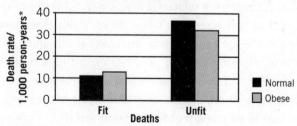

Joint Associations of CRF and % Body Fat with All-Cause Mortality, ACLS 2,603 Adults 60+

*Rates adjusted for age, sex, and exam year.

X. Sui et al., *JAMA* 2007; 298; 2507–16

These data show the risk for death in normal-weight versus obese people who are fit or unfit. In the unfit groups, normal and obese people both have a high risk for death, and it does not seem to matter if you are fat or thin. In the fit groups, both fat and thin people have a much lower risk of death than their counterparts in the unfit groups, with fat but fit people at only slightly more risk than thin fit people. But what I now emphasize is that *fat people who are fit have a low risk of death*.

Steve concludes that a major part of the obesity epidemic is really a couch potato epidemic. Fatness contributes to mortality, but so does lack of exercise. There are not enough data to say which contributes more, but they are compelling enough to require that all future studies of obesity and death adjust carefully for exercise.

These are important conclusions for the average fat adult. Most dieting is a scam, a $59 billion scam last year in America. You can take off 5 percent of your weight in one month by following any diet on the best-seller list. The problem is that 80 percent to 95 percent of people will regain all that weight or more over the next three to five years, just like I did. Dieting can make you thinner, but it is usually only temporary. It does not make you healthier, however, because for most of us, dieting does not stick.

Exercise, in contrast, is not a scam. A much higher percentage of people who take up exercise stick with it and become permanently fit. Exercise is sticky and self-maintaining, dieting is usually not. Even though it lowers your risk for death, exercise will not make you much thinner, since the average vigorous exerciser loses fewer than five pounds of body weight.

Just as optimism is a subjective health asset for cardiovascular disease, it is clear that exercise is a functional health asset: people who exercise a moderate amount have increased health and low mortality, while couch potatoes have poor health and high mortality. The beneficial effects of exercise on health and illness are finally well accepted even within the most reductionist part of the medical community, a guild very resistant to any treatment that is not a pill or a cut. The surgeon general's 2008 report enshrines the need for adults to do the equivalent of walking 10,000 steps per day. (The real danger point is fewer than 5,000 steps a day, and if this describes you, I want to emphasize that the findings that you are at undue risk for death are—there is no other word for it—compelling.) To take the equivalent of 10,000 steps a day can be done by swimming, running, dancing, weight lifting; even yoga and a host of other ways of moving vigorously.

What we need to discover now are new ways to get more people off the couch. I'm not waiting for new techniques, however. I found one that really works for me. The day after Ray's talk, not only did I buy a pedometer, but I began—for the first time in my life—to walk. And walk. (I gave up swimming, having swum two-thirds of a mile a day for twenty years and failing to find any technique that kept me from being bored out of my skull.) I formed an Internet group of pedometrized walkers. Ray and Steve are in it, and also about a dozen other people from several walks of life, varying in age from seventeen to seventy-eight, from Down syndrome adults to chaired professors. We *report* to each other every night exactly how many steps we walked that day. The day feels like a failure under 10,000. When I find myself before bedtime at only 9,000 steps, I go out and walk around the block before reporting in. We *reinforce* one another for exceptional walking: Margaret Roberts just reported 27,692 steps, and I sent her a "Wow!" We give one another *advice* about exercise: my left ankle really hurt for two weeks, and my fellows told me, correctly, that my sneakers— with their new, expensive insoles—had become too tight. "Buy an airdesk [www.airdesks.com]," Caroline Adams Miller advised me. "That way you can play bridge online and walk on the treadmill at the same time." We have become *friends,* bonded by this common interest. I believe such Internet groups are one new technique that will save lives.

I made a New Year's resolution for 2009: to take 5 million steps, 13,700 per day on average. On December 30, 2009, I crossed the 5 million mark, and got "Wow!" and "What a role model!" from my Internet friends. So effective is this group for exercise that I am now trying this out for dieting. Having failed at dieting once every year for forty years, and knowing that I am among the 80 percent to 95 percent who regain all the weight we lose, I am at it again. I started 2010 at 215 pounds, and I also started reporting my daily caloric intake, as well as my number of steps, every night to my Internet friends. Yesterday I took in 1,703 calories and walked 11,351 steps. Today, February 19, 2010, for the first time in more than twenty years, I weigh less than 200 pounds.

Chapter 10

The Politics and Economics of Well-Being

There is a politics behind positive psychology. It is not a politics of left versus right, however. Left and right are the politics of means—empowering the state versus empowering the individual—but, stripped to essentials, they both advocate similar ends: more material prosperity, more wealth. Positive psychology is a politics that advocates no particular means but rather another end. That end is not wealth or conquest but well-being. Material prosperity matters to positive psychology, but only insofar as it increases well-being.

Beyond Money

What is wealth for? I believe it should be in the service of well-being. But in the eyes of economists, wealth is for producing more wealth, and the success of policy is to be measured by how much added wealth it produces. The dogma of economics is that gross domestic product (GDP) tells us how well a nation is doing. Economics now reigns unchallenged in the policy arena. All daily newspapers have a section devoted to money. Economists hold prominent positions in the capitals of the world. When politicians run for office, they campaign about what they will do, or have done, for the economy. We hear frequent reports on television about unemployment, the Dow Jones average, and the national debt. All this policy clout and media coverage stem from the fact that economic indicators are rigorous, widely available, and updated daily.

At the time of the industrial revolution, economic indicators were a very good approximation of how well a nation was doing. Meeting simple human needs for food, shelter, and clothing was chancy, and satisfying these needs moved in lockstep with more wealth. The more prosperous a society becomes, however, the worse an approximation wealth is to how well that society is doing. Basic goods and services, once scarce, became so widely available that in the twenty-first century, many economically developed nations such as the United States, Japan, and Sweden experience an abundance, perhaps an overabundance, of goods and services. Because simple needs are largely satisfied in modern societies, factors other than wealth now play an enormous role in how well these societies are doing.

In 2004 Ed Diener and I published an article, "Beyond Money," which lays out the shortcomings of the gross domestic product and argues that how well a nation is doing is better measured by how enjoyable, engaging, and meaningful the citizens of that nation find their lives—by measuring their well-being. Today the divergence between wealth and the quality of life has become glaring.

The Divergence Between GDP and Well-Being

Gross domestic product measures the volume of goods and services that are produced and consumed, and any events that increase that volume increase the GDP. It does not matter if those events happen to decrease the quality of life. Every time there is a divorce, the GDP goes up. Every time two automobiles collide, the GDP goes up. The more people who scarf down antidepressants, the more the GDP goes up. More police protection and longer commutes to work raise the GDP even though they may lower the quality of life. Economists, humorlessly, call these "regrettables." Cigarette sales and casino profits are included in the GDP. Some entire industries, such as law, psychotherapy, and drugs, prosper as misery increases. This is not to say that law-yers, psychotherapists, and drug companies are bad, but rather that GDP is blind when it comes to whether it is human suffering or human thriving that increases the volume of goods and services.

This divergence between well-being and gross domestic product can be quantified. Life satisfaction in the United States has been flat for fifty years even though GDP has tripled.

Even scarier, measures of ill-being have not declined as gross domestic product has increased; they have gotten much worse. Depression rates have increased tenfold over the last fifty years in the United States. This is true of every wealthy nation, and, importantly, it is not true of poor nations. Rates of anxiety have also risen. Social connect-edness in our nation has dropped, with declining levels of trust in other people and in governmental institutions, and trust is a major predictor of well-being.

Wealth and Happiness

What exactly is the relationship of wealth to happiness? And the question you really care about: how much of your precious time should you devote to pursuing money if what you want is life satisfaction?

There is an enormous literature on money and happiness that compares whole nations with each other and that also looks closely within a given nation and compares rich people to poor people. There is universal agreement on two points:

1. The more money, the more life satisfaction, as the figure on page 224 shows.

In the graph, each circle is a country, with diameter propor-tional to population. The horizontal axis is national per capita GDP in 2003 (the nearest year for which there are complete data) measured in purchasing power dollars at 2000 prices, while the vertical axis is a country's average life-satisfaction rating. Most of the countries of sub-Saharan Africa are on the bottom left, India and China are the two large circles near the left, the Western European countries appear near the upper right, and the United States is the large country on the top right. Life satisfaction is higher in countries with higher GDP per person. Notice that the slope (at the left) is steepest among poor countries, where more money and more life satisfaction go most strongly together.

2. *But* making more money rapidly reaches a point of diminishing returns on life satisfaction.

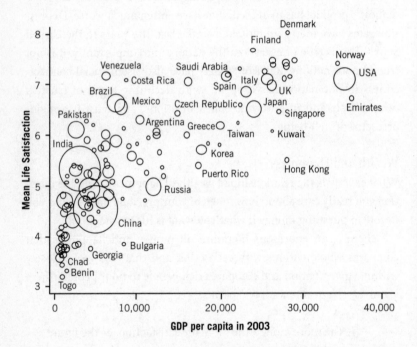

You can see this if you look closely at the figure above, but it is much more obvious when you look within a nation rather than between nations. Below the safety net, increases in money and increases in life satisfaction go up hand in hand. Above the safety net, it takes more and more money to produce an increment in happiness. This is the venerable "Easterlin paradox," and it has been challenged recently by my young colleagues at Penn, Justin Wolfers and Betsey Stevenson. They argue that more and more money will make you happier and happier and that there is no satiation point at all. If true, this would have major implications for policy and for your own life. Here is their clever argument: if you replot the graph above, which shows diminishing returns of increasing wealth on life satisfaction, changing absolute income to log income, lo and behold, the curve becomes a straight line up, with no end in sight. So even though twice as much life satisfaction is produced by a $100 rise in per capita income for poor than for rich nations, a log plot straightens this out.

This is only a conjuring trick, but it is an instructive one. At first glance, you might infer from a never-ending straight line up that if you want to maximize life satisfaction, you should strive to earn more and more money no matter how much money you already have. Or, if public policy is aimed at increasing national happiness, it should create more and more wealth no matter how rich it is already. The trick is that log income has no psychological meaning at all and no implications at all for how you (or governments) should behave about pursuing more wealth. This is because your time is linear (not logarithmic) and precious, because time is money, and because you can choose to use your precious time pursuing happiness in better ways than making more money—particularly when you are already above the safety net. Consider how you might spend your time next year to maximize happiness. If your income is $10,000, and giving up six weekends next year to take a second job will make you an additional $10,000, your net happiness will go up dramatically. If your income is $100,000, and giving up six weekends a year will earn an additional $10,000, your net happiness increase will actually decrease, since the happiness you lose by giving up all that time with family, friends, and pastimes will overwhelm the tiny increment that an additional $10,000 (or even $50,000) would bring. Just how poorly the notion of wealth having no upper limit on happiness fares is exemplified in the table on page 226.

LIFE SATISFACTION FOR VARIOUS GROUPS
(Diener and Seligman, 2004)
Responses to: "You are satisfied with your life," ranging from complete agreement (7) to complete disagreement (1), where 4 is neutral.

Forbes magazine's richest Americans	5.8
Pennsylvania Amish	5.8
Inughuit (Inuit people in northern Greenland)	5.8
African Masai	5.7
Swedish probability sample	5.6
International college student sample (forty-seven nations in 2000)	4.9
Illinois Amish	4.9
Calcutta slum dwellers	4.6
Fresno, California, homeless	2.9
Calcutta pavement dwellers (homeless)	2.9

What? The three hundred richest Americans are no happier than the average Amish or Inuit adult? As for the proposition that happiness rises steadily with log income, what Mr. David Midgley used to say to me in my high school political science class applies: "Correct. No credit."

The measure used in almost all the studies of income and happiness is actually not "How happy are you?" but "How satisfied are you with your life?" In Chapter 1, I dissected the latter question when I discussed why I moved from happiness theory to well-being theory. Your answer to "How satisfied are you with your life?" has two components: what transient mood you happen to be in when you answer and your more abiding evaluation of your life circumstances. A major reason for my giving up happiness theory was that 70 percent of the variance in the answers to this alleged gold standard question was mood, while only 30 percent was evaluation, and I did not think that transient mood should be the be-all and end-all of positive psychology. It also turns out that these two components, mood and judgment, are influenced differentially by income. Increasing income increases the positivity of your evaluation of your life circumstances, but it does not influence your mood very much at all. Further confirmation of this disjunction is found by looking at changes over time within nations. There are fifty-two nations for which substantial time series analyses of subjective well-being (SWB) exist from 1981 to 2007. In forty-five of them, I am pleased to report, SWB has risen. In six, all Eastern European, SWB declined. Importantly, subjective well-being was divided into happiness (mood) and life satisfaction (evaluation), and each was looked at separately. Life satisfaction goes up mostly with income, whereas mood goes up mostly with increased tolerance in the nation. Hence the inference that happiness goes up with income does not bear close scrutiny: the truth is that your judgment that your circumstances are better goes up with income (no surprise), but not your spirits.

When life satisfaction is plotted against income, some very instructive anomalies appear—anomalies that give us hints about what the good life is beyond income. Colombia, Mexico, Guatemala, and the other Latin American countries are a lot happier than they should be given their low gross domestic product. The entire ex-Communist bloc is much unhappier than it should be given its GDP. Denmark, Switzerland, and Iceland, near the top in income, are even happier than their high gross domestic product warrants. Poor people in Calcutta are much happier than poor people in San Diego. Utah is much happier than its income suggests. What these places have in abundance that other places lack gives us clues about what well-being really is.

So I conclude that gross domestic product should no longer be the only serious index of how well a nation is doing. It is not just the alarming divergence between quality of life and GDP that warrants this conclusion. Policy itself follows from what is measured, and if all that is measured is money, all policy will be about getting more money. If well-being is also measured, policy will change to increase well-being. Had Ed Diener and I proposed that measures of well-being replace or supplement GDP thirty years ago, economists would have laughed us out of court. Well-being, they would have said correctly, cannot be measured at all, or at least not with anything like the validity that income can be measured. This is no longer correct, and I will return to this at the very end.

The Financial Downturn

As I write (the first half of 2010), most of the world seems to be recovering from a sudden and frightening financial downturn. I certainly was frightened. Close to retirement age, with a wife and seven children, my life savings were down 40 percent a year and a half ago. What went wrong, and whom can we blame? As stocks plummeted, I heard about the scapegoats: greed, lack of regulation, overpaid CEOs too dumb to understand the derivatives that their smart younger geeks created, Bush and Cheney and Greenspan, short-selling, short-termism, unscrupulous mortgage salesmen, corrupt bond rating services, and Bear Stearns CEO Jimmy Cayne playing bridge while his company burned. My thoughts about each of these (except Jimmy's bridge) are no more informed than those of my readers. Two of the alleged culprits hit close enough to home, however, for me to comment: lousy ethics and too much optimism.

ETHICS VERSUS VALUES

"We're responsible for the recession, Marty. We gave these students their MBA sheepskins, and they went off to Wall Street, creating these disastrous derivatives. They made themselves a bundle, but they knew that in the long run these derivatives would be bad for their companies and bad for the whole national economy." The speaker was my friend Yoram (Jerry) Wind.

Jerry, the Lauder Professor of Marketing at Penn's Wharton School of Business, is a shrewd judge of local university politics and an even shrewder judge of international finance. "The faculty can prevent this from ever happening again. Shouldn't we teach ethics as a serious part of the business curriculum?"

Ethics?

If Jerry's analysis was right, and the downturn was caused by mathematical wizards and greedy salespeople who profited hugely in the short run by selling derivatives that they knew would crash and burn in the long run, would courses in ethics help? Was the problem ignorance of ethical principles? I think this puts more weight on ethics than ethics can bear and not enough weight on values. When a mother rushes into a burning building to save her child, she is not acting from any ethical principle, and this is not an ethical act; she rushes in because the life of her child is overwhelmingly important to her—because she cares about her child. In his marvelous essay "The Importance of What We Care About," Harry Frankfurt, the Princeton philosopher who also wrote the popular essay "On Bullshit," argues that the understanding of what we care about is the great unasked question in philosophy.

Ethics and what we care about are not by any means the same thing. I might be a master of ethical reasoning, a whiz at moral philosophy, but if what I really care about is having sex with little children, my behavior will be beneath contempt. Ethics are the rules you apply to get what you care about. What you care about—your values—is more basic than ethics. There is no philosophical discipline concerned with what we care about, and there is just the same gap in psychology. How does a person come to care about bridge, or breasts, or accumulating money, or greening the world? This is an issue that I have worked on my entire career, and I have not penetrated it well enough.

There are some things we care about instinctively: water, food, shelter, sex. But most of what we care about is learned. Freud called what we learn to care about cathexis: a negative cathexis occurs when some neutral event, such as seeing a snake, co-occurs with a trauma, such as getting your hand smashed in a car door. Snakes become heinous. A positive cathexis occurs when a previously neutral event is paired with ecstasy: a young boy is masturbated by his older sister using her feet. He becomes a foot fetishist, cathected to the female foot, and he makes a satisfactory life by becoming a shoe salesman. Gordon Allport, one of the fathers of the modern study of personality, called this result the "functional autonomy of motives": the fact that stamps, once just small pieces of colored paper of neutral valence, become an obsession for the stamp collector. Allport and Freud observed this, but neither could explain it.

My solution was "prepared" Pavlovian conditioning. Rats that get a bell and a sweet taste paired with foot shock learn to be afraid only of the bell, but they continue to love the sweet taste. When the same bell and sweet taste are paired with stomach sickness, in contrast, they hate sweets thereafter but remain indifferent to the bell. This is called the Garcia effect, after John Garcia, the iconoclastic psychologist who discovered it in 1964 and thereby overthrew the first principle of learning theory and of British associationism: that any stimulus that just happens to be paired with any other stimulus will become associated by the mind. I called the Garcia effect the sauce béarnaise phenomenon, after I came to hate sauce béarnaise when it was followed by the stomach flu, whereas I continued to love *Tristan and Isolde,* the opera that was playing during that dinner. (My critics derided this as the "most publicized meal since the Last Supper.") Learning is biologically selective, with evolutionarily prepared stimuli—taste and illness, but not bell and illness—learned about very readily. Prepared fear conditioning (a picture of a formerly neutral spider paired with a shock to the hand) occurs in one trial, does not readily extinguish when shocks no longer follow the spider, and it defies rationality, remaining full-blown even when the shock electrodes are removed. Easy learning, resistance to extinction, and irrationality are the very properties of cathexis and of the functional autonomy of motives.

I reasoned that prepared learning might not just be species-wide (all monkeys learn to fear snakes in just one viewing of an older monkey scared of a snake), but it might be genetically heritable within a family: specific fears run in families, and identical twins are more concordant for depression—and for almost all personality traits—than fraternal twins. So the disposition to cathect to breasts or to stamps or to the life of the mind or to liberal politics might be biologically prepared and heritable: easily learned, hard to extinguish, and below the cognitive radar. That's my story, quite speculative and incomplete, but I believe it is on the right track, and I'm sticking to it.

So in my view, if Wharton graduates—MBAs who care only about making a quick fortune—are given ten ethics courses, it will have no effect. It is a matter not of ethics but of what they care about. And a course in values would probably not do much good either, since wherever values come from, it is not from lectures and assigned readings.

My conversation with Jerry took place on our way to class; I was guest lecturing in his MBA course on creativity and marketing. It so happened that the weekend before, I was at West Point lecturing to the cadets. The contrast between these two groups is breathtaking. Not in grades or in IQ or in their accomplishments—these are two of the most selective universities in the world—but in what they care about. There is almost no overlap between the values of the two groups. The Wharton MBAs care about making money. The West Point cadets care about serving the nation. The students are selected and they select themselves primarily around this difference in what they care about. If our business schools wish to avoid the economic consequences of greed and short-termism, they have to select their students for a broader moral circle and for long-termism.

If a new course is to be given at Wharton, it should not be about ethics. Rather it should be about "positive business." It would be aimed at broadening what MBAs care about. Getting what we care about—positive accomplishment—is one of the elements of well-being. A course on positive business would argue that well-being comes from five different pursuits: positive emotion, engagement, positive accomplishment, positive relations, and meaning. If you want well-being, you will not get it if you care only about accomplishment. If we want our students to flourish, we must teach that the positive corporation and the individuals therein must cultivate meaning, engagement, positive emotion, and positive relations as well as tending to profit. The new bottom line of the positive corporation in this view is profit . . . plus meaning . . . plus positive emotion . . . plus engagement . . . plus positive human relations.

There is a lesson here as well for those of us who are the victims of the recent economic downturn. As I watched my life savings dwindle day by day, I wondered what would happen to my family's well-being if the stock market collapsed even further. Well-being theory says that there are five routes to well-being: positive emotion, engagement, meaning, relationships, and accomplishment. How would my life in these five realms be diminished by a lot less wealth? My total positive emotion would surely go down, for we purchase a lot of positive emotion: good restaurant meals, theater tickets, massages, a sunny retreat in the dead of winter, and pretty clothes for my daughters. But my meaning and engagement in life would remain unchanged; it derives from belonging to and serving what I believe is larger than I am: in my case, increasing the well-being of the world by writing, research, leadership, and teaching. Less money would not affect that. My close relationships might even improve: cooking together, reading plays as a family, learning massage rather than purchasing massage, evenings by the fire in winter, and making clothes together. Not to be forgotten is the well-replicated finding that experiences bring more well-being than material goods of the same price. Accomplishment would be unaffected: I would write this book even if no one paid me to do so. (In fact, I wrote most of it before I even told my publisher about its existence.)

Change of lifestyle is wrenching, but when stared at hard, I concluded that my own well-being and that of my family would actually not be much reduced. One reason the prospect was so terrifying to me, though, is that I am indirectly a child of the Great Depression. My parents were young adults when it hit, and their view of the future was forever altered. "Martin," they would tell me, "become a doctor. Doctors are always needed; that way you'll never starve." There was no safety net at the time of the 1929 Wall Street crash; people did starve, they went without medicine, and they left school. My mother dropped out of high school to support her parents, and my father took the most secure civil service job he could find at the cost of never fulfilling his great political potential. The recession of 2008–9, even if it had gotten much worse, would have been cushioned by the safety net that every wealthy nation has created since the Great Depression: no one would starve, medical care would be intact, and education would still be free. Knowing this also eased my fears—not at four in the morning, perhaps, but at my other waking hours.

OPTIMISM AND ECONOMICS

Apart from ethics, the other alleged culprit for the economic down-turn that I know something about is optimism. Danny Kahneman is a Princeton professor and the only psychologist who works on well-being to ever win the Nobel Prize. Quite finicky about how he is labeled, he does not call himself a positive psychologist and asks me not to call him one. But I think he is. Danny is ambivalent about optimism. On the one hand, he is not against optimism—he actually calls it the "engine of cap-italism." On the other, he indicts overconfidence and delusional opti-mism, saying, "People do things they have no business doing because they believe they'll be successful." Delusional optimism is a first cousin of Kahneman's "planning fallacy," in which planners chronically under-estimate costs and overestimate benefits, because they ignore the base-line statistics for other projects that resemble theirs. Such optimism, he believes, can be corrected by exercises in which investors systematically remember and rehearse realistically how well similar business ventures have actually fared in the past. This is an exercise analogous to "putting it in perspective": the exercise we use to correct negatively "delusional" pessimism in Comprehensive Soldier Fitness.

Barbara ("I hate hope") Ehrenreich, again. She is not ambivalent about optimism. In her chapter "How Positive Thinking Destroyed the Economy," she places the blame for the downturn of 2008–9 on posi-tive thinking. (She also describes optimism as a critical tool for Stalin-ism's social control but somehow refrains from claiming that optimism was also a critical tool for Hitler and Jabba the Hutt.) Motivational gurus such as Oprah, televangelist Joel Osteen and Tony Robbins, she tells us, revved up the general public into buying more than they could afford to repay. Executive coaches espousing positive thinking infected CEOs with the viral and profitable idea that the economy would grow and grow. Academics—she likens me to the Wizard of Oz—provided the scientific props for these hucksters. What Ehrenreich tells us we need is realism, not optimism. Indeed, cultivating realism, rather than positivity, is the theme of her entire book.

This is vacuous.

The view that the meltdown was caused by optimism seems

180 degrees wrong. Rather, optimism causes the market to go up, and pessimism causes it to go down. I am not an economist, but I think that stocks (and the price of goods generally) go up when people are optimistic about their future worth, and they go down when people are pessimistic about their future worth. (This is like the Bronx diet: want to lose weight, eat less; want to gain weight, eat more.) There is no *real* value of a stock or a derivative that can be independent of the perceptions and expectations of investors. Perceptions about what price that piece of paper will have in the future strongly influence price and value.

REFLEXIVE AND NONREFLEXIVE REALITY

There are two kinds of reality. One kind is not influenced by what human beings think, desire, wish for, or expect. There is an independent reality out there when you are a pilot deciding whether to fly during a thunderstorm. There is an independent reality out there when you are deciding which graduate school to attend: how well you will get along with the professors, whether there is adequate laboratory space, whether you can afford the cost. There is the reality of her rejecting you when you propose marriage. In all of these, your thinking and your wishes do not influence the reality, and I am all for keen realism in these circumstances.

The other kind of reality (George Soros, the businessman and philanthropist, calls it "reflexive reality") is influenced and sometimes even determined by expectations and perceptions. Market price is a reflexive reality that is strongly influenced by perception and expectation. Realism about the price of a stock is always invoked after the fact. (The price crashed, so you are now labeled an overconfident optimist. The price zoomed up, so you are now a genius, and I, who sold too early, am labeled an underconfident pessimist.) How much you are willing to pay is not just a judgment of the real value of stock, you are also judging the market's perception of the future value of the stock. When investors are optimistic about the market's perception about the stock's future price, its price goes up. When investors are very (delusionally) optimistic about the market's perceptions of the stock's future price, its price goes way up. When investors are very pessimistic about the market's perception of the future price of a stock, the price of the stock or the derivative crashes, and the economy melts down.

I hasten to add that optimism and pessimism are not the whole story; some investors are still concerned with fundamentals. In the long run, fundamentals anchor the range of the price a stock brings, with the price fluctuating broadly around the value of the fundamentals, but with the short-run price heavily influenced by optimism and pessimism. But even here I believe that "reality" is reflexive and the value of fundamentals is influenced—even if it is not determined—by the market's expectations of the future value of the fundamentals.

The same is true of derivatives (and of goods and services more generally). Consider real estate derivatives—important instruments of the recent downturn. When investors are optimistic about the ability of a mortgagee to repay his or her loan, the value of the mortgage goes up. The mortgagee's ability to repay, however, is not a real ability either; it too is a perceived ability to repay, largely conditional upon the bank's willingness to foreclose, on the perceived future price of the property, and on the interest rate on the mortgage. When investors are pessimistic about the future price of the property, its value goes down. Credit gets tight. The interest being charged now exceeds the perception of the price the property will bring if sold, and so the willingness to foreclose goes up. So the driving force is the investors' perception of the future price of the property and the perceived ability of the mortgagee to repay. These perceptions are self-fulfilling, and they influence, à la the physicist Werner Heisenberg's uncertainty principle, the inability of a mortgagee to repay the debt. When investors are optimistic about the perceived value of the mortgage, the real estate market goes up.

So the claim that optimism caused the meltdown is pure twaddle. The opposite is the case. Optimism causes stocks to rise; pessimism causes stocks to go down. Viral pessimism caused the economic meltdown.

More formally, the Ehrenreich error confuses optimism that does not influence reality with optimism that does influence reality. In the case of whether there will be a total eclipse of the sun viewable from

Philadelphia next year, my hopes have no influence. However, in the case of the future price of stocks, investors' optimism and pessimism strongly influence the market.

What is really going on in Ehrenreich's exhortation to accept reality is more insidious than misconstrued economics. It's not just that she wants women with breast cancer to accept the "reality" of their diseases, she confuses optimism and hope with "sugar-coating" and "denial of understandable feelings of anger and fear." But eschewing optimism is bad, even potentially lethal, medical advice, because it is not unlikely that optimism will cause a better medical outcome through one of the causal pathways outlined in the last chapter. What Ehrenreich appears to be after is a world in which human well-being follows only from externalities such as class, war, and money. Such a crumbling, Marxist worldview must ignore the enormous number of reflexive realities in which what a person thinks and feels goes on to influence the future. The science of positive psychology (and this book) is entirely about such reflexive realities.

Here is one more important case of a reflexive reality that surely influences your life: how positively you view your spouse. Sandra Murray, professor at the State University of New York at Buffalo, has done an extraordinary set of studies on good marriage. She carefully measures what you think about your spouse: how handsome, how kind, how funny, how devoted, and how smart he is. She poses the very same questions about your spouse to your closest friends, and she derives a discrepancy score: if you think more of your spouse than your friends do, the discrepancy is positive. If you are a "realist" and see your spouse exactly as your friends do, the discrepancy is zero. If you are more pessimistic about him than your friends, the discrepancy is negative. The strength of the marriage is directly a function of how positive the discrepancy is. Spouses with very strong benign illusions about their mates have much better marriages. The mechanism is likely that your spouse knows about your illusions, and he tries to live up to them. Optimism helps love, pessimism hurts. Ehrenreich notwithstanding, the literature puts health squarely in the same corner as marriage: pessimism undermines health, and optimism promotes it.

I am all for realism when there is a knowable reality out there that is not influenced by your expectations. When your expectations influence reality, realism sucks.

PERMA 51

Wealth, as we have seen, contributes substantially to life satisfaction, but not much to happiness or good mood. At the same time, there is a huge disparity between gross domestic product—a good measure of wealth—and well-being. Prosperity in the traditional way of keeping score equals wealth. I want to suggest now a better goal and a better way of keeping score. It combines wealth and well-being, and I call it the "New Prosperity."

When nations are poor, at war, afflicted by famine or plague, or in civil discord, it is natural that their first concerns should be about containing damage and building defenses. These distressing straits describe most nations through most of human history. Under these conditions, gross domestic product has a palpable influence on how well things will turn out. In those few instances when nations are rich, at peace, well fed, healthy, and in civic harmony, something very different happens. Their eyes turn upward.

Florence, Italy, of the midfifteenth century is a beacon. She became very rich by 1450, largely through Medici banking genius. She was at peace, well fed, healthy, and harmonious—at least relative to her past and to the rest of Europe. She considered and debated what to do with her wealth. The generals proposed conquest. Cosimo the Elder, however, won the day, and Florence invested its surplus in beauty. She gave us what two hundred years later was called the Renaissance.

The wealthy nations of the world—North America, the European Union, Japan, and Australia—are at a Florentine moment: rich, at peace, enough food, health, and harmony. How will we invest our wealth? What will our renaissance be?

History, in the hands of the postmodernists, is taught as "one damn thing after another." I believe the postmodernists are misguided and misguiding. I believe that history is the account of human progress and that you have to be blinded by ideology not to see the reality of this progress. Balky, with fits and starts, the moral and economic envelope of recorded history is, nevertheless, upward. As a child of the Great Depression and the Holocaust, I am clear eyed about the terrible obstacles that remain. I am clear eyed about the fragility of prosperity, and of the billions of human beings who do not yet enjoy the flowers of human progress. But it cannot be denied that even in the twentieth century, the bloodiest of all of our centuries, we defeated fascism and communism, we learned how to feed six billion people, and we created universal education and universal medical care. We raised real purchasing power more than fivefold. We extended the life span. We began to curb pollution and care for the planet, and we made huge inroads into racial, sexual, and ethnic injustice. The age of the tyrant is coming to an end, and the age of democracy has taken firm root.

These economic, military, and moral victories are our proud heritage of the twentieth century. What gift will the twenty-first century pass to our posterity?

I was asked this of positive psychology at the first World Congress of the International Positive Psychology Association in June 2009. Approximately 1,500 people—including scientists, coaches, teachers, students, health care workers, and executives—gathered in Philadelphia to listen to speeches about the cutting-edge research and practice of positive psychology. At the board meeting, James Pawelski, the director of Penn's MAPP program, posed this question: "What vision can we articulate that is as grand and inspiring as John Kennedy's of putting a man on the moon? What is our moon shot? What is the long mission of positive psychology?"

At this point, Felicia Huppert, the director of the University of Cambridge's Well-Being Institute, leaned over and slipped me a copy of her paper for the congress. I ended Chapter 1 by telling you about her work, and I will end this book by expanding on its promise: Huppert and Timothy So surveyed 43,000 adults, a representative sample of twenty-three nations. They measured flourishing, which they defined as having high positive emotion, plus being high on any three of the following: self-esteem, optimism, resilience, vitality, self-determination, and positive relationships.

These are stringent criteria for flourishing. Their three core elements (positive emotion, engagement, and meaning) are taken from authentic happiness theory, but with the addition of the other elements—most important, positive relationships—they come close to the elements of well-being theory. I would suggest that accomplishment be added as an element so that being in the upper range of positive emotion, and engagement, and meaning, and positive relationships, and positive accomplishment would be my criteria for flourishing.

Notice that such criteria are not merely subjective. As the measurement of well-being has become an acceptable if not yet a wholly respectable endeavor in social science, there are those, led by my friend Richard Layard, who advocate that the common metric should be happiness—being in a good mood and judging your life as satisfying. We would then evaluate policy by how much happiness it brings. While the metric of happiness is a big improvement over just measuring GDP and, indeed, is what authentic happiness theory advocated, it is inadequate. The first problem is that happiness is a wholly subjective target, and it lacks objective measures. Positive relationships, meaning, and accomplishment have both objective and subjective components: not just how you feel about your relationships, but how these people feel about you; not just your sense of meaning (you could be deluded), but the degree to which you actually belong to and actually serve something larger than you are; not just your pride in what you have done, but whether you have actually met your goals, and where these goals stand in their impact on the people you care about and on the world.

The second problem of using just the happiness metric for policy is that it undercounts the vote of half of the world—introverts and low-positive-affective people. Introverts, on average, do not feel as much positive emotion and do not feel as great elation as extraverts feel when they make a new friend or tour a national park. This means that if we were to decide on whether to build a new park by counting how much additional happiness the park will produce, we will undercount introverts. Measuring how much additional well-being—additional happiness plus engagement plus meaning plus relationships plus accomplishment—that a proposed policy will create is not only more objective, it is more democratic.

I expect to see vigorous debate and great refinement about how exactly to measure the elements of well-being, about how to combine wealth with well-being measures, and about the weight of objective criteria versus subjective criteria. There are thorny questions with very real consequences: for example, how to weight income disparity within a nation, how to weight flow versus joy in deriving a positive emotion score, how to weight raising children well, how to weight volunteering, and how to weight green space. In the political and empirical fights that will occur over what should go into a well-being index, it is important to remember that well-being is not the only thing we value as human beings. I do not remotely advocate that well-being should be the only influence on public policy. We value justice, democracy, peace, and tolerance, to name a few other desiderata that might or might not correlate with well-being. But the future calls us to measure and then make policy around well-being rather than just around money. This measurement will be part of our gift to our posterity.

More than just measuring flourishing, our gift will be more flourishing itself. I underscore the downstream benefits of flourishing. Much of this book has been about these downstream effects: when individuals flourish, health, productivity, and peace follow. With this in mind, I now articulate the long mission for positive psychology.

By the year 2051, 51 percent of the people of the world will be flourishing.

Just as I understand the huge benefits of achieving this, I understand how hugely challenging it is. It will be aided, but only a bit, by psychologists in one-on-one coaching or therapy sessions. It will be aided by positive education, in which teachers embed the principles of well-being into what they teach, and the depression and anxiety of their students drop and their students' happiness rises. It will be aided by the teaching of resilience in the army, by which post-traumatic stress disorder will lower, resilience will increase, and post-traumatic growth will become more common. These young soldiers, equipped with better psychological fitness, will become better citizens. It will be aided by positive business, in which the goal of commerce will not be solely profit but also better relationships and more meaning. It will be aided by government being judged by how much it increases not just GDP but also the well-being of the governed. It will also be aided—perhaps crucially—by positive computing.

But even with positive computing, this will not be enough to achieve 51 percent. More than half the population of the world lives in China and India. These two great nations are consumed now with growing their gross domestic products, and so the importance of well-being must also take root there. The very first positive psychology congresses took place in China and India in August 2010. How the ethic of building flourishing in addition to wealth might happen in Asia, I cannot foresee, but I am mindful of contagion: happiness turns out to be more contagious than depression, and upward spirals around positive goals will occur.

Friedrich Nietzsche analyzed human growth and human history in three stages. The first, he calls the "Camel." The Camel just sits there, moans, and takes it. The first four millennia of recorded history are the Camel. The second, he calls the "Lion." The Lion says "no." "No" to poverty, "no" to tyranny, "no" to plague, "no" to ignorance. Western politics since 1776, or even since the drafting of the Magna Carta in 1215, can be seen as the uphill struggle to say "no." This has undeniably been working.

What if the Lion really worked? What if humanity could actually say "no" successfully to all the disabling conditions of life? What then? Nietzsche tells us that there is a third stage of development: the "Child Reborn." The Child asks, "To what can we say 'yes'?" What can every human being affirm?

We can all say "yes" to more positive emotion.
We can all say "yes" to more engagement.
We can all say "yes" to better relationships.
We can all say "yes" to more meaning in life.
We can all say "yes" to more positive accomplishment.

We can all say "yes" to more well-being.

APPENDIX:
SIGNATURE STRENGTHS TEST

I will now describe each of the twenty-four strengths. My description will be simple and brief, just enough to have you recognize the strengths. For my purposes now, I want to tell you just enough so that you have the strength clearly in mind. At the end of each description of the twenty-four strengths, there is a self-rating scale for you to fill out. It consists of two of the most discriminating questions from the complete questionnaire,* which can be found on the website www.authentichappiness.org. Your answers will roughly rank order your strengths in the same way as the website.

Wisdom and Knowledge

The first virtue cluster is wisdom. The five routes to displaying wisdom and its necessary antecedent, knowledge, are the strengths in this cluster. I have arranged them from the most developmentally basic, curiosity, up to the most mature, perspective.

1. Curiosity/Interest in the World

Curiosity about the world entails openness to experience and flexibility about matters that do not fit one's preconceptions. Curious people do not simply tolerate ambiguity; they like it and are intrigued by it. Curiosity can either be specific (for example, only about polyantha roses) or global; a wide-eyed approach to everything. Curiosity is actively engaging novelty, and the passive absorption of information does not display this strength (for instance, couch potatoes clicking

---

*The questionnaire is the work of the Values-in-Action (VIA) Institute under the direction of Christopher Peterson and Martin Seligman. Funding for this work has been provided by the Manuel D. and Rhoda Mayerson Foundation. Both this adaptation and the longer version on the website are copyrighted by VIA.

their TV remotes). The opposite end of the dimension of curiosity is being easily bored.

If you are not going to use the website to take the Strengths Questionnaire, please answer the following two questions:

a) The statement "I am always curious about the world" is

Very much like me	5
Like me	4
Neutral	3
Unlike me	2
Very much unlike me	1

b) "I am easily bored" is

Very much like me	1
Like me	2
Neutral	3
Unlike me	4
Very much unlike me	5

Total your score for these two items and write it here. _____
This is your curiosity score.

2. Love of Learning

You love learning new things, whether you are in a class or on your own. You always loved school, reading, and museums—anywhere and everywhere there is an opportunity to learn. Are there domains of knowledge in which you are *the* expert? Is your expertise valued by people in your social circle or by the larger world? Do you love learning about these domains, even in the absence of any external incentives to do so? For example, postal workers all have zip code expertise, but this knowledge reflects a strength only if it has been acquired for its own sake.

a) The statement "I am thrilled when I learn something new" is

Very much like me	5
Like me	4

Neutral   3
Unlike me   2
Very much unlike me   1

b) "I never go out of my way to visit museums" is
Very much like me   1
Like me   2
Neutral   3
Unlike me   4
Very much unlike me   5

Total your score for these two items and write it here. _____
This is your love of learning score.

3. Judgment/Critical Thinking/Open-Mindedness

Thinking things through and examining them from all sides are important aspects of who you are. You do not jump to conclusions, and you rely only on solid evidence to make your decisions. You are able to change your mind.

By judgment, I mean the exercise of sifting information objectively and rationally, in the service of the good for self and others. Judgment in this sense is synonymous with critical thinking. It embodies reality orientation and is the opposite of the "logical" errors that plague so many depressives: for example, overpersonalization ("It's always my fault") and black-or-white thinking. The opposite of this strength is thinking in ways that favor and confirm what you already believe. This is a significant part of the healthy trait of not confusing your own wants and needs with the facts of the world.

a) The statement "When the topic calls for it, I can be a highly rational thinker" is
Very much like me   5
Like me   4
Neutral   3
Unlike me   2
Very much unlike me   1

b) "I tend to make snap judgments" is

Very much like me	1
Like me	2
Neutral	3
Unlike me	4
Very much unlike me	5

Total your score for these two items and write it here. _____
This is your judgment score.

4. Ingenuity/Originality/Practical Intelligence/Street Smarts

When you are faced with something you want, you are outstanding at finding novel yet appropriate behavior to reach that goal. You are rarely content with doing something the conventional way. This strength category includes what people mean by creativity, but I do not limit it to traditional endeavors within the fine arts. This strength is also called "practical intelligence," or, more bluntly, common sense. Or even more bluntly, street smarts.

a) "I like to think of new ways to do things" is

Very much like me	5
Like me	4
Neutral	3
Unlike me	2
Very much unlike me	1

b) "Most of my friends are more imaginative than I am" is

Very much like me	1
Like me	2
Neutral	3
Unlike me	4
Very much unlike me	5

Total your score for these two items and write it here. _____
This is your ingenuity score.

5. Social Intelligence/Personal Intelligence/Emotional Intelligence

Social and personal intelligence is knowledge of self and others. You are aware of the motives and feelings of others, and you can respond well to them. Social intelligence is the ability to notice differences among others, especially with respect to their moods, temperament, motivations, and intentions—and then to act upon these distinctions. This strength is not to be confused with merely being introspective, psychologically minded, or ruminative; it shows up in socially skilled action.

Personal intelligence consists of finely tuned access to your own feelings and the ability to use that knowledge to understand and guide your behavior. Taken together, Daniel Goleman has labeled these strengths "emotional intelligence." This set of strengths is likely fundamental to other strengths such as kindness and leadership.

Another aspect of this strength is niche finding: putting oneself in settings that maximize one's skills and interests. Have you chosen your work, your intimate relations, and your leisure to put your best abilities into play—every day if possible? Do you get paid for doing what you are truly best at? The Gallup Corporation found that workers could readily answer the question "Does your job allow you every day to do what you do best?" Consider Michael Jordan, so mediocre as a baseball player, and the niche he chose in basketball. In order to find your niche, you have to be able to identify what you do best, whether these are strengths and virtues on the one hand or talents and abilities on the other.

a) "No matter what the social situation, I am able to fit in" is

Very much like me	5
Like me	4
Neutral	3
Unlike me	2
Very much unlike me	1

b) "I am not very good at sensing what other people are feeling" is

Very much like me	1
Like me	2

Neutral	3
Unlike me	4
Very much unlike me	5

Total your score for these two items and write it here. _____
This is your social intelligence score.

6. Perspective

I use the label "perspective" to describe the most mature strength in this category: wisdom. Others seek you out to draw on your experience to help them solve problems and gain perspective. You have a way of looking at the world that makes sense to others and yourself. Wise people are the experts in what is most important, and knottiest, in life.

a) "I am always able to look at things and see the big picture" is

Very much like me	5
Like me	4
Neutral	3
Unlike me	2
Very much unlike me	1

b) "Others rarely come to me for advice" is

Very much like me	1
Like me	2
Neutral	3
Unlike me	4
Very much unlike me	5

Total your score for these two items and write it here. _____
This is your perspective score.

Courage

The strengths that make up courage reflect the open-eyed exercise of will toward uncertain worthy ends in the face of strong adversity. This virtue is universally admired, and every culture has heroes who exemplify this virtue. I include valor, perseverance, and integrity as three ubiquitous routes to this virtue.

7. Valor and Bravery

You do not shrink from threat, challenge, pain, or difficulty. Valor is more than bravery under fire, when one's physical well-being is threatened. It refers as well to intellectual or emotional stances that are unpopular, difficult, or dangerous. Over the years, investigators have distinguished between moral valor and physical valor or bravery. Another way to slice the valor pie is based on the presence or absence of fear.

The brave person is able to uncouple the emotional and behavioral components of fear, resisting the behavioral response of flight and facing the fearful situation despite the discomfort produced by subjective and physical reactions. Fearlessness, boldness, and rashness are not valor; it is facing danger, despite fear, that marks valor.

The notion of valor has broadened over history from battlefield courage, or physical courage, to now include moral courage and psychological courage. Moral courage is taking stands that you know are unpopular and are likely to bring you ill fortune. Rosa Parks taking a front seat on a Montgomery, Alabama, bus in 1955 is an American exemplar. Whistle-blowing is another. Psychological courage includes the stoic and even cheerful stance needed to face serious ordeals and persistent illness without the loss of dignity.

a) "I have taken frequent stands in the face of strong opposition" is

Very much like me	5
Like me	4
Neutral	3
Unlike me	2
Very much unlike me	1

b) "Pain and disappointment often get the better of me" is

Very much like me	1
Like me	2
Neutral	3

Unlike me	4
Very much unlike me	5

Total your score for these two items and write it here. _____
This is your valor score.

8. Perseverance/Industry/Diligence

You finish what you start. The industrious person takes on difficult projects and finishes them. He or she "gets it out the door" and does so with good cheer and minimal complaint. You do what you say you will do and sometimes more, never less. At the same time, perseverance does not mean dogged or obsessive persistence of unattainable goals. The truly industrious person is flexible, realistic, and not perfectionistic. Ambition has both positive and negative meanings, but its desirable aspects belong in this strength category.

a) "I always finish what I start" is

Very much like me	5
Like me	4
Neutral	3
Unlike me	2
Very much unlike me	1

b) "I get sidetracked when I work" is

Very much like me	1
Like me	2
Neutral	3
Unlike me	4
Very much unlike me	5

Total your score for these two items and write it here. _____
This is your perseverance score.

9. Integrity/Genuineness/Honesty

You are an honest person, not only by speaking the truth but by living your life in a genuine and authentic way. You are down to earth and without pretense; you are a "real" person. By integrity and genuineness, I mean more than just telling the truth to others; I mean representing yourself—your intentions and commitments—to others and to yourself in a sincere fashion, whether by word or deed. "To thine own self be true . . . and thou canst not then be false to any man" (William Shakespeare).

a) "I always keep my promises" is

Very much like me	5
Like me	4
Neutral	3
Unlike me	2
Very much unlike me	1

b) "My friends never tell me I'm down to earth" is

Very much like me	1
Like me	2
Neutral	3
Unlike me	4
Very much unlike me	5

Total your score for these two items and write it here. ____
This is your integrity score.

Humanity and Love

The strengths here are displayed in positive social interaction with other people: friends, acquaintances, family members, and also strangers.

10. Kindness and Generosity

You are kind and generous to others, and you are never too busy to do a favor. You enjoy doing good deeds for others, even if you do not know them well. How frequently do you take the interests of another human being at least as seriously as your own? All the traits in this category have at their core the acknowledgment of other people's worth, a worth that can equal or even transcend your own. The "kindness" category encompasses various ways of relating to another person that are guided by that person's best interests, and these may override your own immediate wishes and needs. Are there other people—family members, friends, fellow workers, or even strangers—for whom you assume responsibility? Empathy and sympathy are useful components of this strength. Shelley Taylor, psychology professor at UCLA, in discussing the masculine response to adversity as fight and flight, split off this category as the feminine response to threat, and called it "tending and befriending."

a) "I have voluntarily helped a neighbor in the last month" is

Very much like me	5
Like me	4
Neutral	3
Unlike me	2
Very much unlike me	1

b) "I am rarely as excited about the good fortune of others as I am about my own" is

Very much like me	1
Like me	2
Neutral	3
Unlike me	4
Very much unlike me	5

Total your score for these two items and write it here. _____
This is your kindness score.

11. Loving and Allowing Oneself to Be Loved

You value close and intimate relations with others. Do the people that you have deep and sustained feelings about feel the same way about you? If so, this strength is in evidence. This strength is more than the Western notion of romance. (It is fascinating that arranged marriages in traditional cultures do better than the romantic marriages of the West.) And I also disavow a "more is better" approach to intimacy. None is a bad thing, but after one, a point of rapidly diminishing returns sets in.

It is more common, particularly among men, to be able to love than to let themselves be loved—at least in our culture. George Vaillant is the custodian of a sixty-year study of the lives of the men in the Harvard classes of 1939 to 1944. These men are now in their eighties, and George interviews them every five years. In his latest round of interviews, a retired physician ushered George into his study to show him a collection of grateful testimonial letters that his patients had sent him on the occasion of his retirement five years before. "You know, George," he said with tears streaming down his cheeks, "I have not read them." This man displayed a lifetime of loving others but no capacity at all for receiving love.

a) "There are people in my life who care as much about my feelings and well-being as they do about their own" is

Very much like me	5
Like me	4
Neutral	3
Unlike me	2
Very much unlike me	1

b) "I have trouble accepting love from others" is

Very much like me	1
Like me	2
Neutral	3
Unlike me	4
Very much unlike me	5

Total your score for these two items and write it here. _____
This is your loving and being loved score.

Justice

These strengths show up in civic activities. They go beyond your one-on-one relationships to how you relate to larger groups, such as your family, your community, the nation, and the world.

12. Citizenship/Duty/Teamwork/Loyalty

You excel as a member of a group. You are a loyal and dedicated teammate, you always do your share, and you work hard for the success of the group. This cluster of strengths reflects how well you work in a group. Do you pull your own weight? Do you value the group goals and purposes even when they differ from your own? Do you respect those who are rightfully in positions of authority, like teachers or coaches (other than Bobby Knight)? Do you meld your identity with that of the group? This strength is not mindless and automatic obedience, but at the same time, I do want to include respect for authority, an unfashionable strength that many parents wish to see their children develop.

a) "I work at my best when I am part of a group" is

Very much like me	5
Like me	4
Neutral	3
Unlike me	2
Very much unlike me	1

b) "I hesitate to sacrifice my self-interest for the benefit of groups I am in" is

Very much like me	1
Like me	2
Neutral	3
Unlike me	4
Very much unlike me	5

Total your score for these two items and write it here. _____
This is your citizenship score.

13. Fairness and Equity

You do not let your personal feelings bias your decisions about other people. You give everyone a chance. Are you guided in your day-to-day actions by larger principles of morality? Do you take the welfare of others, even those you do not know personally, as seriously as your own? Do you believe that similar cases should be treated similarly? Can you easily set aside personal prejudices?

    a) "I treat all people equally, regardless of who they might be" is

Very much like me	5
Like me	4
Neutral	3
Unlike me	2
Very much unlike me	1

    b) "If I do not like someone, it is difficult for me to treat him or her fairly" is

Very much like me	1
Like me	2
Neutral	3
Unlike me	4
Very much unlike me	5

Total your score for these two items and write it here. _____
This is your fairness score.

14. Leadership

You do a good job organizing activities and seeing to it that they happen. The humane leader must first of all be an effective leader, attending to getting the group's work done while maintaining good relations among group members. The effective leader is additionally humane when he or she handles intergroup relations. "With malice toward none and charity toward all. With firmness in the right." For example, a humane national leader forgives enemies and includes them in the same broad moral circle that his or her followers enjoy. He or she is free from the weight of history, acknowledges responsibility for mistakes, and is peaceable. Think of Nelson Mandela on the one hand versus Slobodan Milosevic on the other. All of the characteristics of humane leadership at the global level have ready counterparts among leaders of other sorts: military commanders, CEOs, union presidents, police chiefs, principals, den mothers, and even student council presidents.

a) "I can always get people to do things together without nagging them" is

Very much like me	5
Like me	4
Neutral	3
Unlike me	2
Very much unlike me	1

b) "I am not very good at planning group activities" is

Very much like me	1
Like me	2
Neutral	3
Unlike me	4
Very much unlike me	5

Total your score for these two items and write it here. _____
This is your leadership score.

Temperance

As a core strength, temperance refers to the appropriate and moderate expression of your appetites and wants. The temperate person does not suppress motives but waits for opportunities to satisfy them so that harm is not done to self or others.

15. Self-Control

You can easily hold your desires, needs, and impulses in check when it is appropriate. It is not enough to know what is correct; you must also be able to put this knowledge into action. When something bad happens, can you regulate your emotions yourself? Can you repair and neutralize your negative feelings on your own? Can you generate positive emotions on your own without support from the environment?

a) "I control my emotions" is

Very much like me	5
Like me	4
Neutral	3
Unlike me	2
Very much unlike me	1

b) "I can rarely stay on a diet" is

Very much like me	1
Like me	2
Neutral	3
Unlike me	4
Very much unlike me	5

Total your score for these two items and write it here. _____
This is your self-control score.

16. Prudence/Discretion/Caution

You are a careful person. You do not say or do things you might regret later. Prudence is waiting until all the votes are in before embarking on a course of action. Prudent individuals are farsighted and deliberative. They are good at resisting impulses about short-term goals for the sake of longer-term success. Especially in a dangerous world, caution is a strength that parents wish their children to display: "Just don't get hurt," on the playground, in an automobile, at a party, in a romance, or by a career choice.

a) "I avoid activities that are physically dangerous" is

Very much like me	5
Like me	4
Neutral	3
Unlike me	2
Very much unlike me	1

b) "I sometimes make poor choices in friendships and relationships" is

Very much like me	1
Like me	2
Neutral	3
Unlike me	4
Very much unlike me	5

Total your score for these two items and write it here. _____
This is your prudence score.

17. Humility and Modesty

You do not seek the spotlight, preferring to let your accomplishments speak for themselves. You do not regard yourself as special, and others recognize and value your modesty. You are unpretentious. Humble people see their own aspirations, their personal victories and defeats, as pretty unimportant. In the larger scheme of things, what you have accomplished and what you have suffered does not amount to much. The modesty that follows from these beliefs is not just a display, but rather an eye into your being.

a) "I change the subject when people pay me compliments" is

Very much like me	5
Like me	4
Neutral	3
Unlike me	2
Very much unlike me	1

b) "I often brag about my accomplishments" is

Very much like me	1
Like me	2
Neutral	3
Unlike me	4
Very much unlike me	5

Total your score for these two items and write it here. _____
This is your humility score.

Transcendence

I use *transcendence* for the final cluster of strengths. This term is not popular throughout history—*spirituality* is the label of choice—but I wanted to avoid confusion between one of the specific strengths, spirituality, with the nonreligious strengths in this cluster, like enthusiasm and gratitude. By transcendence, I mean emotional strengths that reach outside and beyond you to connect you to something larger and more permanent: to other people, to the future, to evolution, to the divine, or to the universe.

18. Appreciation of Beauty and Excellence

You stop and smell the roses. You appreciate beauty, excellence, and skill in all domains: nature and art, mathematics and science, and in everyday things. Appreciation of beauty in art, or in nature, or just in living is an ingredient of the good life. When intense, it is accompanied by the unfashionable emotions of awe and wonder. Witnessing virtuosity in sports or witnessing acts of human moral beauty or virtue provokes the kindred emotion of elevation.

a) "In the last month, I have been thrilled by excellence in music, art, drama, film, sport, science, or mathematics" is

Very much like me	5
Like me	4
Neutral	3
Unlike me	2
Very much unlike me	1

b) "I have not created anything of beauty in the last year" is

Very much like me	1
Like me	2
Neutral	3
Unlike me	4
Very much unlike me	5

Total your score for these two items and write it here. _____
This is your appreciation of beauty score.

19. Gratitude

You are aware of the good things that happen to you, and you never take them for granted. You always take the time to express your thanks. Gratitude is an appreciation of someone else's excellence in moral character. As an emotion, it is a sense of wonder, thankfulness, and appreciation for life itself. We are grateful when people do well by us, but we can also be more generally grateful for good acts and good people: for example, "How wonderful life is while you're in the world," as Elton John once sang. Gratitude can also be directed toward impersonal and nonhuman sources—God, nature, animals—but it cannot be directed toward the self. When in doubt, remember that the word comes from the Latin, *gratia*, which means grace.

a) "I always say thank you, even for little things" is

Very much like me	5
Like me	4
Neutral	3
Unlike me	2
Very much unlike me	1

b) "I rarely stop and count my blessings" is

Very much like me	1
Like me	2
Neutral	3
Unlike me	4
Very much unlike me	5

Total your score for these two items and write it here. _____
This is your gratitude score.

20. Hope/Optimism/Future-Mindedness

You expect the best in the future, and you plan and work in order to achieve it. Hope, optimism, and future-mindedness are a family of strengths that represent a positive stance toward the future. Expecting that good events will occur, feeling that these will ensue if you try hard, and planning for the future sustain good cheer in the here and now and galvanize a goal-directed life.

a) "I always look on the bright side" is

Very much like me	5
Like me	4
Neutral	3
Unlike me	2
Very much unlike me	1

b) "I rarely have a well-thought-out plan for what I want to do" is

Very much like me	1
Like me	2
Neutral	3
Unlike me	4
Very much unlike me	5

Total your score for these two items and write it here. _____
This is your optimism score.

21. Spirituality/Sense of Purpose/Faith/Religiousness

You have strong and coherent beliefs about the higher purpose and meaning of the universe. You know where you fit in the larger scheme. Your beliefs shape your actions and are a source of comfort to you. After a half century of neglect, psychologists are again studying spirituality and religiosity in earnest, no longer able to ignore their importance to people of faith. Do you have an articulate philosophy of life, religious or secular, that locates your being in the larger universe? Does life have meaning for you by virtue of attachment to something larger than you are?

a) "My life has a strong purpose" is

Very much like me	5
Like me	4
Neutral	3

Unlike me   2
Very much unlike me   1

b) "I do not have a calling in life" is
Very much like me   1
Like me   2
Neutral   3
Unlike me   4
Very much unlike me   5

Total your score for these two items and write it here. _____
This is your spirituality score.

22. Forgiveness and Mercy

You forgive those who have done you wrong. You always give people a second chance. Your guiding principle is mercy and not revenge. Forgiveness represents a set of prosocial changes that occur within an individual who has been offended or hurt by someone else. When people forgive, their basic motivations or actions regarding the transgressor become more positive (for example, benevolent, kind, generous) and less negative (vengeful, avoidant). It is useful to distinguish between forgivingness, which is a readiness or proneness to forgive, and forgiveness, which can be thought of as changes vis-à-vis a specific transgressor and a specific transgression.

a) "I always let bygones be bygones" is
Very much like me   5
Like me   4
Neutral   3
Unlike me   2
Very much unlike me   1

b) "I always try to get even" is
Very much like me   1
Like me   2
Neutral   3

Unlike me	4
Very much unlike me	5

Total your score for these two items and write it here. ____
This is your forgiveness score.

23. Playfulness and Humor

You like to laugh and bring smiles to other people. You can easily see the light side of life. Up to this point, our list of strengths sounds grimly righteous: kindness, spirituality, valor, and ingenuity. Cotton Mather or Girolamo Savonarola in the guise of social science. The last two strengths, however, are the most fun. Are you playful? Are you funny?

a) "I always mix work and play as much as possible" is

Very much like me	5
Like me	4
Neutral	3
Unlike me	2
Very much unlike me	1

b) "I rarely say funny things" is

Very much like me	1
Like me	2
Neutral	3
Unlike me	4
Very much unlike me	5

Total your score for these two items and write it here. ____
This is your humor score.

24. Zest/Passion/Enthusiasm

You are a spirited person. You throw yourself body and soul into the activities you undertake. Do you wake up in the morning looking forward to the day? Is the passion that you bring to activities infectious? Do you feel inspired?

a) "I throw myself into everything I do" is

Very much like me	5
Like me	4
Neutral	3
Unlike me	2
Very much unlike me	1

b) "I mope a lot" is

Very much like me	1
Like me	2
Neutral	3
Unlike me	4
Very much unlike me	5

Total your score for these two items and write it here. _____
This is your zest score.

Summary

At this point, you will have gotten your scores as well as their meaning and norms from the website, or you will have scored each of your twenty-four strengths in the book yourself. If you are not using the website, write your score for each of the twenty-four strengths in the spaces below, and then rank them from highest to lowest.

Wisdom and Knowledge

1. Curiosity _____
2. Love of learning _____
3. Judgment _____
4. Ingenuity _____
5. Social intelligence _____
6. Perspective _____

Courage

7. Valor _____
8. Perseverance _____
9. Integrity _____

APPENDIX: SIGNATURE STRENGTHS TEST

Humanity and Love

10. Kindness ____
11. Loving ____

Justice

12. Citizenship ____
13. Fairness ____
14. Leadership ____

Temperance

15. Self-control ____
16. Prudence ____
17. Humility ____

Transcendence

18. Appreciation of Beauty ____
19. Gratitude ____
20. Hope ____
21. Spirituality ____
22. Forgiveness ____
23. Humor ____
24. Zest ____

Typically you will have five or fewer scores of 9 or 10, and these are your highest strengths—at least as you self-reported on them. Circle them. You will also have several low scores in the 4-to-6 range (or lower), and these are your weaknesses.

THANKS AND ACKNOWLEDGMENTS

This book began because it was too hot to go out. The seven of us were on the Greek island of Santorini in July 2009, and it was 110 degrees. Mandy and the five kids rushed out every morning to tour. I stayed in the air-conditioned room and wondered what to do. I did not intend to write a book, but I had been refining my thinking about what happiness is for a decade and had been engaged in eight large projects that stemmed from positive psychology. And it all converged to a single point: 51—that in the year 2015, 51 percent of the world's population will be flourishing. So I began to put this all on paper, to see if what the decade had wrought hung together. The first chapter just flowed out of me.

"I don't have an audience in mind," I told Mandy.

"Just write it for yourself, " she responded, going off to the beach. Within a week, the first chapter was done, and the eight projects started to cohere into chapters: What Well-Being Is; Depression, Prevention, and Therapy; Master's of Applied Positive Psychology; Positive Education; Comprehensive Soldier Fitness; Achievement and Intelligence; Positive Health; 51.

This is how I organize my gratitude and the acknowledgments.

My debt to some people is sweeping, and their inspiration pervades the whole: Robert Nozick, Peter Madison, Byron Campbell, Ernie Steck, Bob Olcott, Miss Eldred (her first name could not be found in the archives of Public School 16 of Albany, New York), Richard Solomon, and Paul Rozin set the stage for positive psychology long ago when, as a young person, I was fortunate to have them as teachers. Hans Eysenck, Ray Fowler, Mike Csikszentmihalyi, Steve Maier, Jack

THANKS AND ACKNOWLEDGMENTS

Rachman, Chris Peterson, Ed Diener, Richard Layard, Aaron Beck, Albert Stunkard, and Barry Schwartz have been my mentors later in life. I can feel their influence in every chapter.

Marie Forgeard, a prize graduate student, did a smashing job on the end notes and gave the entire manuscript a thorough reading. My special thanks to her.

The opening chapter on the theory of well-being and the call to 51, which is the last chapter and the whole point, owes debts to Eranda Jayawickreme, Corey Keyes, Richard Layard, Martha Nussbaum, Dan Chirot, Senia Maymin, Denise Clegg, Philip Streit, Danny Kahneman, Barbara Ehrenreich (total disagreement does not cancel gratitude), Felicia Huppert, Paul Monaco, the Dalai Lama, Doug North, Timothy So, Ilona Boniwell, James Pawelski, Antonella Della Fave, Geoff Mulgan, Anthony Seldon, Jon Haidt, Don Clifton, Dan Gilbert, Robert Biswas-Diener, Jerry Wind, Tomas Sanders, Linda Stone, and Yukun Zhao. Judith Ann Gebhardt thought up the acronym PERMA, an acronym that may outlive much of the rest of positive psychology.

The chapter on drugs, psychotherapy, and prevention owes particular debts to Tayyab Rashid, Acacia Parks, Tom Insel, Rob DeRubeis, Steve Schueller, Afroze Rashid, Steve Hollon, Judy Garber, Karen Reivich, and Jane Gillham.

The chapter on the master's of applied positive psychology would not have been possible without the labors of James Pawelski, Debbie Swick, and the 150 graduates of MAPP. Special thanks go to Derrick Carpenter, Caroline Adams Miller, Shawna Mitchell, Angus Skinner, Yakov Smirnoff, David Cooperrider, Michelle McQuaid, Bobby Dauman, Dave Shearon, Gail Schneider, Aren Cohen, Pete Worrell, Carl Fleming, Jan Stanley, Yasmin Headley (who emblematically sold her Mercedes to pay the tuition), Aaron Boczowski, Marie-Josee Salvas, Elaine O'Brien, Dan Bowling, Kirsten Cronlund, Tom Rath, Reb Rebele, Leona Brandwene, Gretchen Pisano, and Denise Quinlain.

The positive education chapter owes huge debts to Karen Reivich, Stephen Meek, Charlie Scudamore, Richard Layard, Mark Linkins, Randy Ernst, Matthew White, and the students, staff, and teachers of the Geelong Grammar School. Thanks also to Amy Walker, Justin Robinson, Elaine Pearson, Joy and Philip Freier, Ben Dean, Sandy MacKinnon, Hugh Kempster, David Levin, Doug North, Ellen Cole, Dominic Randolph, Jonathan Sachs, J. J. Cutuli, Trent Barry, Rosie Barry, Matt Handbury, Tony Strazerra, Debbie Cling, John Hendry, Lisa Paul, Frank Mosca, Roy Baumeister, Barbara Fredrickson, Diane Tice, Jon Ashton, Kate Hayes, Judy Saltzberg, and Adele Diamond.

"Army Strong" would not have happened without Rhonda Cornum (my hero), Karen Reivich, George Casey, and Darryl Williams. Thanks also to Paul Lester, Sharon McBride, Jeff Short, Richard Gonzales, Stanley Johnson, Lee Bohlen, Breon Michel, Dave Szybist, Valorie Burton, Katie Curran, Sean Doyle, Gabe Paoletti, Gloria Park, Paul Bliese, John and Julie Gottman, Richard Tedeschi, Richard McNally, Paul McHugh, Paul Monaco, Jill Chambers, Mike Fravell, Bob Scales, Eric Schoomaker, Richard Carmona, Carl Castro, Chris Peterson, Nansook Park, Ken Pargament, Mike Matthews, Pat Sweeney, Patty Shinseki, Donna Brazil, Dana Whiteis, Mary Keller, Judy Saltzberg, Sara Algoe, Barbara Fredrickson, John Cacioppo, Norman Anderson, Gary VandenBos, Shelly Gable, Peter Schulman, Deb Fisher, and Ramin Sedehi.

The chapter on intelligence and success leans heavily with profound gratitude and evident admiration on the work of its central character, Angela Lee Duckworth. I also thank Anders Ericsson, John Sabini, Jane Drache, Alan Kors, Darwin Labarthe, and Sheldon Hackney.

The positive health chapter owes debts to Darwin Labarthe, Paul Tarini, Chris Peterson, Steve Blair, Ray Fowler, Arthur Barsky, John Cacioppo, David Sloan Wilson, Ed Wilson, Julian Thayer, Arthur Rubenstein, Elaine O'Brien, Sheldon Cohen, Monte Mills, Barbara Jacobs, Julie Boehm, Caroline Adams Miller, Paul and John Thomas, and my Internet walk group.

I have spent the last forty-five years at my academic home, the University of Pennsylvania, and I have drawn every kind of support from my colleagues and students here: first, Peter Schulman, who is my right arm, Linda Newsted, Karen Reivich, Jane Gillham, Rachel Abenavoli, Denise Clegg, Derek Freres, Andrew Rosenthal, Judy Rodin, Sam Preston, Amy Gutmann, Mike Kahana, Rebecca Bushnell, David Brainard, Ramin Sedehi, Richard Schultz, David Balamuth, Gus Hartman, Frank Norman, Angela Duckworth, and Ed Pugh. I am presently the Zellerbach Family Professor of Psychology and was previously the Robert Fox Leadership Professor of Psychology, and I am grateful to all the Zellerbachs and to Bob Fox for this support.

Positive psychology has been generously funded by Atlantic Philanthropies, the Annenberg Foundation, and especially Kathleen Hall Jamieson, the U.S. Department of Education, the U.S. Department of the Army, the National Institute of Mental Health, Jim Hovey, the Gallup Foundation, the Hewlett-Packard Foundation, the Young Foundation, the Robert Wood Johnson Foundation (especially Paul Tarini), Neal Mayerson of the Mayerson Foundation, and the John Templeton Foundation, with special thanks to Jack Templeton, Arthur Schwartz, Mary Anne Myers, Kimon Sargeant, and Barnaby Marsh.

Positive psychology has been constructively reported by Ben Carey, Stacey Burling, Claudia Wallis, Joshua Wolf Shenk, Rhea Farberman, and Cecilia Simon, among many others, and I am very grateful for such responsible press.

To Leslie Meredith, my hardworking and unfailingly enthusiastic editor, Martha Levin, publisher, Dominick Anfuso, editor in chief, and to Richard Pine, agent without parallel and close friend, my high thanks.

To my seven children, Jenny, Carly, Darryl, Nikki, Lara, David, and Amanda, just for their patience with a father who is married to his work. My highest thanks go to the love of my life and my life companion, Mandy McCarthy Seligman.

NOTES

Preface

1 *If anything changes in the practitioner, it is a personality shift toward depression:* K. S. Pope and B. G. Tabachnick, "Therapists as Patients: A National Survey of Psychologists' Experiences, Problems, and Beliefs," *Professional Psychology: Research and Practice* 25 (1994): 247–58. Research has shown that psychotherapists and psychologists have high rates of depression. In a survey of about five hundred psychologists, Pope and Tabachnick found that 61 percent of their sample reported at least one episode of depression during their career, 29 percent had experienced suicidal feelings, and 4 percent had actually attempted suicide.

American Psychological Association, *Advancing Colleague Assistance in Professional Psychology* (February 10, 2006). Retrieved October 15, 2009, from www.apa.org/practice/acca_monograph.html. In 2006 the APA's Board of Professional Affairs' Advisory Committee on Colleague Assistance (ACCA) issued a report on distress and impairment in psychologists. The report pointed out that depending on how depression is measured, its lifetime prevalence in psychologists ranges from 11 percent to 61 percent. In addition to depression, mental health practitioners are exposed to high levels of stress, burnout, substance abuse, and vicarious traumatization.

See also P. L. Smith and S. B. Moss, "Psychologist Impairment: What Is It, How Can It Be Prevented, and What Can Be Done to Address It?" *Clinical Psychology: Science and Practice* 16 (2009): 1–15.

2 *At this moment, several thousand people around the world:* The International Positive Psychology Association (IPPA) currently counts more than three thousand members from over seventy countries around the world. Approximately 45 percent of the association's members are academic researchers and practicing psychologists. The next 20 percent (called associates) are practitioners involved in putting positive psychology research into practice in applied contexts (schools, businesses, and so on). The next 25 percent are students interested in positive psychology. The remaining 10 percent (affiliates) include people who are simply interested in the field. More details about IPPA can be found at www.ippanetwork.org.

One of several active Internet groups worth joining is friends-of-pp@lists.apa.org.

NOTES

Chapter 1: What Is Well-Being?

5   *Judy zoomed at an astonishingly young age:* "Judith Rodin: Early Career Awards for 1977," *American Psychologist* 33 (1978): 77–80. Judy Rodin won the American Psychological Association's Early Career Award in 1977. This article summarizes her early accomplishments.

Judy Rodin has also recently been selected by *U.S. News & World Report* as one of America's best leaders for her work as head of the Rockefeller Foundation: D. Gilgoff, "Judith Rodin: Rockefeller Foundation Head Changes the Charity and the World," *U.S. News & World Report,* October 22, 2009.

Throughout her career, she has authored or coauthored more than two hundred academic articles and twelve books, including *The University and Urban Renewal: Out of the Ivory Tower and into the Streets* (Philadelphia: University of Pennsylvania Press, 2007).

5   *we even managed to collaborate on a study investigating the correlation of optimism with a stronger immune system:* L. Kamen-Siegel, J. Rodin, M. E. P. Seligman, and J. Dwyer, "Explanatory Style and Cell-Mediated Immunity in Elderly Men and Women," *Health Psychology* 10 (1991): 229–35. In collaboration with Leslie Kamen-Siegel, we found that a pessimistic explanatory style predicted lower immunocompetence in a sample of twenty-six older adults (aged sixty-two to eighty-two years old), controlling for other factors such as current health, depression, medication, weight changes, sleep habits, and alcohol use. Our study, as well as the relation between optimism and the immune system, is discussed further in Chapter 9.

6   *the princes and princesses of ethnopolitical violence, attended:* the conference report is available at www.ppc.sas.upenn.edu/chirot.htm.

7   *the volume* Ethnopolitical Warfare: D. Chirot and M. E. P. Seligman, eds., *Ethnopolitical Warfare: Causes, Consequences, and Possible Solutions* (Washington, DC: American Psychological Association, 2001).

7   *the medical anthropologist Mel Konner:* Mel Konner is the Samuel Candler Dobbs Professor of Anthropology at Emory University, in Atlanta. Among other books, he is the author of: M. Konner, *The Tangled Wing: Biological Constraints on the Human Spirit* (New York: Holt, Rinehart, Winston, 1982). More information on Mel Konner's life and work is available on his website, at www.melvinkonner.com.

8   *Charles Feeney:* Atlantic Philanthropies was in 2006 the third most generous foundation in the United States (giving out a half billion dollars in grants), surpassed only by the Ford and Gates Foundations. For more information on Chuck Feeney's career and philanthropic activities, see J. Dwyer, "Out of Sight, Till Now, and Giving Away Billions," *New York Times,* September 26, 2007.

C. O'Clery, *The Billionaire Who Wasn't: How Chuck Feeney Secretly Made and Gave Away a Fortune Without Anyone Knowing* (New York: Public Affairs, 2007).

8   *It contained some very fine science:* Our 2000 progress report for the Humane Leadership Project can be found at www.ppc.sas.upenn.edu/hlprogressreport.htm#Research.

9   *Thales thought that everything was water:* Thales of Miletus (ca. 624 B.C.–ca. 546 B.C.) is considered by many to be the first philosopher in the Greek tradition. A central claim to Thales' theory is the belief that the world

NOTES

started from water, and that water is the principle of all things. For more information on Thales, see B. Russell, *A Western History of Philosophy* (London: George Allen and Unwin, 1945).

9   *Aristotle thought that all human action was to achieve happiness:* Aristotle, *Nichomachean Ethics* (New York: Oxford University Press, 1998).

9   *Nietzsche thought that all human action was to get power:* F. Nietzsche, *The Will to Power* (New York: Vintage, 1968).

9   *Freud thought that all human action was to avoid anxiety:* S. Freud, *Inhibitions, Symptoms, and Anxiety* (New York and London: W. W. Norton, 1959).

9   *when there are too few variables to explain the rich nuances of the phenomenon in question, nothing at all is explained:* D. Gernert, "Ockham's Razor and Its Improper Use," *Cognitive Systems:* 133–38. A critical discussion of the misuse and limitations of the principle of parsimony.

9   happiness, *which is so overused:* D. M. Haybron, *The Pursuit of Unhappiness: The Elusive Psychology of Well-Being* (New York: Oxford University Press, 2008). A review of the various meanings of happiness.

10   *"People try to achieve just for winning's own sake":* Senia pointed out that although achievement can lead to desirable outcomes and is also often accompanied by positive emotion, achievement can be intrinsically motivating as well.

11   *a far cry from what Thomas Jefferson declared that we have the right to pursue:* A. De Tocqueville, *Democracy in America* (New York: Perennial Classics, 2000). In *Democracy in America,* Tocqueville explained that Jefferson's concept of happiness was one that involved self-restraint in order to achieve long-term fulfillment. Jeffersonian happiness is therefore much closer to enduring well-being than transient pleasure.

D. M. McMahon, *Happiness: A History* (New York: Atlantic Monthly Press, 2006). The best source on the historical evolution of the concept of happiness.

11   *if you ask people who are in flow what they are thinking and feeling, they usually say, "nothing":* M. Csikszentmihalyi, *Creativity: Flow and the Psychology of Discovery and Invention* (New York: Harper Perennials, 1997). Mihalyi Csikszentmihalyi used the example of the creative process to describe the relationship between flow and positive emotion. In his words: "When we are in flow, we do not usually feel happy—for the simple reason that in flow we feel only what is relevant to the activity. Happiness is a distraction. The poet in the middle of writing or the scientist working out equations does not feel happy, at least not without losing the thread of his or her thought. It is only after we get out of flow, at the end of a session or in moments of distraction within it, that we might indulge in feeling happy. And then there is a rush of well-being, of satisfaction that comes when the poem is completed or the theorem is proved."

A. Delle Fave and F. Massimini, "The Investigation of Optimal Experience and Apathy: Developmental and Psychosocial Implications," *European Psychologist* 10 (2005): 264–74.

11   *There are no shortcuts to flow. On the contrary, you need to deploy your highest strengths and talents to meet the world in flow:* M. Csikszentmihalyi, K. Rathunde, and S. Whalen, *Talented Teenagers: The Roots of Success and Failure* (New York: Cambridge University Press, 1997). Csikszentmihalyi, Rathunde, and Whalen found that the development of talent in a group of American teenagers

was linked to the ability to use their concentration abilities, to commit to the development of their skills, and to experience flow.

12   *Hence, the importance of identifying your highest strengths and learning to use them more often in order to go into flow:* M. E. P. Seligman, T. A. Steen, N. Park, and C. Peterson, "Positive Psychology Progress: Empirical Validation of Interventions," *American Psychologist* 60 (2005): 410–21. This idea was first presented in *Authentic Happiness* (2002). In subsequent research, we found that learning to use their signature strengths in a new way made people happier (and less depressed), and that this effect lasted for up to six months after our intervention. Using your highest strengths, however, is not a necessary condition for going into flow: I go into flow when I get a back massage. Using your highest strength is at most only a contributing condition to flow. You can identify your highest strengths by taking the Values in Action survey at www.authentichappiness.org.

12   *Human beings, ineluctably, want meaning and purpose in life:* V. Frankl, *Man's Search for Meaning* (London: Random House / Rider, 2004). A stirring portrait of just how ineluctable the pursuit of meaning is.

13   *a widely researched self-report measure that asks on a 1-to-10 scale how satisfied you are with your life:* E. Diener, R. Emmons, R. Larsen, and S. Griffin. "The Satisfaction with Life Scale," *Journal of Personality Assessment* 49 (1985): 71–75.

13   *how much life satisfaction people report is itself determined by how good we feel at the very moment we are asked:* R. Veenhoven, "How Do We Assess How Happy We Are? Tenets, Implications, and Tenability of Three Theories" (paper presented at conference on New Directions in the Study of Happiness: United States and International Perspectives, University of Notre Dame, South Bend, IN, October 2006).

M. Schwarz and F. Strack, "Reports of Subjective Well-Being: Judgmental Processes and Their Methodological Implications," in *Foundations of Hedonic Psychology: Scientific Perspectives on Enjoyment and Suffering,* eds. D. Kahneman, E. Diener, and N. Schwarz (New York: Russell Sage Foundation, 1999), pp. 61–84.

14   *Introverts are much less cheery than extroverts:* for example, see P. Hills and M. Argyle, "Happiness, Introversion-Extraversion and Happy Introverts," *Personality and Individual Differences* 30 (2001): 595–608.

W. Fleeson, A. B. Malanos, and N. M. Achille, "An Intraindividual Process Approach to the Relationship Between Extraversion and Positive Affect: Is Acting Extraverted as 'Good' as Being Extraverted?" *Journal of Personality and Social Psychology* 83 (2002): 1409–22.

14   *any theory that aims to be more than a happiology:* C. Peterson, *A Primer in Positive Psychology* (New York: Oxford University Press, 2006). In *A Primer in Positive Psychology,* Christopher Peterson noted that the positive psychology movement has unfortunately often been associated with Harvey Ball's clichéd smiley face when featured in the media. Peterson pointed out how misleading this iconography is: "a smile is not an infallible indicator of all that makes life worth living. When we are highly engaged in fulfilling activities, when we are speaking from our hearts, or when we are doing something heroic, we may or may not be smiling, and we may or may not be experiencing pleasure in the moment. All of these are central concerns to positive psychology, and they fall outside the realm of happiology" (p. 7).

15 *the topic is a* construct—*well-being*—*which in turn has several measurable elements, each a real thing, each contributing to well-being,* but none defining well-being: E. Diener, E. M. Suh, R. E. Lucas, and H. L. Smith, "Subjective Well-Being: Three Decades of Progress," *Psychological Bulletin* 125 (1999): 276–302. See this source for more information on the multifaceted nature of subjective well-being.

16 *Many people pursue it for its own sake:* E. L. Deci and R. M. Ryan, *Intrinsic Motivation and Self-Determination in Human Behavior* (New York: Plenum Press, 1985). In other words, the element is intrinsically motivating, as defined by Deci and Ryan.

17 *Abraham Lincoln, a profound melancholic, may have, in his despair, judged his life to be meaningless:* J. Shenk, *Lincoln's Melancholy* (New York: Houghton Mifflin, 2005). A splendid emotional biography of Lincoln.

17 *Jean-Paul Sartre's existentialist play* No Exit: J.-P. Sartre, *No Exit and Three Other Plays* (New York: Vintage, 1949).

18 *Some will even cheat to win:* R. Wolff, *The Lone Wolff: Autobiography of a Bridge Maverick* (New York: Masterpoint Press, 2007). An excellent book on expert bridge and why some experts cheat.

19 *John D. Rockefeller:* R. Chernow, *Titan: The Life of John D. Rockefeller, Sr.* (New York: Vintage, 1998). An outstanding biography of his winning in the first half of his life and then his philanthropy in the second half.

19 Chariots of Fire: D. Putnam, J. Eberts, D. Fayed, and J. Crawford (producers), and H. Hudson (director), *Chariots of Fire* (motion picture), 1981. Burbank, CA: Warner Home Video.

20 *Robert White had published a heretical article:* R. W. White, "Motivation Reconsidered: The Concept of Competence," *Psychological Review* 66 (1959): 297–333.

20 *all of them took place around other people:* H. T. Reis and S. L. Gable, "Toward a Positive Psychology of Relationships," in *Flourishing: Positive Psychology and the Life Well-Lived,* eds. C. L. M. Keyes and J. Haidt (Washington, DC: American Psychological Association, 2003), pp. 129–59. In a review of the evidence, Reis and Gable concluded that good relationships with others may be the single most important source of life satisfaction and emotional well-being across people of all ages and cultures. I am especially indebted to Corey Keyes for his foresighted use of the term and the concept of "flourishing," which antedates my own usage. Although I use the term in a different sense—PERMA—Corey's work has been an inspiration to me.

20 *My friend Stephen Post:* S. Post, J. Neimark, and O. Moss, *Why Good Things Happen to Good People* (New York: Broadway Books, 2008).

20 *doing a kindness produces the single most reliable momentary increase in well-being:* M. E. P. Seligman, T. A. Steen, N. Park, and C. Peterson, "Positive Psychology Progress: Empirical Validation of Interventions," *American Psychologist* 60 (2005): 410–21. In recent research, we found that, among five different positive psychology exercises, the gratitude visit (as described in *Authentic Happiness*) produced the largest positive changes in happiness (and decreases in depressive symptoms), and this effect lasted for a month. In the gratitude visit exercise, participants are asked to write and deliver a letter of gratitude in person to someone who had been especially kind to them but had never been properly thanked.

S. Lyubomirsky, K. M. Sheldon, and D. Schkade, "Pursuing Happiness: The Architecture of Sustainable Change," *Review of General Psychology* 9 (2005): 111–31. Sonja Lyubomirsky and colleagues have also found that asking students to perform five acts of kindness per week over six weeks resulted in an increase in well-being, especially if they performed their five acts of kindness all in one day.

21   *the master strength is the capacity to* be *loved:* D. M. Isaacowitz, G. E. Vaillant, and M. E. P. Seligman, "Strengths and Satisfaction Across the Adult Lifespan, *International Journal of Aging and Human Development* 57 (2003): 181–201. In 2000 we held a meeting in Glasbern, Pennsylvania, to refine the VIA taxonomy of strengths and virtues. More than twenty-five researchers gathered to discuss which strengths should be included. Love—almost implicitly defined as the capacity to love—had always figured high on our list. George Vaillant chastised us for ignoring the capacity to *be* loved. For Vaillant, the capacity to be loved is the master strength. Vaillant's insight came from his seminal work on the Grant Study, an almost seventy-year (and ongoing) longitudinal investigation of the developmental trajectories of Harvard College graduates. (This study is also referred to as the Harvard Study.) In a study led by Derek Isaacowitz, we found that the capacity to love and be loved was the single strength most clearly associated with subjective well-being at age eighty.

21   *loneliness is such a disabling condition:* J. T. Cacioppo and W. Patrick, *Loneliness: Human Nature and the Need for Social Connection* (New York: W. W. Norton, 2008); J. T. Cacioppo, L. C. Hawkley, J. M. Ernst, M. Burleson, G. G. Berntson, B. Nouriani, and D. Spiegel, "Loneliness Within a Nomological Net: An Evolutionary Perspective," *Journal of Research in Personality* 40 (2006): 1054–85. According to Cacioppo and Patrick, social cooperation has been a driving force in the evolution of human behavior. The converse, loneliness, extracts a significant toll from its sufferers by raising stress levels and causing negative cycles of self-defeating behaviors. For instance, Cacioppo and colleagues found that lonely (compared to nonlonely) young adults are higher in anxiety, anger, negative mood, as well as fear of negative evaluation. They are also lower in optimism, social skills and support, positive mood, extraversion, emotional stability, conscientiousness, agreeableness, and sociability.

D. W. Russell, "The UCLA Loneliness Scale (Version 3): Reliability, Validity, and Factor Structure," *Journal of Personality Assessment* 66 (2006). Loneliness can be measured using the UCLA Loneliness Scale, a twenty-item questionnaire.

22   *if they did not bring about positive emotion or engagement or meaning:* R. F. Baumeister and M. R. Leary, "The Need to Belong: Desire for Interpersonal Attachments as a Fundamental Human Motivation," *Psychological Bulletin* 117 (1995): 497–529. A review of the research on the determinants and consequences of the human drive to engage in social relationships (or "need to belong").

22   *the big brain is a social problem solver:* N. Humphrey, *The Inner Eye: Social Intelligence in Evolution* (New York: Oxford University Press, 1986).

22   *The eminent British biologist and polemicist Richard Dawkins:* R. Dawkins, *The Selfish Gene* (New York: Oxford University Press, 1976).

23   *what others are thinking and feeling:* The issue of group selection—pros and cons—is a complicated theoretical one. The main objection to group selection is the "free rider" problem. Imagine a group that wins out because some of

its members have altruism and cooperation along with the hive emotions. They do well in battle, but those members who are the uncooperative cowards among them do even better than the courageous cooperators. These free riders survive and reproduce on the backs (and over the dead bodies) of the brave. The selfish free riders will eventually crowd out the self-sacrificing genetically, and so the entire groups' altruistic edge will fall apart. The most ingenious counter to the free rider problem is that morality and religion are a counteradaptation with a heritable basis among human beings that nullifies the advantage of being a free rider. Selfish free riders are condemned by morality and religion and so lose their reproductive edge. Hence the universality of moral and religious systems among our species. Versions of this argument can be found in Charles Darwin's *Descent of Man* (1871), Chapter 5; in David Sloan Wilson's *Evolution for Everyone* (2007); and most convincingly in Jon Haidt's *The Righteous Mind: Why Good People Are Divided by Politics and Religion* (2011), Chapter 9.

23   *the group is a primary unit of natural selection:* D. S. Wilson, and E. O. Wilson, "Rethinking the Theoretical Foundation of Sociobiology," *Quarterly Review of Biology* 82 (2007): 327–48.

24   *You go into flow when your highest strengths are deployed to meet the highest challenges that come your way:* M. Csikszentmihalyi, *Finding Flow in Everyday Life* (New York: Basic Books, 1997). The precise balance between skills and challenges determines whether an individual will enter flow (or the states of control, relaxation, boredom, apathy, worry, and anxiety). Flow corresponds to the optimal combination of high skills and high challenges, per Csikszentmihalyi.

25   *Richard Layard argues:* R. Layard, *Happiness* (New York: Penguin, 2005).

26   *why we choose to have children:* N. Powdthavee, "Think Having Children Will Make You Happy?" *The Psychologist* 22 (2009): 308-11. A substantial literature measuring life satisfaction and happiness consistently finds less, or at best no more, among parents than non-parents.

J. Senior, "All Joy and No Fun," *New York Magazine*, July 4, 2010. Jennifer Senior sets out the controversy well, and captures my view: "Happiness is best defined in the ancient Greek sense: leading a productive, purposeful life. And the way we take stock of that life, in the end, isn't by how much fun we had, but what we did with it. (Seligman has seven children.)"

26   Brave New World: A. Huxley, *Brave New World* (New York: Harper and Brothers, 1932). Aldous Huxley's unforgettable dystopia.

26   *subjective and objective measures of positive emotion, engagement, meaning:* E. Jayawickreme and M. E. P. Seligman, "The Engine of Well-Being" (manuscript in preparation, 2010). Eranda Jayawickreme and I have contrasted well-being theory with the other major theories of well-being in a recent manuscript, "The Engine of Well-Being." There are three kinds of theories: wanting, liking, and needing theories. The first—*wanting theories*—dominates mainstream economics and behavioral psychology and says that an individual achieves well-being when he is able to fulfill his "desires," where "desires" are defined objectively. In economic terms, well-being is tied to satisfying one's preferences. There is no subjective *requirement*, no need for satisfying your preferences to lead to pleasure or satisfaction. Positive reinforcement, similarly, is based on instrumental choice (an objective preference measure), with no subjective com-

ponent, and so constitutes a wanting theory. Well-being in reinforcement theory is approximated by how much positive reinforcement and how little punishment (both behavioral measures of preference) one obtains. People and animals strive to get what they want because such behavior is positively reinforcing, not because it satisfies any particular need or drive, and not because it engenders any subjective state of liking.

Liking theories are the hedonic accounts of happiness in philosophy and psychology that center on subjective reports of positive emotion, life satisfaction, and happiness. Subjective well-being is the combination of general satisfaction with life, satisfaction with specific domains of life, current mood, and current positive and negative emotion. Subjective well-being is perhaps the most widely used theory in the psychology of happiness, and well-being is typically assessed by asking an individual, "How satisfied are you with your life?" The answer includes both momentary emotions along with a cognitive evaluation of how life is going.

Needing theories catalogue the objective list of goods required for well-being or for a happy life. They do not completely discount what people choose (wanting) and how people feel about their choices (liking), but contend that what people need is more central to well-being. These theories include the objective-list accounts of Amartya Sen and Martha Nussbaum, the hierarchy-of-needs approach of Abraham Maslow, and the eudemonic approaches of Carolyn Ryff, Ed Deci, and Rich Ryan. Ryff's sustained, creative work on eudemonic approaches to well-being is important as a counterweight to purely subjective approaches.

Veenhoven and Cummins are the progenitors of the engine approach: R. A. Cummins, "The Second Approximation to an International Standard for Life Satisfaction," *Social Indicators Research* 43 (1998): 307–34; R. Veenhoven, "Quality-of-Life and Happiness: Not Quite the Same," in G. DeGirolamo, et al., eds., *Health and Quality-of-Life* (Rome: Il Pensierro Scientifico, 1998).

Parfit (1984), as well as Dolan, Peasgood, and White (2006), first made the valuable distinction among needing, wanting, and liking theories: P. Dolan, T. Peasgood, and M. White, *Review of Research on the Influences on Personal Well-Being and Application to Policy Making* (London: DEFRA, 2006); D. Parfit, *Reasons and Persons* (Oxford: Clarendon Press, 1984).

My friend and colleague Ed Diener, the first of the modern positive psychologists, is the giant in the field of subjective well-being: E. Diener, E. Suh, R. Lucas, and H. Smith, "Subjective Well-Being: Three Decades of Progress," *Psychological Bulletin* 125 (1999): 276–302.

The major theoretical papers on objective list theory (or needing theory) include: A. K. Sen, *Development as Freedom* (Oxford: Oxford University Press, 1999); A. H. Maslow, *Toward a Psychology of Being* (New York: Van Nostrand, 1968); M. C. Nussbaum, "Capabilities as Fundamental Entitlements: Sen and Social Justice," *Feminist Economics* 9 (2003): 33–59; C. D. Ryff, "Happiness Is Everything, or Is It? Explorations on the Meaning of Psychological Well-Being," *Journal of Personality and Social Psychology* 57 (1989): 1069–81; C. D. Ryff, "Psychological Well-Being in Adult Life," *Current Directions in Psychological Science* 4 (1995): 99–104; R. M. Ryan and E. L. Deci, "On Happiness and Human Potentials: A Review of Research on Hedonic and Eudaimonic Well-Being," *Annual Review of Psychology* 52 (2001): 141–66.

26   *Felicia Huppert and Timothy So of the University of Cambridge have defined and measured flourishing in each of twenty-three European Union nations:* T. So and F. Huppert, "What Percentage of People in Europe Are Flourishing and What Characterizes Them?" (July 23, 2009). Retrieved October 19, 2009, from www.isqols2009.istitutodeglinnocenti.it/Content_en/Huppert.pdf. So and Huppert used the latest round of the European Social Survey, which incorporates a well-being module, to measure flourishing in a sample of around forty-three thousand adults (all above sixteen years old) in the twenty-three countries of the European Union. Aside from between-nations differences, they found that higher flourishing is associated with higher education levels, higher income, and being married. General health is also moderately associated with flourishing, although only a third of individuals with good self-reported health are flourishing. Flourishing was found to decline with age, although not linearly so. Indeed, people over sixty-five years of age in certain countries (for instance, Ireland) show the highest rates of flourishing. Middle-aged people show the lowest rates.

So and Huppert also tested the relationship between life satisfaction and flourishing to determine how much the two concepts overlap. Consistent with well-being theory, the two measures correlated only modestly ($r = .32$). In other words, many people who are satisfied with their lives are not flourishing, and vice versa. This finding reinforces the notion that measures of life satisfaction (a unitary construct) are not adequate to assess well-being and flourishing (both multifaceted constructs).

28   *"moon-shot goal":* In May 1961, President John F. Kennedy announced the then implausible goal of putting humans on the moon by the end of that decade. There is nothing like a huge goal to galvanize the best.

28   *Public policy follows only from what we measure—and until recently, we measured only money, gross domestic product (GDP):* P. Goodman, "Emphasis on Growth Is Called Misguided," *New York Times,* September 23, 2009. As explained by Nobel Prize–winning economist Joseph Stiglitz: "What you measure affects what you do. If you don't measure the right thing, you don't do the right thing." Governments around the world are starting to consider the idea that indicators other than the GDP are needed in order to address the needs of their citizens. In 2008 French president Nicolas Sarkozy commissioned a report from renowned economists Joseph Stiglitz, Amartya Sen, and Jean-Paul Fitoussi, asking for the creation of a new measure of economic growth that would take into account, among other factors, social well-being. As a result of the recent economic turmoil, Sarkozy felt that the old-fashioned measures of economic growth are giving citizens the impression that they are being manipulated. The resulting Commission on the Measurement of Economic Performance and Social Progress (CMEPSP) recently released its first report, supporting Sarkozy's initiative and proposing alternative measurement strategies. The full text of the commission's first report can be found at: www.stiglitz-sen-fitoussi.fr.

This report and much subsequent action is tied to objective list theory and is not incompatible with well-being theory and its goal of flourishing. The essential difference, however, is that flourishing takes subjective variables at least as seriously as objective ones. The economist-dominated developments are quite skeptical about subjective indicators of human progress.

Chapter 2: Creating Your Happiness: Positive Psychology Exercises That Work

31 *You will be happier and less depressed one month from now:* M. E. P. Seligman, T. A. Steen, N. Park, and C. Peterson, "Positive Psychology Progress: Empirical Validation of Interventions," *American Psychologist* 60 (2005): 410–21. This has been shown by our first randomized, controlled study conducted on the Internet, described here.

31 *many aspects of human behavior do not change lastingly:* M. E. P. Seligman and J. Hager, eds., *The Biological Boundaries of Learning* (New York: Appleton-Century-Crofts, 1992); M. E. P. Seligman, *What You Can Change . . . and What You Can't* (New York: Vintage, 1993). The extent to which any behavior can be learned is a long-standing debate. The evidence suggests that we are hardwired to learn certain things easily, but not others. This debate was the topic of my very first book, *The Biological Boundaries of Learning.* As a result, interventions targeting modifiable behaviors will be much more likely to succeed than those targeting more intractable ones. This was the topic of *What You Can Change . . . and What You Can't.* Common examples of modifiable behaviors include sexual dysfunction, mood, and panic attacks (if provided with the right intervention). Examples of things that are much harder to change are weight, sexual orientation, and alcoholism.

31 *I did the watermelon diet for thirty days:* To reinforce this point, there isn't a single scientific study looking at the effectiveness of the watermelon diet. That's never a good sign. Anecdotal reports of unpleasant side effects and overall ineffectiveness, however, abound on the Internet.

31 *like 80 percent to 95 percent of dieters, I regained all that weight (and more) within three years:* For a recent review of the effectiveness of dieting, see T. Mann, J. Tomiyama, E. Westling, A.-M. Lew, B. Samuels, and J. Chatman. "Medicare's Search for Effective Obesity Treatments: Diets Are Not the Answer," *American Psychologist* 62 (2007): 200–33; L. H. Powell, J. E. Calvin III, and J. E. Calvin Jr., "Effective Obesity Treatments," *American Psychologist* 62 (2007): 234–46. Mann, et al., pointed out that although many studies have shown that certain diets work (at least in the short term), their conclusions should be interpreted with caution, as methodological problems may have biased their results.

Another review by Powell and colleagues compared different kinds of treatment for obesity (dieting, drugs, gastric surgery) and found that overall, dieting and drugs had a consistent significant effect on weight. The average weight loss in these studies was, however, only seven pounds! These so-called effective treatments for obesity are therefore no panaceas. Interestingly though, the authors pointed out that even small amounts of weight loss had significant effects on other markers of health (blood pressure, diabetes, and so on). The results of gastric surgery are much better. So while we cannot dismiss the advantage of losing even a small amount of weight, the results still clearly show that substantial weight loss by dieting is very difficult to achieve.

31 *a study of lottery winners, who were happier for a few months after their windfall but soon fell back to their habitual level of grouchiness or cheerfulness:* P. Brickman, D. Coates, and R. Janoff-Bulman, "Lottery Winners and Accident Victims: Is Happiness Relative?" *Journal of Personality and Social Psychology* 36 (1978): 917–27. In this classic study, Brickman and colleagues demonstrated that

lottery winners are not happier than nonwinners, thus suggesting that lottery winners adapt to their new situation. However, another finding from the same study put into question the notion that we are always able to adapt to a set-point level of happiness. Indeed, Brickman and colleagues also examined the levels of happiness of a group of people with paraplegia. These subjects bounced back from their initial misery but never quite caught up with controls. This study therefore suggested that happiness may be more difficult to increase than to decrease.

32   *If we trade up successfully, we stay on the hedonic treadmill, but we will always need yet another shot:* E. Diener, R. E., Lucas, and C. N. Scollon, "Beyond the Hedonic Treadmill," *American Psychologist* 6 (2006): 305–14. Diener and colleagues made five revisions to the hedonic treadmill model to reflect our current understanding of happiness, including whether or not it can be improved.

First they argue that people's set points are not neutral (against previous findings). In other words, most people are happy most of the time (as shown by Diener and Diener, 1996), and they revert back to this "happy" set point after events. Second, people differ in their set points. In other words, some people are generally happier than others, for both genetic and environmental reasons. Third, people also differ in the degree to which they adapt to external events (and revert back to their set points). Fourth, it doesn't make sense to talk about one set point of happiness. Instead, there are multiple set points which correspond to the various components of well-being (which allows for the adaptation of the hedonic treadmill theory to well-being theory). Finally, and most important, set points can be changed under certain conditions. The fact that citizens of different countries report differing levels of happiness is evidence that environmental circumstances do affect well-being. In particular, wealth and human rights appear to be strong predictors of national well-being (Diener, Diener, and Diener, 1995).

In the words of Diener and colleagues (2006), the hedonic treadmill theory asks us to "Imagine that individuals living in a cruel dictatorship where crime, slavery, and inequality are rampant are as satisfied with their lives as people living in a stable democracy where crime is minimal." The research shows that, fortunately, there is no need to imagine that this would be true. It is false.

E. Diener and C. Diener, "Most People Are Happy," *Psychological Science* 7 (1996): 181–85.

E. Diener, M. Diener, and C. Diener, "Factors Predicting the Subjective Well-Being of Nations," *Journal of Personality and Social Psychology* 69 (1995): 851–64.

32   *which are just bogus?:* S. Lyubomirsky, *The How of Happiness: A Scientific Approach to Getting the Life You Want* (London: Penguin, 2007). A good self-help manual that separates scientific advice from unfounded myths on how to become happier.

32   *"naughty thumb of science":* e. e. cummings, "O Sweet Spontaneous Earth," *Complete Poems, 1904–1962* (New York: Norton, 1994), p. 58. I use this quote often in lectures, and it always surprises me how few members of the audience are acquainted with the marvelous poem.

32   *There is a gold standard for testing therapies—random-assignment, placebo-controlled studies:* J. B. Persons and G. Silberschatz, "Are Results of Randomized Controlled Trials Useful to Psychotherapists?" *Journal of Consulting and Clinical Psychology* 66 (1998): 126–35. For an entertaining debate on the useful-

ness of RCTs for clinicians, see the following discussion between Jacqueline Persons and George Silberschatz. Persons argued that clinicians cannot provide top quality care without reading the findings from RCTs. Silberschatz, on the other hand, explained that RCTs do not address the issues and concerns of practicing clinicians because they lack external validity.

M. E. P. Seligman, "The Effectiveness of Psychotherapy: The Consumer Reports Study," *American Psychologist* 50 (1995): 965–74. Elsewhere, I have argued that efficacy studies (such as RCTs) do have certain drawbacks: treatments have a fixed duration (usually around twelve weeks), treatment delivery is not flexible, and subjects are assigned to a group and are therefore consigned to a more passive role. They are also somewhat nonrepresentative of many "real-life" patients who enter treatment with high comorbidity. Finally, outcomes tend to focus on symptom reduction as opposed to general decreases in impairment. I therefore argued that the ideal study should combine features of both efficacy and effectiveness studies, so that the scientific rigor of RCTs can be augmented with the real-life relevance of effectiveness studies.

34 *The odds are that you will be less depressed, happier, and addicted to this exercise:* M. E. P. Seligman, T. A. Steen, N. Park, and C. Peterson, "Positive Psychology Progress: Empirical Validation of Interventions," *American Psychologist* 60 (2005): 410–21.

34 *It was all book learning, and they could never know craziness itself:* Admittedly, some courageous teachers have attempted to provide an experiential perspective in their Abnormal Psychology courses, but the ethical considerations are tricky.

F. E. Rabinowitz, "Creating the Multiple Personality: An Experiential Demonstration for an Undergraduate Abnormal Psychology Class," in *Handbook of Demonstrations and Activities in the Teaching of Psychology,* vol. 3, *Personality, Abnormal, Clinical-Counseling, and Social* (2nd ed.), eds. M. E. Ware and D. E. Johnson (Mahwah, NJ: Erlbaum, 2000).

D. Wedding, M. A. Boyd, and R. M. Niemec, *Movies and Mental Illness: Using Films to Understand Psychopathology* (New York: McGraw-Hill, 1999). Less controversial than direct experiences, teachers can use carefully chosen movies to communicate the subjective experience of mental illness. This volume suggests relevant movies.

D. L. Rosenhan, "On Being Sane in Insane Places," *Science* 179 (1973): 250–58. I long for the good old days before institutional review boards (IRB) made bold experimentation impossible. I was a pseudopatient with David Rosenhan in 1972. We got ourselves admitted to mental hospitals and observed how we were treated. It was one of the most rewarding experiences of my life. Unlike the rest of the pseudopatients, I was treated splendidly. It was a fine way to be exposed to craziness from the inside, but no IRB would allow the study today because we deceived the psychiatrists and the patients about our identities. This is Rosenhan's original research report.

35 *Dr. Ben Dean:* www.mentorcoach.com.

38 *Two of the exercises* [. . .] *markedly lowered depression three months and six months later:* M. E. P. Seligman, T. A. Steen, N. Park, and C. Peterson, "Positive Psychology Progress: Empirical Validation of Interventions," *American Psychologist* 60 (2005): 410–21.

39 *This questionnaire was developed by Chris Peterson, a professor at the University of Michigan:* C. Peterson and N. Park, "Classifying and Measuring Strengths of Character," in *Handbook of Positive Psychology* (2nd ed.), eds. C. R. Snyder and S. J. Lopez (New York: Oxford University Press, 2009).

For more information on the specific strengths, see C. Peterson and M. E. P. Seligman, eds., *The VIA Classification of Strengths and Virtues* (Washington, DC: American Psychological Association, 2003).

40 *at appropriate places throughout this book:* T. Rashid and M. Seligman, *Positive Psychotherapy* (New York: Oxford, 2001). Includes the complete exposition of these exercises.

40 *they stayed nondepressed for the year that we tracked them:* M. E. P. Seligman, T. Rashid, and A. C. Parks, "Positive Psychotherapy," *American Psychologist* 61 (2006): 774–88.

40 *Dr. Tayyab Rashid created positive psychotherapy:* on this topic, see the following publications:

T. Rashid and A. Anjum, "Positive Psychotherapy for Children and Adolescents," in *Depression in Children and Adolescents: Causes, Treatment, and Prevention*, eds. J. R. Z. Abela and B. L. Hankin (New York: Guilford Press, 2007).

M. E. P. Seligman, T. Rashid, and A. C. Parks, "Positive Psychotherapy," *American Psychologist* 61 (2006): 774–88.

T. Rashid, "Positive Psychotherapy," in *Positive Psychotherapy, Perspective Series*, ed. S. J. Lopez (London: Blackwell Publishing, forthcoming).

R. Cummins, "Subjective Well-Being, Homeostatically Protected Mood and Depression: A Synthesis," *Journal of Happiness Studies* 11 (2010): 1–17.

C. Harmer, G. Goodwin, and P. Cowen, "Why Do Antidepressants Take So Long to Work?" *British Journal of Psychiatry* 195 (2009): 102–8.

41 *Rashid and Seligman, 2011:* T. Rashid and M. E. P. Seligman, *Positive Psychotherapy: A Treatment Manual* (New York: Oxford University Press, forthcoming).

See also A. Wood and S. Joseph, "The Absence of Positive Psychological (Eudemonic) Well-Being as a Risk Factor for Depression: A Ten-Year Cohort Study," *Journal of Affective Disorders* 122 (2010): 213–17.

C. Harmer, U. O'Sullivan, and E. Favaron, et al., "Effect of Acute Antidepressant Administration on Negative Affective Bias in Depressed Patients," *American Journal of Psychiatry* 166 (2009): 1178–84.

41 *We introduce forgiveness as a powerful tool:* Perhaps the best illustration of this idea is the story of Kim Phuc, the Vietnamese woman who was famously photographed at age nine running naked on the streets of Trang Bang after a napalm attack by South Vietnamese forces. Her essay "The Long Road to Forgiveness" (2008) has been featured on NPR's *This I Believe* series. More information on Kim Phuc's story can be found in the following biography: D. Chong, *The Girl in the Picture: The Story of Kim Phuc, the Photograph, and the Vietnam War* (New York: Viking Penguin, 1999).

42 *Satisficing is encouraged over maximizing:* B. Schwartz, A. Ward, J. Monterosso, S. Lyubomirsky, K. White, and D. R. Lehman, "Maximizing Versus Satisficing: Happiness Is a Matter of Choice," *Journal of Personality and Social Psychology* 83 (2002): 1178–97.

B. Schwartz, *The Paradox of Choice: Why More Is Less* (New York: Harper-Collins, 2004).

Barry Schwartz, the Dorwin Cartright Professor of Social Theory and Social Action at Swarthmore College, is the leading researcher on the costs and benefits of using satisficing versus maximizing strategies during decision making. In particular, maximizers endure psychological costs when they are faced with an increased number of options (as they will always attempt to improve their situation rather than be content with their current one). In a series of seven studies conducted with Sonja Lyubomirsky (among other authors), Schwartz showed that maximizing (measured as an individual difference variable) is associated with lower levels of happiness, optimism, self-esteem, and life satisfaction but with higher levels of depression, perfectionism, and regret.

43   *55 percent of patients in positive psychotherapy, 20 percent in treatment as usual, and only 8 percent in treatment as usual plus drugs achieved remission:* M. E. P. Seligman, T. Rashid, and A. C. Parks, "Positive Psychotherapy," *American Psychologist* 61 (2006): 774–88. Note that the treatment-as-usual condition in this study consisted of an integrative and eclectic approach to therapy delivered by licensed psychologists and social workers, and graduate interns.

43   Time *magazine ran a cover story on positive psychology:* C. Wallis, "The New Science of Happiness," *Time,* January 17, 2005.

Chapter 3: The Dirty Little Secret of Drugs and Therapy

45   *depression is the most costly disease in the world:* World Health Organization, *Global Burden of Disease: 2004 Update* (2008). Retrieved October 20, 2009, from www.who.int/healthinfo/global_burden_disease/GBD_report_2004update_full .pdf. In 2004 the WHO estimated that unipolar depression had the highest number of years lost to disability (YLDs) of all diseases. Depression is at the top of the list for both males (twenty-four million YLDs) and females (forty-one million YLDs), as well as for both high (ten million YLDs) and middle- to low-income countries (fifty-five million YLDs). In all regions of the world, neuropsychiatric illnesses (of all types) are the leading cause of disability, accounting for approximately one-third of all YLDs (among adults aged fifteen and over).

45   *the treatments of choice are drugs and psychotherapy:* Kaiser Permanente Care Management Institute, *Depression Clinical Practice Guidelines* (Oakland, CA: Kaiser Permanente Care Management Institute, 2006).

45   *On average, treating a case of depression costs about $5,000 per year, and there are around ten million such cases annually in America:* www.allaboutdepression.com/gen_01.html; http://mentalhealth.about.com/b/2006/07/17/depression-treatment-can-be-expensive.htm.

45   *Antidepressant drugs are a multibillion-dollar industry:* IMS Health, *Top 15 Global Therapeutic Classes* (2008). Retrieved October 26, 2009, from www.imshealth.com/deployedfiles/imshealth/Global/Content/StaticFile/Top_Line_Data/Global_Top_15_Therapy_Classes.pdf. In 2008 global sales for antidepressants amounted to more than $20 billion. Antidepressants were at the time the eighth most prescribed class of drugs in the world.

45   *as effective as therapy and drugs:* M. E. P. Seligman, T. Rashid, and A. C. Parks, "Positive Psychotherapy," *American Psychologist* 61 (2006): 774–88.

46   *both have given up the notion of cure:* J. Moncrieff, *The Myth of the Chemical Cure: A Critique of Psychiatric Drug Treatment* (London: Palgrave Mac-

Millan, 2009). For more on the notion of cure in psychiatry, see Joanna Mon-crieff's controversial book.

For a review of Dr. Moncrieff's book, see A. Yawar, "Book Review: The Fool on the Hill," *Lancet* 373 (2009): 621–22.

46   *only brief treatment is reimbursed by insurance companies:* S. A. Glied and R. G. Frank, "Shuffling Towards Parity: Bringing Mental Health Care Under the Umbrella," *New England Journal of Medicine* 359 (2008): 113–15; C. L. Barry, R. G. Frank, and T. G. McGuire, "The Costs of Mental Health Parity: Still an Impediment?" *Health Affairs* 25 (2006): 623–34. In spite of the progress made during recent years, mental illness still is not on an equal footing with other medical conditions in terms of insurance coverage. For a discussion of the current problems in the debate about mental health parity, see Glied and colleagues. For a critique of the notion that establishing mental health parity would increase spending and would be unsustainable, see Barry, et al.

46   *There are two kinds of medications: cosmetic drugs and curative drugs:* C. King and L. N. P. Voruganti, "What's in a Name? The Evolution of the Nomen-clature of Antipsychotic Drugs," *Journal of Psychiatry & Neuroscience* 27 (2007): 168–75. Many factors affect clinicians' and patients' perceptions of what drugs do and how they work. Simple factors—such as the name of the drug—can influence these perceptions. In a review paper, Caroline King and Lakshmi Voruganti examine the history and influence of the names given to drugs used to treat psychosis. The researchers explain why a multitude of different terms were used throughout the past century (from tranquilizer, to ataractic, to neuroleptic, to antischizophrenic, to antipsychotic, to serotonin-dopamine agonists, and so on). They conclude that although psychiatry has come a long way in understanding the mechanisms of action of psychotropic medications, the nomenclature system is still incredibly vague and promotes misunderstandings about what drugs actually do. A similar commentary could be made about the class of drugs we currently call the antidepressants.

46   Every single drug on the shelf of the psychopharmacopoeia is cosmetic: S. D. Hollon, M. E. Thase, and J. C. Markowitz, "Treatment and Prevention of Depression," *Psychological Science in the Public Interest* 3 (2002): 39–77. According to Hollon and colleagues, the bulk of the evidence shows that antidepressants have only symptom suppressive (rather than curative) effects. Once treatment is terminated, patients are at a high risk for recurrence.

46   *a defense called "flight into health":* W. B. Frick, "Flight into Health: A New Interpretation," *Journal of Humanistic Psychology* 39 (1999): 58–81. A historical review and critique (from a humanistic perspective) of the concept of "flight into health."

47   *Almost always, the effects are what is technically called "small":* I. Kirsch, T. J. Moore, A. Scoboria, and S. S. Nicholls, "The Emperor's New Drugs: An Analysis of Antidepressant Medication Data Submitted to the U.S. Food and Drug Administration," *Prevention and Treatment* (July 15, 2002). Retrieved October 26, 2009, from http://psycnet.apa.org/journals/pre/5/1/23a.html. In 2002 Kirsch and colleagues published a review of studies investigating the efficacy of the six most prescribed antidepressants approved between 1987 and 1999 (fluoxetine, parox-etine, sertraline, venlafaxine, nefadozone, and citalopram). Results showed that the overall difference between drug and placebo, although significant, was only

NOTES

approximately a 2-point difference on the Hamilton Depression Scale. Most clinicians would agree that such a difference is trivial. Results, moreover, did not differ for low or high doses of the medication.

S. D., Hollon, R. J. DeRubeis, R. C. Shelton, and B. Weiss, The Emperor's New Drugs: Effect Size and Moderation Effects," *Prevention and Treatment* (July 15, 2002). Retrieved October 26, 2009, from http://psycnet.apa.org/index .cfm?fa=fulltext.journal&jcode=pre&vol=5&issue=1&format=html&page=28c& expand=1. In a commentary of Kirsch's review, Hollon and colleagues proposed that the small effect described may be misleading, because it obscures the fact that different drugs may work for different people, and that potential effects are therefore dampened by taking into account the effect of the drug on everyone. Effect sizes based on the average patient may therefore underestimate the drug-placebo difference for those who do respond.

For another review of the size of the effect of antidepressant medication, see J. Moncrieff and I. Kirsch, "Efficacy of Antidepressants in Adults," *British Medical Journal* 331 (2005): 155–57.

47 *for each you get a 65 percent relief rate, accompanied by a placebo effect that ranges from 45 percent to 55 percent:* In their review of the efficacy of antidepressants, Kirsch et al. (see previous note) found that 82 percent of drug effects can be accounted for by placebo effects. In other words, only 18 percent of the drug response can be traced to the pharmacological effects of the medication. The authors argue that, moreover, these 18 percent could also be due to the breaking of the blind before the end of the study, as people are cued by side effects that they are probably in the active treatment condition and not in the control condition.

47 *so high is the placebo response that in half the studies on which the U.S. Food and Drug Administration (FDA) based its official approval of the antidepressant drugs, there was no difference between placebo and drug:* As described by Kirsch and colleagues (2002; see previous note), the FDA requires two positive findings (in other words, significant differences between placebo and drug) from two controlled clinical trials in order to approve a drug, even if other additional trials show negative findings. For example, the drug Celexa (citalopram) was approved on the basis of two positive findings and three negative findings.

47 *the effects were nonexistent:* J. Fournier, R. DeRubeis, S. Hollon, S. Dimidjian, J. Amsterdam, R. Shelton, and J. Fawcett, "Antidepressant Drug Effects and Depression Severity: A Patient-Level Meta-Analysis," *Journal of the American Medical Association* 303 (2010): 47–53.

48 *Every single drug has exactly the same property: once you stop taking it, you are back to square one, and recurrence and relapse are the rule:* S. D. Hollon, M. E. Thase, and J. C. Markowitz, "Treatment and Prevention of Depression," *Psychological Science in the Public Interest* 3 (2002): 39–77.

48 *Shelly Gable, professor of psychology at the University of California at Santa Barbara, has demonstrated that how you celebrate is more predictive of strong relations than how you fight:* S. L. Gable, H. T. Reis, E. A. Impett, and E. R. Asher, "What Do You Do When Things Go Right? The Intrapersonal and Interpersonal Benefits of Sharing Good Events," *Journal of Personality and Social Psychology* 87 (2004): 228–45.

S. L. Gable, G. C. Gonzaga, and A. Strachman, "Will You Be There for Me

When Things Go Right? Supportive Responses to Positive Events Disclosures," *Journal of Personality and Social Psychology* 9 (2006): 904–17.

51   *there is another, more realistic approach to these dysphorias: learning to function well even if you are sad or anxious or angry—in other words,* dealing with it: S. C. Hayes, Acceptance and Commitment Therapy, Relational Frame Theory, and the Third Wave of Behavioral and Cognitive Therapies," *Behavior Therapy* 35 (2004): 639–65. The so-called third wave of behavioral and cognitive therapies shares the idea that patients may be better off dealing with their problems rather than trying to get rid of them. Steven Hayes, the architect of Acceptance and Commitment Therapy (ACT, pronounced as one word), explains how clients can lose sight of what their ultimate goals are, and how acceptance, or "dealing with it," can help them do just that: "Typically, an anxiety-disordered person wants to get rid of anxiety. It could be experienced as invalidating to refuse to work directly on that desired outcome. At another level, however, the anxious client wants to get rid of anxiety in order to do something such as living a vital human life. Lack of anxiety is not the ultimate goal—it is a means to an end. Since often it has failed as a means, ACT suggests abandoning that means [...] The larger message thus is validating (trust your experience) and empowering (you can live a powerful life from here, without first winning a war with your own history)" (p. 652).

For another review of ACT, see S. C. Hayes, J. B. Luoma, F. W. Bond, A. Masuda, and J. Lillis, "Acceptance and Commitment Therapy: Model, Processes, and Outcomes," *Behaviour Research and Therapy* 44 (2006): 1–25.

Another "third wave therapy," Mindfulness-Based Cognitive Therapy (MBCT), also emphasizes the importance of acceptance in the therapeutic process: Z. V. Segal, J. M. G. Williams, and J. G. Teasdale, *Mindfulness-Based Cognitive Therapy for Depression* (New York: Guilford Press, 2002).

51   *most personality traits are highly heritable, which* [. . .] *Dysphorias often, but not always, stem from these personality traits:* J. C. Loehlin, R. R. McCrae, and P. T. Costa, "Heritabilities of Common and Measure-Specific Components of the Big Five Personality Factors," *Journal of Research in Personality* 32 (1998): 431–53. One twin study by Loehlin and colleagues looked at the heritability of the Big Five factor traits and showed that approximately 50 percent to 60 percent of the variance in extraversion, openness, agreeableness, conscientiousness, and neuroticism is genetic in origin. Forty percent to 50 percent of the variance appears to derive from the unique individual environment, while none of the variance seems to stem from shared environmental influences.

See also J. Harris, *The Nurture Assumption* (New York: Free Press, 1998), and S. Pinker, *The Blank Slate: The Denial of Human Nature and Modern Intellectual Life* (New York: Viking, 2002).

53   *Abraham Lincoln:* R. P. Basler, M. D. Pratt, and L. A. Dunlap, *The Collected Works of Abraham Lincoln* (9 vols.) (New Brunswick, NJ: Rutgers University Press, 1953). In a letter addressed to his law partner John T. Stuart on January 23, 1841, Lincoln describes the intense depressive episode he went through: "I am now the most miserable man living. If what I feel were equally distributed to the whole human family, there would not be one cheerful face on the earth. Whether I shall ever be better I cannot tell; I awfully forebode I shall not. To remain as I am is impossible; I must die or be better, it appears to me."

About Lincoln's biography, as previously cited: R. C. White, *Lincoln: A Biography* (New York: Random House, 2009).

The best of the books that I have read about Lincoln's emotional life is J. W. Shenk, *Lincoln's Melancholy* (Boston: Houghton-Mifflin, 2005).

53   *Winston Churchill*: G. Rubin, *Forty Ways to Look at Winston Churchill: A Brief Account of a Long Life* (New York: Random House, 2004). For an account of Winston Churchill's depression, see Chapter 11, "Churchill as Depressive: The 'Black Dog?'" Winston's Churchill's productivity in light of his impairment has been used as a communication tool to decrease stigma among mental ill persons in the United Kingdom. Recently, the largest severe mental illness charity in the UK (Rethink) commissioned a statue of Churchill wearing a straitjacket. Fittingly, the statue was called "Black Dog," the name Churchill himself gave to his depression. In spite of the good intentions behind this initiative, the statue caused a lot of controversy, perhaps because the straitjacket carries very negative connotations of backward treatment for the mentally ill. However, the leaders of Rethink replied that the straitjacket was used as a metaphor illustrating how mental illness can act as a straitjacket to deny work, social, and other opportunities to sufferers.

C. London, A. Scriven, and N. Lalani, "Sir Winston Churchill: Greatest Briton Used as an Antistigma Icon," *Journal of the Royal Society for the Promotion of Health* 126 (2006): 163–64.

53   *Lincoln came close to killing himself in January 1841*: J. W. Shenk, *Lincoln's Melancholy* (Boston: Houghton-Mifflin, 2005). As a home-schooling parent, I have had the privilege of teaching American history to my children. In the last iteration, when the kids were eight, ten, and twelve, I spent three years teaching the presidents. After the first year, we got through James Buchanan. When we started Abraham Lincoln, the kids said, "Whoa, this is one awesome dude." So we spent an entire year on Abraham Lincoln, using Carl Sandburg's marvelous biography, *Abraham Lincoln: The Prairie Years and the War Years* (New York: Mariner Books, 2002).

55   *"An A for 'applied'"*: I was not present, of course, so my narration is from hearsay.

55   *Even though Penn was founded by Benjamin Franklin to teach both the "applied" and the "ornamental"*: B. Franklin, *Proposals Relating to the Education of Youth in Pensilvania* (1749). In the words of Franklin himself: "As to their studies, it would be well if they could be taught every Thing that is useful, and every Thing that is ornamental: But Art is long, and their Time is short. It is therefore propos'd that they learn those Things that are likely to be most useful and most ornamental. Regard being had to the several Professions for which they are intended."

56   Tractatus Logico-Philosophicus: L. Wittgenstein, *Tractatus Logico-Philosophicus* (New York: Routledge Classics, 1921/2001).

56   Philosophical Investigations: L. Wittgenstein, *Philosophical Investigations* (Malden, MA: Blackwell, 1953/2009). In a poll of five thousand teachers of philosophy asked to name the five most important works of philosophy of the twentieth century, Wittgenstein's *Philosophical Investigations* was the runaway winner. (*Tractatus* also made it among the five most important philosophy books of the century, ranked fourth behind Heidegger's *Being and Time* and Rawls's *A Theory of Justice*.) Incidentally, *Philosophical Investigations* was published posthu-

mously. Wittgenstein did not deign to publish himself; his students published his thoughts from their classroom notes.

D. Lackey, "What Are the Modern Classics? The Baruch Poll of Great Philosophy in the Twentieth Century," *Philosophical Forum* 30 (1999), 329–46.

56   *Just as important as Wittgenstein's ideas was the fact that he was a spellbinding teacher:* R. Monk, *Wittgenstein: The Duty of Genius* (New York: Penguin, 1990). When Wittgenstein returned to Cambridge to teach in 1929, his *Tractatus* had become legendary, and he was met at the railway station by the elite of England's intelligentsia. John Maynard Keynes (one of Wittgenstein's friends) commented in a letter to his wife, "Well, God has arrived. I met him on the 5.15 train."

For more on Wittgenstein's teaching style, see A. T. Gasking and A. C. Jackson, "Wittgenstein as Teacher," in *Ludwig Wittgenstein: The Man and His Philosophy,* ed. K. T. Fann (New York: Delta, 1967), pp. 49–55.

57   *Walter Kaufmann, the charismatic teacher of Nietszche:* W. Kaufmann, *Nietszche: Philosopher, Psychologist, Antichrist* (Princeton, NJ: Princeton University Press, 1950).

57   (*This event is re-created in David Edmonds and John Eidinow's gripping* Wittgenstein's Poker): D. Edmonds and J. Eidinow, *Wittgenstein's Poker: The Story of a Ten-Minute Argument Between Two Great Philosophers* (New York: HarperCollins, 2001).

58   *I did my PhD with white rats:* M. E. P. Seligman, "Chronic Fear Produced by Unpredictable Electric Shock," *Journal of Comparative and Physiological Psychology* 66 (1968): 402–11.

59   *Then in his mideighties and almost blind, Jerry is a walking history of American psychology:* D. Bakhurst and S. G. Shanker, eds., *Jerome Bruner: Language, Culture, Self* (London: Sage Publications, 2001). An overview of Jerome Bruner's work and its legacy.

60   *This is, indeed, the logic of the artificial intelligence endeavor:* J. McCarthy, M. Minsky, N. Rochester, and C. Shannon, *A Proposal for the Dartmouth Summer Research Project on Artificial Intelligence* (1955). Retrieved August 2, 2010, from www-formal.stanford.edu/jmc/history/dartmouth/dartmouth.html. The 1956 Dartmouth conference is largely credited as the time of birth of artificial intelligence. In the said proposal leading to the conference, the researchers asserted that "Every aspect of learning or any other feature of intelligence can be so precisely described that a machine can be made to simulate it."

61   *benefits were not specific to any one kind of therapy or to any one kind of disorder:* M. E. P. Seligman, "The Effectiveness of Psychotherapy: The Consumer Reports Study," *American Psychologist* 50 (1995): 965–74.

Chapter 4: Teaching Well-Being: The Magic of MAPP

63   Derrick Carpenter: Derrick Carpenter graduated from the MAPP program in 2007. He received his B.S. in mathematics from MIT and subsequently worked as a research coordinator at the University of Pennsylvania, studying perceptual learning and mathematics education. Derrick is an avid rower and cyclist, and is interested in the connection between sports and positive psychology. Derrick has a monthly column on *Positive Psychology News Daily* (positivepsychology news.com).

64 *the master of applied positive psychology:* for more information about the program, go to www.sas.upenn.edu/lps/graduate/mapp.

64 *Dr. James Pawelski:* James Pawelski is the director of education and a senior scholar at the Positive Psychology Center. He is also adjunct associate professor of religious studies at the University of Pennsylvania. Pawelski earned his PhD in philosophy in 1997. He is the author of *The Dynamic Individualism of William James,* in which he presents a major new interpretation and application of the work of this seminal philosopher and psychologist. He currently studies the philosophical underpinnings of positive psychology, the philosophy and psychology of character development, and the development, application, and assessment of interventions in positive psychology. He is also the founding executive director of the International Positive Psychology Association (IPPA).

For more information on James Pawelski and his work, see http://james pawelski.com and J. O. Pawelski, *The Dynamic Individualism of William James* (Albany, NY: SUNY Press, 2007).

64 *Debbie Swick:* Deborah Swick is the associate director of education of the Positive Psychology Center at the University of Pennsylvania. She obtained her MBA from Vanderbilt University. In addition to directing the MAPP program, Debbie Swick is also one of the associate executive directors of the International Positive Psychology Association.

65 *Tom Rath:* Tom Rath is the author of the best-selling business books *How Full Is Your Bucket?, StrengthsFinder 2.0,* and *Strengths Based Leadership.* His latest best seller, with Jim Harter, is *Well Being: the Five Essential Elements* (Washington, DC: Gallup, 2010). Also see T. Rath and D. O. Clifton, *How Full Is Your Bucket?* (New York: Gallup Press, 2004); T. Rath, *StrengthsFinder 2.0* (New York: Gallup Press, 2007); T. Rath and B. Conchie, *Strengths Based Leadership* (New York: Gallup Press, 2008).

65 *Yakov Smirnoff:* famous comedian and painter. For more information about the current activities of Yakov Smirnoff, see www.yakov.com/branson.

65 *Senia Maymin:* Senia Maymin is currently pursuing her PhD at Stanford University's Graduate School of Business. She is also the publisher and editor in chief of *Positive Psychology News Daily* (PPND), a gold mine of information about positive psychology research and applications. Most authors featured on PPND (http://positivepsychologynews.com) are graduates of the MAPP programs at the University of Pennsylvania or at the University of East London.

66 *the laboratory genius of positive psychology:* B. L. Fredrickson, *Positivity: Groundbreaking Research Reveals How to Embrace the Hidden Strength of Positive Emotions, Overcome Negativity, and Thrive* (New York: Random House, 2009). Overview of Barbara Fredrickson's work on positive emotions.

66 *Barb began by detailing her "broaden-and-build" theory of positive emotion:* B. L. Fredrickson, "The Role of Positive Emotions in Positive Psychology: The Broaden-and-Build Theory of Positive Emotions," *American Psychologist* 56 (2001): 218–26.

B. L. Fredrickson and C. Branigan, "Positive Emotions Broaden the Scope of Attention and Thought-Action Repertoires," *Cognition & Emotion* 19 (2005): 313–32.

66 *"Companies with better than a 2.9:1 ratio for positive to negative statements are flourishing":* B. L. Fredrickson and M. F. Losada, "Positive Affect and the Complex Dynamics of Human Flourishing, *American Psychologist* 60 (2005):

678–86. Fredrickson and Losada had previously found similar results for individuals. They asked 188 subjects to complete a survey to determine whether they were flourishing. These subjects then provided daily reports of positive and negative emotions over the span of a month. The mean ratio of positive to negative affect was found to lie above 2.9 for flourishing individuals, and below for those not flourishing.

For another discussion of the role of positive emotions in organizational settings, see B. L. Fredrickson, "Positive Emotions and Upward Spirals in Organizational Settings," in *Positive Organizational Scholarship*, eds. K. Cameron, J. Dutton, and R. Quinn (San Francisco: Berrett-Koehler, 2003): 163–75.

67   *"call this the 'Losada ratio'"*: M. Losada, "The Complex Dynamics of High Performance Teams," *Mathematical and Computer Modeling* 30 (1999): 179–92; M. Losada and E. Heaphy: "The Role of Positivity and Connectivity in the Performance of Business Teams: A Nonlinear Dynamics Model," *American Behavioral Scientist* 47 (2004): 740–65.

67   *"Law is the profession with the highest depression, suicide, and divorce rates"*: W. W. Eaton, J. C. Anthony, W. Mandel, and R. Garrison, "Occupations and the Prevalence of Major Depressive Disorder," *Journal of Occupational and Environmental Medicine* 32 (1990): 1079–87. In a 1990 study, researchers from Johns Hopkins University compared the prevalence of clinical depression in 104 occupations. Lawyers topped the list, with a prevalence of depression approximating four times that of the general population.

P. J. Schiltz, "On Being a Happy, Healthy, and Ethical Member of an Unhappy, Unhealthy, and Unethical Profession," *Vanderbilt Law Review* 52 (1999): 871–951. Schiltz gives an excellent overview and commentary on the research showing higher rates of depression, anxiety, alcoholism, drug abuse, suicide, divorce, and poor physical health among lawyers and/or law students. He offers three explanations for these findings: the long hours worked, the money at stake, and the competitiveness of the profession. Finally, Schiltz gives advice on how to stay sane and ethical without giving up on being a lawyer.

K. M. Sheldon and L. S. Krieger, "Understanding the Negative Effects of Legal Education on Law Students: A Longitudinal Test of Self-Determination Theory," *Personality and Social Psychology Bulletin* 33 (2007): 883–97. Sheldon and Krieger recently investigated the psychological processes underlying the decline of well-being in law students enrolled at two different law schools. At both schools, the students' well-being declined over three years. In one of the two schools, however, students reported that the faculty encouraged a higher sense of perceived autonomy in students. As a result, the decline in their well-being was less steep than that of the students at the other school. Perceived autonomy support also predicted a higher GPA, better bar exam results, and more self-determined motivation for finding a first job after graduation.

67   *John Gottman computed the same statistic*: J. M. Gottman, "The Roles of Conflict Engagement, Escalation, and Avoidance in Marital Interaction: A Longitudinal View of Five Types of Couples," *Journal of Consulting and Clinical Psychology* 61 (1993): 6–15; J. M. Gottman, *What Predicts Divorce: The Relationship Between Marital Processes and Marital Outcomes* (Hillsdale, NJ: Erlbaum, 1994).

69   *The "basic rest and activity cycle":* N. Kleitman, "Basic Rest-Activity Cycle in Relation to Sleep and Wakefulness," in *Sleep: Physiology and Pathology,* ed. A. Kales (Philadelphia: Lippincott, 1969), pp. 33–38. Nathaniel Kleitman, the father of sleep research, coined this term.

70   *I fear that coaching has run wild:* G. B. Spence, M. J. Cavanagh, and A. M. Grant, "Duty of Care in an Unregulated Industry: Initial Findings on the Diversity and Practices of Australian Coaches," *International Coaching Psychology Review* 1 (2006): 71–85. An Australian perspective on the role of coaches and problems created by the lack of regulation of the profession.

For a review of the literature on executive coaching (the area where most of the research is currently accumulating), see S. Kampa-Kokesch and M. Z. Anderson, "Executive Coaching: A Comprehensive Review of the Literature," *Consulting Psychology Journal: Practice and Research* 53 (2001): 205–28.

70   *Positive psychology can provide both:* M. E. P. Seligman, "Coaching and Positive Psychology," *Australian Psychologist* 42 (2007): 266–67.

For an example of coaching based on positive psychology, see R. Biswas-Diener and B. Dean, *Positive Psychology Coaching: Putting the Science of Happiness to Work for Your Clients* (Hoboken, NJ: John Wiley & Sons, 2007).

C. Kauffman, D. Stober, and A. Grant, "Positive Psychology: The Science at the Heart of Coaching," in *The Evidence Based Coaching Handbook,* eds. D. R. Stober and A. M. Grant (Hoboken, NJ: John Wiley & Sons, 2006), pp. 219–54.

70   *interventions and measurements that work:* Three good examples that have good empirical validation in addition to those detailed in this book are Michael Frisch's Quality of Life Therapy, Solution-Focused Therapy, and Acceptance and Commitment Therapy (ACT).

M. Frisch, *Quality of Life Therapy* (New York: Wiley, 2005).

W. Gingerich, "Solution-Focused Brief Therapy: A Review of the Outcome Research," *Family Process,* 39 (2004): 477–98.

S. Hayes, K. Strosahl, and K. Wilson, *Acceptance and Commitment Therapy* (New York: Guilford, 1999).

71   *and you know when to refer a client to someone who is more appropriately trained:* S. Berglas, "The Very Real Dangers of Executive Coaching," *Harvard Business Review* (June 2002): 87–92. A case of coaching gone awry.

72   *goal-setting theory:* E. A. Locke and G. P. Latham, "Goal Setting Theory," in *Motivation: Theory and Research,* eds. H. F. O'Neil and M. E. Drillings (Hillsdale, NJ: Erlbaum, 1994), pp. 13–29; E. A. Locke and G. P. Latham, "Building a Practically Useful Theory of Goal Setting and Task Motivation: A 35-Year Odyssey," *American Psychologist* 57 (2002): 705–17; E. A. Locke, "Motivation by Goal Setting," in *Handbook of Organizational Behavior,* ed. R. Golembiewski (New York: Marcel Dekker, 2001).

72   Creating Your Best Life: C. A. Miller and M. Frisch, *Creating Your Best Life: The Ultimate Life List Guide* (New York: Sterling, 2009).

72   *Appreciative Inquiry:* D. L. Cooperrider, D. Whitney, and J. M. Stavros, *Appreciative Inquiry Handbook: For Leaders of Change,* 2nd ed. (Bedford Heights, OH: Lakeshore Communications, 2007); D. L. Cooperrider and D. Whitney, *Appreciative Inquiry: A Positive Revolution in Change* (San Francisco: Berrett-Koehler, 2005). For the latest on research about Appreciative Inquiry.

72   *corporations use 360:* J. W. Smither, M. London, R. R. Reilly, "Does Performance Improve Following Multisource Feedback? A Theoretical Model, Meta-Analysis, and Review of Empirical Findings," *Personnel Psychology* 58 (2005): 33–66. A review of the effectiveness of 360 feedback.

73   *married adults [. . .] tend to be healthier and live longer than their single counterparts:* R. H. Coombs, "Marital Status and Personal Well-Being: A Literature Review," *Family Relations* 40 (1991): 97–102. A review of the benefits of marriage; S. Stack and J. R. Eshleman, "Marital Status and Happiness: A 17-Nation Study," *Journal of Marriage and the Family* 60 (1998): 527–36. The benefits of marriage, moreover, do not seem to depend on cultural factors.

75   *Sociologists distinguish among a job, a career, and a calling:* A. Wrzesniewski, C. R. McCauley, P. Rozin, and B. Schwartz, "Jobs, Careers, and Callings: People's Relations to Their Work," *Journal of Research in Personality* 31 (1997): 21–33.

75   Groundhog Day: T. Albert (producer) and H. Ramis (producer and director), *Groundhog Day* (motion picture), USA: Columbia Pictures (1993).

76   The Devil Wears Prada: W. Finerman and K. Rosenfelt (producers) and D. Frankel (director). *The Devil Wears Prada* (motion picture), USA: 20th Century Fox (2006).

76   The Shawshank Redemption: N. Marvin (producer) and F. Darabont (director), *The Shawshank Redemption* (motion picture), USA: Columbia Pictures (1994).

76   Chariots of Fire: D. Putnam and D. Fayed (producers) and H. Hudson, *Chariots of Fire* (motion picture), USA: Warner Bros. and the Ladd Company (1981).

76   Sunday in the Park with George: M. Brandman (producer) and T. Hughes (director), *Sunday in the Park with George* (video), USA: Image Entertainment (1986).

76   Field of Dreams: L. Gordon and C. Gordon (producers) and P. A. Robinson (director), *Field of Dreams* (motion picture), USA: Universal Studios (1989).

76   Shoeless Joe: W. P. Kinsella, *Shoeless Joe* (New York: Houghton Mifflin, 1982).

76   Close Encounters: J. Phillips and M. Phillips (producers) and S. Spielberg (director), *Close Encounters of the Third Kind* (motion picture), USA: Columbia Pictures (1977).

Chapter 5: Positive Education: Teaching Well-Being to Young People

79   *depression is about ten times more common now than it was fifty years ago:* P. J. Wickramaratne, M. M. Weissman, P. J. Leaf, and T. R. Holford, "Age, Period, and Cohort Effects on the Risk of Major Depression: Results from Five United States Communities," *Journal of Clinical Epidemiology* 42 (1989): 333–43.

79   *Now the first onset is below age fifteen:* P. M. Lewinsohn, P. Rohde, J. R. Seeley, and S. A. Fischer, "Age-Cohort Changes in the Lifetime Occurrence of Depression and Other Mental Disorders," *Journal of Abnormal Psychology* 102 (1993): 110–20. By the end of high school, around 20 percent of adolescents report having already experienced a depressive episode.

79   *While there is controversy about whether this rises to the scary appellation* epidemic: E. J. Costello, A. Erkanli, and A. Angold. "Is There an Epidemic of Child or Adolescent Depression?" *Journal of Child Psychology and Psychiatry* 47 (2006): 1263–71. In a meta-analysis of twenty-six epidemiological studies conducted between 1965 and 1996, Costello and colleagues did not find cohort effects in the rates of depression. They suggested that results from other studies showing rising prevalence might have been biased by the use of retrospective recall. The public perception of an "epidemic" may also be due to the fact that depression had previously been underdiagnosed by clinicians.

For another discussion of the effect of birth cohort as well as gender on the prevalence of depression, see J. M. Twenge and S. Nolen-Hoeksema, "Age, Gender, Race, Socioeconomic Status, and Birth Cohort Differences on the Children's Depression Inventory: A Meta-Analysis," *Journal of Abnormal Psychology* 111 (2002): 578–88.

79   *This is a paradox:* G. E. Easterbrook, *The Progress Paradox: How Life Gets Better While People Feel Worse* (New York: Random House, 2003); G. E. Easterbrook, "Life Is Good, So Why Do We Feel So Bad?" *Wall Street Journal,* June 13, 2008.

79   *Progress has not been limited to the material:* See for instance *Latest Findings on National Air Quality: Status and Trends Through 2006* (Research Triangle Park, NC: U.S. Environmental Protection Agency, 2006); T. D. Snyder, S. A. Dillow, and C. M. Hoffman, *Digest of Education Statistics, 2007* (Washington, DC: U.S. Department of Education, 2008); H. Schuman, C. Steeh, I. Bobo, and M. Krysan, *Racial Attitudes in America: Trends and Interpretations* (Cambridge, MA: Harvard University Press, 1997).

79   *Happiness has gone up only spottily, if at all:* R. Inglehart, R. Foa, C. Peterson, and C. Welzel, "Development, Freedom, and Rising Happiness: A Global Perspective (1981–2007)," *Perspectives on Psychological Science* 3 (2007): 264–85.

80   *the Old Order Amish of Lancaster County:* J. A. Egeland and A. M. Hostetter, "Amish Study: I. Affective Disorders Among the Amish, 1976–1980," *American Journal of Psychiatry* 140 (1983): 56–61.

80   *Positive mood produces broader attention:* B. L. Fredrickson and C. Branigan, "Positive Emotions Broaden the Scope of Attention and Thought-Action Repertoires," *Cognition & Emotion* 19 (2005): 313–32; A. Bolte, T. Goschke, and J. Kuhl, "Emotion and Intuition: Effects of Positive and Negative Mood on Implicit Judgments of Semantic Coherence," *Psychological Science* 14 (2003): 416–21; G. Rowe, J. B. Hirsh, A. K. Anderson, and E. E. Smith, "Positive Affect Increases the Breadth of Attentional Selection," *Proceedings of the National Academy of Sciences of the United States of America* 104 (2007): 383–88.

80   *more creative thinking:* A. M. Isen, K. A. Daubman, and G. P. Nowicki, "Positive Affect Facilitates Creative Problem-Solving," *Journal of Personality and Social Psychology* 52 (1987): 1122–31; C. A. Estrada, A. M. Isen, and M. J. Young, "Positive Affect Improves Creative Problem Solving and Influences Reported Source of Practice Satisfaction in Physicians," *Motivation and Emotion* 18 (1994): 285–99.

80   *and more holistic thinking:* A. M. Isen, A. S. Rosenzweig, and M. J. Young, "The Influence of Positive Affect on Clinical Problem Solving," *Medical Decision Making* 11 (1991): 221–27; J. Kuhl, "Emotion, Cognition, and Motivation: II. The Functional Significance of Emotions in Perception, Memory, Problem-Solving, and Overt Action," *Sprache and Kognition* 2 (1983): 228–53; J. Kuhl, "A Functional-Design Approach to Motivation and Self-Regulation: The Dynamics of Personality Systems Interactions," in *Handbook of Self-Regulation,* eds. M. Boekaerts, P. R. Pintrich, and M. Zeidner (San Diego: Academic Press, 2000), pp. 111–69.

80   *in contrast to negative mood, which produces narrowed attention:* A. Bolte, T. Goschke, and J. Kuhl, "Emotion and Intuition: Effects of Positive and Negative Mood on Implicit Judgments of Semantic Coherence," *Psychological Science* 14 (2003): 416–21.

82   *A meta-analysis of all the studies:* S. M. Brunwasser and J. E. Gillham, "A Meta-Analytic Review of the Penn Resiliency Programme" (paper presented at the Society for Prevention Research, San Francisco, CA, May 2008).

82   *in the first PRP study, the program halved the rate of moderate to severe depressive symptoms through two years of follow-up:* J. E. Gillham, K. J. Reivich, L. H. Jaycox, and M. E. P. Seligman, "Prevention of Depressive Symptoms in Schoolchildren: Two-Year Follow-Up," *Psychological Science* 6 (1995): 343–51.

82   *In a medical setting, PRP prevented depression and anxiety disorders:* J. E. Gillham, J. Hamilton, D. R. Freres, K. Patton, and R. Gallop, "Preventing Depression Among Early Adolescents in the Primary Care Setting: A Randomized Controlled Study of the Penn Resiliency Program," *Journal of Abnormal Child Psychology* 34 (2006): 203–19.

82   *benefits on parents' reports of adolescents' conduct problems three years after their youngsters completed the program:* J. J. Cutuli, "Preventing Externalizing Symptoms and Related Features in Adolescence" (unpublished honors thesis, University of Pennsylvania, 2004); J. J. Cutuli, T. M. Chaplin, J. E. Gillham, K. J. Reivich, and M. E. P. Seligman, "Preventing co-occurring depression symptoms in adolescents with conduct problems: The Penn Resiliency Program," *New York Academy of Sciences* 1094 (2006): 282–86.

82   *Penn Resiliency Program works equally well for children of different racial/ethnic backgrounds:* S. M. Brunwasser and J. E. Gillham, "A Meta-Analytic Review of the Penn Resiliency Programme" (paper presented at the Society for Prevention Research, San Francisco, CA, May 2008).

83   *PRP's effectiveness varies considerably across studies:* J. E. Gillham, S. M. Brunwasser, and D. R. Freres, "Preventing Depression Early in Adolescence: The Penn Resiliency Program," in *Handbook of Depression in Children and Adolescents,* eds. J. R. Z. Abela and B. L. Hankin (New York: Guilford Press, 2007), pp. 309–32.

83   *The fidelity of curriculum delivery is critical:* J. E. Gillham, J. Hamilton, D. R. Freres, K. Patton, and R. Gallop, "Preventing Depression Among Early Adolescents in the Primary Care Setting: A Randomized Controlled Study of the Penn Resiliency Program," *Journal of Abnormal Child Psychology* 34 (2006): 203–19.

83   *We tested students' strengths:* using the VIA classification described by C. Peterson and M. E. P. Seligman, *Character Strengths and Virtues: A Handbook and Classification* (New York: Oxford University Press/Washington, DC: American Psychological Association, 2004).

85   *The positive psychology program improved the strengths of curiosity, love of learning, and creativity:* M. E. P. Seligman, R. M. Ernst, J. Gillham, K. Reivich, and M. Linkins, "Positive Education: Positive Psychology and Classroom Interventions," *Oxford Review of Education* 35 (2009): 293–311.

85   *The positive psychology program improved social skills:* M. E. P. Seligman, R. M. Ernst, J. Gillham, K. Reivich, and M. Linkins, "Positive Education: Positive Psychology and Classroom Interventions," *Oxford Review of Education* 35 (2009): 293–311.

86   *"What is the Geelong Grammar School":* For more information about the school, see www.ggs.vic.edu.au.

89   *the ABC model:* A. Ellis, *Reason and Emotion in Psychotherapy* (New York: Lyle Stuart, 1962); see also M. E. P. Seligman, *Learned Optimism: How to Change Your Mind and Your Life* (New York: Pocket Books, 1992).

90   *students learn "real-time resilience":* K. Reivich and A. Shatte, *The Resilience Factor: 7 Essential Skills for Overcoming Life's Inevitable Obstacles* (New York: Broadway, 2003).

90   *active-constructive responding:* E. L. Gable, H. T. Reis, E. A. Impett, and E. R. Asher, "What Do You Do When Things Go Right? The Intrapersonal and Interpersonal Benefits of Sharing Positive Events," *Journal of Personality and Social Psychology* 87 (2004): 228–45.

90   *a 3:1 Losada positive-to-negative ratio:* B. L. Fredrickson and M. F. Losada, "Positive Affect and the Complex Dynamics of Human Flourishing," *American Psychologist* 60 (2005): 678–86.

90   *Shakespeare's* King Lear: W. Shakespeare, *King Lear* (London: Arden, 2007).

90   *Arthur Miller's* Death of a Salesman: A. Miller, *Death of a Salesman* (New York: Viking Press, 1996).

90   *Franz Kafka's* Metamorphosis: F. Kafka, *The Metamorphosis* (Cheswold, DE: Prestwick House, 2005).

90   *Student preparation for these speeches:* M. E. P. Seligman, R. M. Ernst, J. Gillham, K. Reivich, and M. Linkins, "Positive Education: Positive Psychology and Classroom Interventions," *Oxford Review of Education* 35 (2009): 293–311.

91   *Elementary teachers start each day with "What went well?":* J. M. F. Eades, *Classroom Tales: Using Storytelling to Build Emotional, Social, and Academic Skills Across the Primary Curriculum* (London: Jessica Kingsley, 2005).

Chapter 6: GRIT, Character, and Achievement: A New Theory of Intelligence

102   *he died suddenly at age fifty-nine in 2005:* M. Silver, "John P. Sabini (1947–2005)," *American Psychologist* 6 (2006): 1025.

102   *it is a legitimate form of moral sanction but at a less punitive level than legal sanction:* J. P. Sabini and M. Silver, "Moral Reproach and Moral Action," *Journal for the Theory of Social Behaviour* 8 (1978): 103–23.

102   Summerbridge Cambridge: N. J. Heller, "Students-Turned-Teachers Help Middle Schoolers Get Ahead in School," *Harvard Crimson*, July 25, 2003. The Summerbridge programs are now known as the Breakthrough Collaborative programs throughout the United States (and Summerbridge Cambridge is now known as Breakthrough Cambridge). For more information, see www.break throughcollaborative.org.

103   *Character had long since gone out of fashion in social science:* The decline in psychologists' interest for the notion of character can be traced back to the work of Gordon Allport, one of the founding fathers of the study of personality in the United States. Allport borrowed from John Watson, another psychologist, the distinction between "character" (the self viewed from a moral perspective) and "personality" (the objective self). According to Allport (1921), "psychologists who accept Watson's view have no right, strictly speaking, to include character study in the province of psychology. It belongs rather to social ethics." Personality is a morally neutral version of character and thus more appropriate to objective science. Allport urged psychologists to study personality traits and leave character to the province of philosophy.

For a review of Allport's work on character and personality, see I. A. M. Nicholson, "Gordon Allport, Character, and the 'Culture of Personality,' 1897–1937," *History of Psychology* 1 (1998): 52–68.

For Allport's original work on the distinction between character and personality, see G. Allport, "Personality and Character," *Psychological Bulletin* 18 (1921): 441–55; G. Allport, "Concepts of Traits and Personality," *Psychological Bulletin* 24 (1927): 284–93; G. Allport and P. Vernon, "The Field of Personality," *Psychological Bulletin* 27 (1930): 677–730.

103   *"better angels of our nature":* Lincoln's inaugural address can be found at www.bartleby.com/124/pres31.html, as well as in *Inaugural Addresses of the Presidents of the United States* (Washington, DC: U.S. Government Printing Office, 2001).

103   *The Haymarket Square riot in 1886 in Chicago was a turning point:* P. Avrich, *The Haymarket Square Tragedy* (Princeton, NJ: Princeton University Press, 1984).

104   *Almost the entire history of twentieth-century psychology:* K. S. Bowers, "Situationism in Psychology: An Analysis and a Critique," *Psychological Review* 80 (1973): 307–36.

104   *giving up character as an explanation of human misbehavior in favor of the environment:* J. Sabini and M. Silver, "Lack of Character? Situationism Critiqued," *Ethics* 115 (2005): 535–62. Discusses the impact of situationism on the notion of character and on the study of virtue ethics.

107   *Together they created Wilson Lodge: University of Chicago Magazine,* May–June 2010. Today this brave reaction is also being emulated by University of Chicago professor Sian Beilock, who established a house system for female math and science students to keep them focused on their discipline and encouraged to stay the course. Goheen, incidentally, had snatched up the torch that a previous Princeton president, Woodrow Wilson, dropped in his futile battle against the club system around the turn of the twentieth century.

107   *Dickie Freeman and Joel Kupperman, two of the prodigies who starred in* Quiz Kids: R. D. Feldman, *Whatever Happened to the Quiz Kids? The Perils and Profits of Growing Up Gifted* (Lincoln, NE: iUniverse.com, 2000). Ruth Duskin Feldman followed up on the *Quiz Kids* contestants and later published this volume describing their long-term outcomes, including the achievements of some (for example, Nobel Prize winner James Watson) and the failure of others to realize their potential.

108   *IQ correlates almost as high as +.50 with how fast people can do this:* I. J. Deary, G. Der, and G. Ford, "Reaction Times and Intelligence Differences: A Population-Based Cohort Study," *Intelligence* 29 (2001): 389–99. Deary and colleagues, for instance, tested nine hundred Scottish subjects in their fifties, and found a correlation of .49 between a measure of intelligence and a four-choice reaction-time test.

109   *people say she has "great intuitions":* M. E. P. Seligman and M. Kahana, "Unpacking Intuition: A Conjecture," *Perspectives on Psychological Science* 4 (2009): 399–402. Intuitions may be a form of enhanced recognition memory (which leads to great speed and the feeling of "automaticity"). This conjecture proposed by Michael Kahana and me implies that intuition may be teachable—for instance, through the use of tools such as massive virtual simulation.

The psychological literature on intuition has also been readably summarized by M. Gladwell, *Blink: The Power of Thinking Without Thinking* (New York: Little, Brown, 2005).

110   *achievement = skill × effort:* A. L. Duckworth, "Achievement = Talent × Effort" (forthcoming). Angela defines *skill* as the rate of change in achievement per unit effort (in other words, how fast someone can learn something within a defined period, also called the "instantaneous" rate of change). Effort can be most simply thought of as time on task (if that time is spent in a state of high concentration!). Angela's theory of achievement also takes into account one additional variable: talent. While most people use the terms *skill* and *talent* interchangeably, Angela differentiates the two constructs by defining talent as the rate of change in skill per unit effort. In other words, talent is the rate of change of the successive instantaneous rates of change. We consider individuals who can learn faster and better over the long term to be more talented. In contrast, individuals who do not show such acceleration in learning (or even show deceleration) may be skilled but would probably be referred to as less talented.

111   *when I should have been reading every word:* G. Salomon and T. Globerson. "Skill May Not Be Enough: The Role of Mindfulness in Learning and Transfer," *International Journal of Educational Research* 11 (1987): 623–37. Salomon and Globerson noted that there is often a gap between what people *can* do and what they *actually* do. They suggest that the notion of mindfulness (in other words, slowness) explains why some individuals realize their full potential and others do not. The authors explain that "increased mindfulness is apparently important where automaticity of skill is not enough" (p. 630). Thus, depending on the type of task and the amount of information already on automatic, a slow, mindful attitude toward learning may be required to succeed.

111   *the legendary William K. Estes:* A. F. Healy, "APF Gold Medal Awards and Distinguished Teaching of Psychology Award: William K. Estes," *American Psychologist* 47 (1992): 855–57.

111   *the greatest of the mathematical learning theorists:* W. K. Estes, "Towards a Statistical Theory of Learning," *Psychological Review* 57 (1950): 94–107. His seminal article.

Almost a half century later, Bower reviewed the major influence of this article on the field of psychology: G. H. Bower, "A Turning Point in Mathematical Learning Theory," *Psychological Review* 101 (1994): 290–300.

111   *Søren Kierkegaard's* Fear and Trembling: S. Kierkegaard, *Fear and Trembling* (New York: Classic Books, 2009).

112   *Walter Mischel's classic marshmallow study:* W. Mischel, Y. Shoda, and M. I. Rodriguez, "Delay of Gratification in Children," *Science* 244 (1989): 933–38.

112   *the seed crystal around which the cascade of school failure begins:* C. Blair and A. Diamond, "Biological Processes in Prevention and Intervention: Promotion of Self-Regulation and the Prevention of Early School Failure," *Development and Psychopathology* 20 (2008): 899–911.

113   *Tools of the Mind kids score higher on tests that require executive function:* A. Diamond, W. S. Barnett, J. Thomas, and S. Munro, "Preschool Program Improves Cognitive Control," *Science* 318 (2007): 1387–88.

See also the coverage of this finding in the popular media: P. Tough, "Can the Right Kinds of Play Teach Self-Control?" *New York Times,* September 25, 2009.

115   *time and effort you spend in deliberate practice:* K. A. Ericsson and P. Ward, "Capturing the Naturally Occurring Superior Performance of Experts in the Laboratory," *Current Directions in Psychological Science* 16 (2007): 346–50.

116   *Self-discipline outpredicts IQ for academic success by a factor of about 2:* A. L. Duckworth and M. E. P. Seligman, "Self-Discipline Outdoes IQ in Predicting Academic Performance of Adolescents," *Psychological Science* 16 (2005): 939–44.

117   *This also solves one of the perennial riddles about the gap in school achievement between girls and boys:* A. L. Duckworth and M. E. P. Seligman, "Self-Discipline Gives Girls the Edge: Gender in Self-Discipline, Grades, and Achievement Test Scores," *Journal of Educational Psychology* 98 (2006): 198–208.

118   *Self-discipline did the same thing for weight gain that it did for grades:* A. L. Duckworth, E. Tsukayama, and A. B. Geier, "Self-Controlled Children Stay Leaner in the Transition to Adolescence," *Appetite* 54 (2010): 304–8; E. Tsukayama, S. L. Toomey, M. S. Faith, and A. L. Duckworth, "Self-Control as a Protective Factor against Overweight Status in the Transition from Childhood to Adolescence," *Archives of Pediatrics and Adolescent Medicine* 164 (2010): 631–5.

118   *Roy Baumeister, believes it is the queen of all the virtues:* For overviews of Baumeister's work on self-control, see R. F. Baumeister, M. Gailliot, C. N. DeWall, and M. Oaten, "Self-Regulation and Personality: How Interventions Increase Regulatory Success, and How Depletion Moderates the Effects of Traits on Behavior," *Journal of Personality* 74 (2006): 1773–1801; R. F. Baumeister, K. D. Vohs, and D. M. Tice, "The Strength Model of Self-Control," *Current Directions in Psychological Science* 16 (2007): 351–55.

118   *the combination of very high persistence and high passion for an objective:* A. L. Duckworth, C. Peterson, M. D. Matthews, and D. R. Kelly, "Grit: Perseverance and Passion for Long-Term Goals," *Journal of Personality and Social Psychology* 92 (2007): 1087–1101.

119   *Charles Murray* [. . .] *in his magnum opus,* Human Accomplishment: C. Murray, *Human Accomplishment* (New York: HarperCollins, 2003).

120   *William Shockley* [. . .] *found this pattern in the publication of scientific papers:* W. Shockley, "On the Statistics of Individual Variations of Productivity in Research Laboratories," *Proceedings of the Institute of Radio Engineers* 45 (1957): 279.

121   *the following scale:* A. L. Duckworth and P. D. Quinn, "Development and Validation of the Short Grit Scale (Grit-S)," *Journal of Personality Assessment* 91 (2009): 166–74.

125   *As psychiatrist Dr. Ed Hallowell says:* E. M. Hallowell and P. S. Jensen, *Superparenting for ADD: An Innovative Approach to Raising Your Distracted Child* (New York: Random House, 2008).

Chapter 7: Army Strong: Comprehensive Soldier Fitness

127   *the legendary George Casey:* E. Schmitt, "The Reach of War: Man in the News—George William Casey Jr.: A Low-Key Commander with 4 Stars to Tame the Iraqi Furies," *New York Times,* July 5, 2004. A short biographical profile written upon George Casey's nomination as commander of the multinational force in Iraq.

127   *author of the brilliant essay "Clausewitz and World War IV," in the* Armed Forces Journal: R. H. Scales, "Clausewitz and World War IV," *Armed Forces Journal* (2006). Retrieved November 12, 2009, from www.armedforces journal.com/2006/07/1866019.

128   *Richard Carmona, the surgeon general of the United States:* R. Pear, "Man in the News: A Man of Many Professions—Richard Henry Carmona," *New York Times,* March 27, 2002. A short biographical profile.

128   *"We spend two trillion dollars every year on health":* A. Sisko, C. Truffer, S. Smith, S. Keehan, J. Cylus, J. A. Poisal, M. K. Clemens, and J. Lizonitz, "Health Spending Projections Through 2018: Recession Effects Add Uncertainty to the Outlook," *Health Affairs* 28 (2009): w346–w57. To make things worse, national health spending may increase up to $4.4 trillion per year by 2018, according to experts' projections.

128   *"seventy-five percent of this goes to treating chronic disease":* Centers for Disease Control and Prevention, *Chronic Disease Overview page.* Retrieved November 12, 2009, from www.cdc.gov/nccdphp/overview.htm.

129   *"in combat for years to come":* G. Casey, "Comprehensive Soldier Fitness: A Vision for Psychological Resilience in the United States Army," *American Psychologist* (forthcoming). Much of the material describing CSF is adapted from a special issue of the *American Psychologist*; guest editors, Martin Seligman and Mike Matthews. General Casey's article is the lead article.

129   *GAT:* C. Peterson, N. Park, and C. Castro, "Assessment: The Global Assessment Tool," *American Psychologist* (forthcoming). Some of the ideas and some of the wording in this section are derived from these authors.

130   *creation of psychological tests:* J. E. Driskell and B. Olmstead, "Psychology and the Military: Research Applications and Trends," *American Psychologist* 44 (1989): 43–54.

See also T. W. Harrell, "Some History of the Army General Classification Test," *Journal of Applied Psychology* 77: 875–78. The AGCT is the successor to the alpha and beta tests used during World War I.

130   *the Aviation Psychology Program:* J. C. Flanagan, *The Aviation Psychology Program in the Army Air Forces* (Washington, DC: U.S. Government Printing Office, 1948).

130   *procedures for selecting and classifying flying personnel:* J. C. Flanagan, "The Selection and Classification Program for Aviation Cadets (Aircrew—Bom-bardiers, Pilots, and Navigators)," *Journal of Consulting Psychology* 6 (1942): 229–39.

133   *"catastrophization" items, a cognitive thinking trap:* as defined and described by A. T. Beck, A. J. Rush, B. F. Shaw, and G. Emery, *Cognitive Therapy of Depression* (New York: Guilford Press, 1979).

135   *this may reduce the stigma surrounding mental health services:* T. M. Greene-Shortbridge, T. W. Britt, and C. A. Castro, "The Stigma of Mental Health Problems in the Military," *Military Medicine* 2 (2007): 157–61. The issue of reducing stigma among soldiers around mental health issues is critical and timely, as highlighted in this article by Colonel Carl Castro and colleagues.

137   *The Soldier Fitness Tracker assesses soldiers:* M. Fravell, K. Nasser, and R. Cornum, "The Soldier Fitness Tracker: Global Delivery of Comprehensive Soldier Fitness," *American Psychologist* (forthcoming). Some of the ideas and some of the wording in this section are derived from these authors.

138   *Here are the Global Assessment Tool scores for a male lieutenant:* This example is from C. Peterson, N. Park, and C. Castro, "Assessment: The Global Assessment Tool," *American Psychologist* (forthcoming). Some of the ideas and some of the wording in this section are derived from these authors.

139   *Emotional fitness module:* S. Algoe and B. Fredrickson, "Emotional Fitness and the Movement of Affective Science from Lab to Field," *American Psychologist* (forthcoming). Some of the ideas and some of the wording in this section are derived from these authors.

140   *regard them as "resource builders":* B. L. Fredrickson, "The Role of Positive Emotions in Positive Psychology: The Broaden-and-Build Theory of Positive Emotions," *American Psychologist* 56 (2001): 218–26.

142   *Family fitness module:* J. M. Gottman and J. S. Gottman, "The Comprehensive Soldier Fitness Program: Family Skills Component," *American Psychologist* (forthcoming). Some of the ideas and some of the wording in this section are derived from these authors.

142   *The majority of suicides by our soldiers in Iraq involve a failed relationship with a spouse or partner:* United States Medical Corps Mental Health Advisory Team, *Fifth Annual Investigation* (MHAT-V) (2008). The report is available at www.armymedicine.army.mil/reports/mhat/mhat_v/Redacted1-MHATV-4-FEB-2008-Overview.pdf.

143   *Social fitness module:* J. Cacioppo, H. Reis, and A. Zautra, "Social Resilience: The Protective Effects of Social Fitness," *American Psychologist* (forthcoming).

143   *"this would be natural selection":* C. R. Darwin, *The Descent of Man, and Selection in Relation to Sex* (Lawrence, KS: Digireads.com, 2009), p. 110.

143   *the devastating effects of loneliness itself:* J. T. Cacioppo and W. Patrick, *Loneliness: Human Nature and the Need for Social Connection* (New York: W. W. Norton, 2008). See Chapter 9.

144   The Selfish Gene: R. Dawkins, *The Selfish Gene* (New York: Oxford University Press, 1976).

144   *This convoluted argument flies in the face of ordinary altruism:* H. Gintis, S. Bowles, R. Boyd, and E. Fehr, "Explaining Altruistic Behavior in Humans," *Evolution and Human Behavior* 24 (2003): 153–72. A review of the various theories that have been invoked to explain altruism.

144   *Christians hiding Jews in their attics:* several psychologists have tried to find out what distinguished "righteous gentiles" who protected Jews during World War II from others. See for example M. P. Oliner and S. P. Oliner, *The Altruistic Personality: Rescuers of Jews in Nazi Europe* (New York: Free Press, 1988); E. Midlarsky, S. F. Jones, and R. P. Corley, "Personality Correlates of Heroic Rescue During the Holocaust," *Journal of Personality* 73 (2005): 907–34; K. R. Monroe, "Cracking the Code of Genocide: The Moral Psychology of Rescuers, Bystanders, and Nazis During the Holocaust," *Political Psychology* 29 (2008): 699–736.

144   *"Born to be good":* D. Keltner, *Born to Be Good: The Science of a Meaningful Life* (New York: W. W. Norton, 2009).

145   *the most forceful advocates of group selection:* as cited earlier, D. S. Wilson and E. O. Wilson, "Rethinking the Theoretical Foundation of Sociobiology," *Quarterly Review of Biology* 82 (2007): 327–48; see also E. Sober and D. S. Wilson, *Unto Others: The Evolution and Psychology of Unselfish Behavior* (Cambridge, MA: Harvard University Press, 1998).

145   *consider the lowly chicken:* D. S. Wilson, *Evolution for Everyone* (New York: Random House, 2007).

145   *egg production does indeed become massive:* C. Goodnight and L. Stevens, "Experimental Studies of Group Selection: What Do They Tell Us About Group Selection in Nature?" *American Naturalist* 150 (1997): S59–79.

145   *factories, fortresses, and systems of communication:* E. O. Wilson, "One Giant Leap: How Insects Achieved Altruism and Colonial Life," *Bioscience* 58 (2008): 17–25.

146   *allowing us to empathize:* M. Iacoboni, "Imitation, Empathy, and Mirror Neurons," *Annual Review of Psychology* 60 (2009): 653–70. A review of the evidence on the role of mirror neurons in empathy; see also S. Blakeslee, "Cells That Read Minds," *New York Times,* January 10, 2006.

146   *Happiness was even more contagious than loneliness or depression:* J. H. Fowler and N. A. Christakis, "Dynamic Spread of Happiness in a Large Social Network: Longitudinal Analysis over 20 Years in the Framingham Heart Study," *British Medical Journal* 337 (2008): a2338.

148   *Karen Reivich and I wanted to predict:* D. C. Rettew, K. Reivich, C. Peterson, D. A. Seligman, and M. E .P. Seligman, "Professional Baseball, Basketball, and Explanatory Style: Predicting Performance in the Major League" (unpublished manuscript).

149   *Spiritual fitness module:* K. Pargament and P. Sweeney, "Building Spiritual Fitness in the Army," *American Psychologist* (forthcoming). Some of the ideas and some of the wording in this section are derived from these authors.

149   *spirituality goes hand in hand with:* for reviews of the many benefits of spirituality, see D. G. Myers, "The Funds, Friends, and Faith of Happy People," *American Psychologist* 55 (2000): 56–67; D. G. Myers, "Religion and Human

Flourishing," in *The Science of Subjective Well-Being*, eds. M. Eid and R. J. Larsen (New York: Guilford Press, 2008), pp. 323–43; G. E. Vaillant, *Spiritual Evolution: A Scientific Defense of Faith* (New York: Broadway Books, 2008); E. A. Greenfield, G. E. Vaillant, N. E. Marks, "Do Formal Religious Participation and Spiritual Perceptions Have Independent Linkages with Diverse Dimensions of Psychological Well-Being?" *Journal of Health and Social Behavior* 50 (2009): 196–212.

149   *Hugh Thompson's:* H. C. Kelman and V. L. Hamilton, *Crimes of Obedience: Towards a Social Psychology of Authority and Responsibility* (New Haven, CT: Yale University Press, 1990). See Chapter 1.

150   *Ken Pargament:* K. I. Pargament, *Spiritually Integrated Psychotherapy: Understanding and Addressing the Sacred* (New York: Guilford, 2007); K. I. Pargament, *The Psychology of Religion and Coping: Theory, Research, Practice* (New York: Guilford Press, 1997). Ken Pargament is the author of two books on spirituality and psychology.

151   openness to alternate viewpoints: K. Pargament and P. Sweeney, "Building Spiritual Fitness in the Army," *American Psychologist* (forthcoming).

Chapter 8: Turning Trauma into Growth

152   *Shell shock and combat fatigue:* J. D. Kinzie and R. R. Goetz, "A Century of Controversy Surrounding Posttraumatic Stress-Spectrum Syndromes: The Impact on DSM-III and DSM-IV," *Journal of Traumatic Stress* 9 (1996): 159–79. A comprehensive description of the history of the post-traumatic stress disorder diagnosis and the controversies surrounding it.

152   *Kai Erikson, son of the famed psychologist Erik Erikson, wrote a landmark book about this disaster:* K. T. Erikson, *Everything in Its Path: Destruction of Community in the Buffalo Creek Flood* (New York: Simon & Schuster, 1978).

153   *Wilbur, his wife, Deborah, and their four children managed to survive:* The stories of the Buffalo Creek disaster are from M. Seligman, E. Walker, and D. Rosenhan. *Abnormal Psychology*, 4th ed. (New York: W. W. Norton, 2001, pp. 183–84).

155   *Here from the fourth edition are the latest criteria for diagnosing a case of PTSD:* American Psychiatric Association, *Diagnostic and Statistical Manual of Mental Disorders*, 4th ed., text revision (Washington, DC: American Psychiatric Association, 1994).

156   *Here is a composite case of PTSD from the Iraq War:* M. J. Friedman, "Posttraumatic Stress Disorder Among Military Returnees from Afghanistan and Iraq," *American Journal of Psychiatry* 163 (2006): 586–93.

157   *with as many as 20 percent of the soldiers said to be afflicted:* C. S. Milliken, J. L. Auchterlonie, and C. W. Hoge, "Longitudinal Assessment of Mental Health Problems Among Active and Reserve Component Soldiers Returning from Iraq," *Journal of the American Medical Association* 298 (2007): 2141–48. In a study of almost 90,000 soldiers having served in Iraq, Charles Milliken and colleagues found that 20.3 percent of active-duty soldiers required mental health treatment six months after returning home. Among reserve component soldiers, this figure reached 42.4 percent.

C. W. Hoge, A. Terhakopian, C. A. Castro, S. C. Messer, and C. C. Engel, "Association of Posttraumatic Stress Disorder with Somatic Symptoms, Health Care Visits, and Absenteeism Among Iraq War Veterans," *American Journal of Psychiatry*

164 (2007): 150–53. Charles Hoge and colleagues also surveyed over 2,800 Iraq veterans and found that 17 percent met criteria for PTSD. The disorder was associated with poorer health, more absenteeism from work, and more severe physical symptoms overall. These results held even when analyses controlled for physical injuries.

C. W. Hoge, C. A. Castro, C. S. Messer, D. McGurk, D. I. Cotting, and R. L. Koffman, "Combat Duty in Iraq and Afghanistan, Mental Health Problems and Barriers to Care," *New England Journal of Medicine* 351 (2004): 13–22. Finally, in a previous study of more than 6,000 soldiers, Charles Hoge and colleagues found that the rate of PTSD in soldiers deployed to Iraq (16 percent to 17 percent) was higher than the rate of those deployed to Afghanistan (11 percent). This difference was explained by the fact that exposure to combat was greater in soldiers deployed to Iraq. These statistics will therefore probably change as the U.S. military strategy focuses more on Afghanistan. This study also highlighted that veterans' perception of stigma was a barrier to receiving proper care for their PTSD symptoms.

157 *resilience—a relatively brief episode of depression plus anxiety, followed by a return to the previous level of functioning:* as explained by A. C. McFarlane and R. Yehuda, "Resilience, Vulnerability, and the Course of Posttraumatic Reactions," in *Traumatic Stress*, eds. B. A. van der Kolk, A. C. McFarlane, and L. Weisaeth (New York: Guilford Press, 1996), pp. 155–81.

G. Bonanno, "Loss, Trauma, and Human Resilience: Have We Underestimated the Human Capacity to Thrive After Extremely Aversive Events?" *American Psychologist* 59 (2004): 20–28; G. Bonanno, "Resilience in the Face of Potential Trauma," *Current Directions in Psychological Science* 14 (2005): 135–38; G. Bonanno, *The Other Side of Sadness* (New York: Basic Books, 2009). In two studies, George Bonanno from Columbia University reviewed the evidence demonstrating that most people exposed to trauma do not develop PTSD. Because early studies of trauma focused on individuals seeking treatment (and therefore experiencing psychological problems), Bonanno argues that researchers have grossly underestimated the potential for human resilience. Until recently, resilience was therefore considered to be the exception—or worse, a pathological state (in other words, the individual is not "working through" his or her problems). Bonanno also makes a useful distinction between *recovery* (returning to pretrauma functioning levels after having experienced significant symptoms) and *resilience* (the ability to maintain a stable equilibrium in the face of adverse events). According to him, resilience is even more common than recovery.

R. C. Kessler, A. Sonnega, E. Bromet, M. Hughes, and C. B. Nelson, "Posttraumatic Stress Disorder in the National Comorbidity Survey," *Archives of General Psychiatry* 52 (1995): 1048–60. Epidemiological studies of the prevalence of PTSD in trauma-exposed populations have confirmed that recovery and/or resilience are the norm, not the exception. In a landmark study using data from the National Comorbidity Survey (NCS), Kessler and colleagues noted that although 50 percent to 60 percent of the U.S. population is exposed to trauma at some point, only about 8 percent will meet full criteria for PTSD.

S. Galea, H. Resnick, J. Ahern, J. Gold, M. Bucuvalas, D. Kilpatrick, J. Stuber, and D. Vlahov, "Posttraumatic Stress Disorder in Manhattan, New York City, After the September 11th Terrorist Attacks," *Journal of Urban Health: Bulletin of the New York Academy of Medicine* 73 (2002): 340–52; S. Galea, D. Vlahov,

H. Resnick, J. Ahern, E. Susser, J. Gold, M. Bucuvalas, and D. Kilpatrick, "Trends of Probable Post-Traumatic Stress Disorder in New York City After the September 11 Terrorist Attacks," *American Journal of Epidemiology* 158 (2003): 514–24.

The September 11, 2001, terrorist attacks also provided useful information about the rates of resilience and recovery and PTSD in exposed populations. Sandro Galea and colleagues (2003) conducted surveys in New York City and found that one month after the event, 7.5 percent of Manhattan residents met criteria for PTSD (17.4 percent had subsyndromal symptoms). Six months later, the prevalence dropped to .6 percent (4.7 percent for subsyndromal symptoms). In contrast, 40 percent of Manhattan residents did not exhibit a single PTSD symptom after the attacks (Galea and colleagues, 2002).

157   *less than 10 percent had heard of post-traumatic growth:* P. Sweeney and M. Matthews (personal communication, 2009).

158   *a symptom of normal grief and mourning:* R. M. Glass, "Is Grief a Disease? Sometimes," *Journal of the American Medical Association* 293 (2005): 2658–60. A discussion of the difference between normal and pathological grief.

158   *much more susceptible to PTSD:* L. S. Elwood, K. S. Hahn, B. O. Olatunji, and N. L. Williams, "Cognitive Vulnerabilities to the Development of PTSD: A Review of Four Vulnerabilities and the Proposal of an Integrative Vulnerability Model," *Clinical Psychology Review* 29 (2009): 87–100. A review of risk factors associated with PTSD.

158   *were diagnosed with PTSD:* C. A. LeardMann, T. C. Smith, B. Smith, T. S. Wells, and M. A. K. Ryan, "Baseline Self-Reported Functional Health and Vulnerability to Post-Traumatic Stress Disorder After Combat Deployment: Prospective US Military Cohort Study," *British Medical Journal* 338 (2009): b1273.

158   *that kind of money can lead to exaggerated and prolonged symptoms:* B. L. Green, M. C. Grace, J. D. Lindy, G. C. Gleser, A. C. Leonard, and T. L. Kramer, "Buffalo Creek Survivors in the Second Decade: Comparison with Unexposed and Nonlitigant Groups," *Journal of Applied Social Psychology* 20 (1990): 1033–50. This hypothesis has been investigated by Bonnie Green and colleagues, who compared litigant and nonlitigant survivors of the Buffalo Creek disaster on reported symptoms of psychopathology, and found no differences. Both groups of survivors however showed higher rates of anxiety, depression, and hostility than a third group of control (nonexposed) subjects. These results suggest that, in the case of the Buffalo Creek disaster, the financial incentives may not have exacerbated symptoms.

159   *We do not know what effect this substantial incentive is having on the diagnosis of PTSD from our wars:* R. A. Kulka, W. E. Schlenger, J. A. Fairbank, R. L. Hough, B. K. Jordan, and C. R. Marmar, et al., *Trauma and the Vietnam War Generation: Report of Findings from the National Vietnam Veterans Readjustment Study* (New York: Brunner/Mazel, 1990); B. P. Dohrenwend, J. B. Turner, N. A. Turse, B. G. Adams, K. C. Koenen, and R. Marshall, "The Psychological Risks of Vietnam for U.S. Veterans: A Revisit with New Data and Methods," *Science* 313 (2006): 979–82; R. J. McNally, "Can We Solve the Mysteries of the National Vietnam Veterans Readjustment Study?" *Journal of Anxiety Disorders* 21 (2007): 192–200; B. C. Frueh, J. D. Elhai, P. B. Gold, J. Monnier, K. M. Magruder, T. M. Keane, and G. W. Arana, "Disability Compensation Seeking Among Veterans Evaluated for Posttraumatic Stress Disorder," *Psychiatric Services* 54 (2003):

84–91; B. C. Frueh, A. L. Grubaugh, J. D. Elhai, and T. C. Buckley, "U.S. Department of Veterans Affairs Disability Policies for Posttraumatic Stress Disorder: Administrative Trends and Implications for Treatment, Rehabilitation, and Research," *American Journal of Public Health* 97 (2007): 2143–45.

The effect of financial incentives on Vietnam veterans has been extensively studied by Christopher Frueh and colleagues, after the National Vietnam Veterans Readjustment Study (NVVRS) reported that more than 30 percent of all men having served in Vietnam suffered from PTSD at one point or another (Kulka, et al., 1990). Many researchers and historians commented that the NVVRS probably overstated the prevalence of PTSD among Vietnam veterans (for instance, Dohrenwend, et al., 2006; McNally, 2007).

Frueh and colleagues conducted a series of studies investigating the effects of disability payments on PTSD symptom reports among Vietnam veterans. They found, for instance, that veterans who sought disability payments were more likely to report more distress across domains of psychopathology than another group of veterans matched on PTSD diagnoses (and who did not seek compensation). Frueh and colleagues (2007) therefore recommended that the VA disability policies be modified to encourage gainful employment while providing the best possible care and retaining a safety net for veterans who need it.

159   *British soldiers returning from Iraq and Afghanistan:* N. Fear, M. Jones, and D. Murphy, et al., "What Are the Consequences of Deployment to Iraq and Afghanistan on the Mental Health of the UK Armed Forces? A Cohort Study," *Lancet* 375 (2010): 1783–97. Why is there such a large discrepancy between British and U.S. rates of PTSD? Is it different exposure to combat? Is it different disability pay for PTSD? Is it different diagnostic stringencies? Is it different gaming of the medical system for British versus American soldiers? Is it different psychological fitness? No one knows yet.

159   *I have combed the Civil War writings and can find almost no PTSD [. . .] from that horrific epoch:* K. C. Hyams, S. Wignall, and R. Roswell, "War Syndromes and Their Evaluation: From the US Civil War to the Persian Gulf War," *Annals of Internal Medicine* 125 (1996): 398–405; J. M. Da Costa, "On Irritable Heart: A Clinical Study of a Form of Functional Cardiac Disorder and its Consequences," *American Journal of the Medical Sciences* 61 (1871): 17–52. In their review of the various war syndromes that have afflicted American soldiers throughout history, Hyams and colleagues note that soldiers involved in the U.S. Civil War most often suffered from "irritable heart syndrome," a disorder first described by Da Costa. This syndrome included shortness of breath, palpitations, chest pain, headache, and diarrhea, as well as other symptoms, in the absence of an obvious physical condition. Hyams and colleagues rightly point out that these symptoms could have been caused by various physical as well as psychological factors.

159   *My doubts are about overdiagnosis:* D. Dobbs, "The Post-Traumatic Stress Disorder Trap," *Scientific American* (April 2009): 64–69; P. McHugh, *Try to Remember* (New York: Dana, 2008). Richard McNally, from Harvard University, perhaps summarized best the situation (as cited by Dobbs, p. 65): "PTSD is a real thing, without a doubt. But as a diagnosis, PTSD has become so flabby and overstretched, so much a part of the culture, that we are almost certainly mistaking other problems for PTSD and thus mistreating them." The lay reader will

appreciate Dobbs's recent summary of the existing evidence for the causes and consequences of the overdiagnosis of PTSD.

See also Paul McHugh's *Try to Remember* for an insightful portrait of the psychiatric politics around PTSD.

159 *In the long run, they arrive at a higher level of psychological functioning than before:* R. G. Tedeschi and L. G. Calhoun, "Posttraumatic Growth: Conceptual Foundations and Empirical Evidence," *Psychological Inquiry* 15 (2004): 1–18. Reviews the concept of post-traumatic growth.

159 *"What does not kill me makes me stronger":* F. Nietzsche, *Twilight of the Idols: Or How to Philosophize with a Hammer* (London: Penguin Classics, 1990), p. 33.

159 *individuals who'd experienced one awful event had more intense strengths:* C. Peterson, N. Park, N. Pole, W. D'Andrea, and M. E. P. Seligman. "Strengths of Character and Posttraumatic Growth," *Journal of Traumatic Stress* 21 (2008): 214–17.

160 *Rhonda Cornum:* R. Cornum and P. Copeland, *She Went to War: The Rhonda Cornum Story* (New York: Presidio Press, 1992).

161 *PTG module:* R. Tedeschi and R. McNally, "Can We Facilitate Posttraumatic Growth in Combat Veterans?" *American Psychologist* (forthcoming). Some of the ideas and some of the wording in this section are derived from these authors.

161 *often follow tragedy:* R. G. Tedeschi and L. G. Calhoun, "Posttraumatic Growth: Conceptual Foundations and Empirical Evidence," *Psychological Inquiry* 15 (2004): 1–18. These domains of growth have been supported by empirical evidence, as reviewed here.

See also S. Joseph, "Growth Following Adversity: Positive Psychological Perspectives on Posttraumatic Stress," *Psychological Topics* 18 (2009): 335–44.

161 *61.1 percent of imprisoned airmen tortured for years by the North Vietnamese said that they had benefited psychologically:* W. H. Sledge, J. A. Boydstun, and A. J. Rabe, "Self-Concept Changes Related to War Captivity," *Archives of General Psychiatry* 37 (1980): 430–43.

161 *Post-Traumatic Growth Inventory (PTGI):* R. G. Tedeschi and L. G. Calhoun, "The Posttraumatic Growth Inventory: Measuring the Positive Legacy of Trauma," *Journal of Traumatic Stress* 9 (1996): 455–71.

162 *five elements that are known to contribute to post-traumatic growth:* R. G. Tedeschi and L. G. Calhoun, *Facilitating Posttraumatic Growth: A Clinician's Guide* (Mahwah, NJ: Erlbaum, 1999). Richard Tedeschi and Lawrence Calhoun have published a guide to help clinicians maximize the potential for post-traumatic growth in their clients.

See also R. G. Tedeschi and L. G. Calhoun, "A Clinical Approach to Posttraumatic Growth," in *Positive Psychology in Practice*, eds. P. A. Linley and S. Joseph (Hoboken, NJ: Wiley and Sons, 2004), pp. 405–19.

163 *Master Resilience Training:* K. Reivich, M. Seligman, and S. McBride, "Resilience Training," *American Psychologist* (forthcoming). Some of the ideas and some of the wording in this section are derived from these authors. Karen Reivich's creativity and energy is the backbone of this section of the book and of Master Resilience Training generally.

163 *"ordinary schoolteachers can be taught to deliver resilience training effectively to adolescents":* S. M. Brunwasser and J. E. Gillham, "A Meta-Analytic

Review of the Penn Resiliency Programme" (paper presented at the Society for Prevention Research, San Francisco, CA, May 2008).

164   *the author of* Happiness: R. Layard, *Happiness: Lessons from a New Science* (London: Penguin, 2005).

164   *he argues that government policy should be measured not by increases in gross domestic product but by increases in global well-being:* R. Layard, "Well-Being Measurement and Public Policy," in *Measuring the Subjective Well-Being of Nations: National Accounts of Time Use and Well-Being*, ed. A. Krueger (Cambridge, MA: National Bureau of Economic Research, 2008).

164   *"I want to take it to the schools of the United Kingdom":* R. Layard, "The Teaching of Values" (Ashby Lecture, University of Cambridge, Cambridge, England, May 2, 2007). In a lecture delivered at the University of Cambridge in 2007, Layard outlined his ideas on positive education and how it might be incorporated in the British educational system. According to Layard, the effects of a large-scale program should be even larger than those observed in controlled scientific trials "because each child taking the programme would interact with other children who had also taken it. If this applied to all children in a city, it should be possible to modify the whole youth culture of that city."

165   *"you are to make resilience training happen for the whole army":* B. Carey, "Mental Stress Training Is Planned for U.S. Soldiers," *New York Times*, August 17, 2009.

167   *the well-validated program we use to teach civilian teachers:* the Penn Resiliency Program, as reviewed in Chapter 6.

167   *Albert Ellis's ABCDE model:* as described in A. Ellis, J. Gordon, M. Neenan, and S. Palmer, *Stress Counseling: A Rational Emotive Behaviour Approach* (London: Cassell, 1997).

A. Ellis, "Fundamentals of Rational-Emotive Therapy for the 1990s," in *Innovations in Rational-Emotive Therapy*, eds. W. Dryden and L. K. Hill (New York: Sage, 1993).

167   *thinking traps:* another term for cognitive biases or distortions, as described by A. T. Beck, A. J. Rush, B. F. Shaw, and G. Emery, *Cognitive Therapy of Depression* (New York: Guilford Press, 1979).

168   *"icebergs," deeply held beliefs:* also referred to as "core beliefs," as defined in J. S. Beck, *Cognitive Therapy: Basics and Beyond* (New York: Guilford Press, 1995).

J. E. Young, J. L. Rygh, A. D. Weinberger, and A. T. Beck, "Cognitive Therapy for Depression," in *Clinical Handbook of Psychological Disorders: A Step-by-Step Treatment Manual*, 4th ed., ed. D. H. Barlow (New York: Guilford Press, 2008), pp. 250–305.

170   *Gabriele Prati and Luca Pietrantoni:* G. Prati and L. Pietrantoni, "Optimism, Social Support, and Coping Strategies as Factors Contributing to Posttraumatic Growth: A Meta-Analysis," *Journal of Loss and Trauma* 14 (2009): 364–88.

171   *people who habitually acknowledge and express gratitude:* R. A. Emmons, *Thanks! How the New Science of Gratitude Can Make You Happier* (New York: Houghton Mifflin, 2007).

173   *four styles of responding:* E. L. Gable, H. T. Reis, E. A. Impett, and E. R. Asher, "What Do You Do When Things Go Right? The Intrapersonal

and Interpersonal Benefits of Sharing Positive Events," *Journal of Personality and Social Psychology* 87 (2004): 228–45.

173 *Dr. Carol Dweck's work on effective praise:* M. L. Kamins and C. Dweck, "Person Versus Process Praise and Criticism: Implications for Contingent Self-Worth and Coping," *Developmental Psychology* 35 (1999): 835–47.

174 *One poignant area is exploring how they talk to their own families:* Much research has been conducted on the well-being of military families. Examples include L. M. Burrell, G. A. Adams, D. B. Durand, and C. A. Castro, "The Impact of Military Lifestyle Demands on Well-Being, Army, and Family Outcomes," *Armed Forces and Society* 33 (2006): 43–58; B. R. Karney and J. S. Crown, *Families Under Stress: An Assessment of Data, Theory, and Research on Marriage and Divorce in the Military* (Arlington, VA: Rand Corporation, 2007).

175 *"brainwashes" soldiers with positive thinking:* B. Levine, (July 29, 2010). *American Soldiers Brainwashed with "Positive Thinking."* Retrieved August 2, 2010, from www.alternet.org/world/147637/american_soldiers_brainwashed_with_%22positive_thinking%22?page=2.

175 *war on terror:* J. Mayer, *The Dark Side* (New York: Doubleday, 2008), pp. 163–64. In the wildest blog I have seen, Thierry Meyssan (May 20, 2010, voltaire net.org) wrote that I "supervised the torture experiments on Guantánamo prisoners. The navy formed a high-powered medical team. In particular, it invited Professor Seligman to Guantánamo . . . It was he who oversaw the experiments on human guinea pigs. U.S. torturers, under Professor Seligman's supervision, experimented and perfected every single coercive technique." This is wholly false and baseless.

176 *James Mitchell and Bruce Jessen:* S. Shane, "2 U.S. Architects of Harsh Tactics in 9/11's Wake," *New York Times*, August 11, 2009.

181 *The outcome of our training:* P. Lester and S. McBride, "Bringing Science to Bear: An Empirical Assessment of the Comprehensive Soldier Fitness Program," *American Psychologist* (forthcoming). Some of the ideas and some of the wording in this section are derived from these authors.

Chapter 9: Positive Physical Health: The Biology of Optimism

183 *mental health is not just the absence of mental illness:* M. Jahoda, *Current Concepts of Positive Mental Health* (New York: Basic Books, 1958). This idea was proposed long ago by Marie Jahoda's pioneering book *Current Concepts of Positive Mental Health.* She proposed then that "it [is] unlikely that the concept of mental health can be usefully defined by identifying it with the absence of disease [. . .] The absence of disease may constitute a necessary, but not sufficient, criterion for mental health" (pp. 14–15).

C. L. M. Keyes, "Mental Illness and/or Mental Health? Investigating Axioms of the Complete State Model of Health," *Journal of Consulting and Clinical Psychology* 73 (2005): 539–48. Since then, empirical research has supported the idea that mental health and mental illness are not the two ends of one continuum but rather constitute separate dimensions of human functioning. Corey Keyes, therefore, proposed a *two continua* model of mental illness and mental health. Using confirmatory factor analysis, he found strong support for his model in a representative survey of more than three thousand American adults. Keyes found that only around 17 percent of his sample had "complete mental" health (low mental illness and high mental health). Around 10 percent were languishing without suffering from a disorder (low mental illness and low mental health); this group corresponds to those described in Chapter 8 as "not [. . .] mentally ill, but [. . .] stuck and languishing in life." Finally, around 15 percent were mentally healthy while also suffering from a psychological disorder. These last two groups do not fit the traditional model positing a continuum of mental health and illness, and their existence, therefore, supports Keyes's *two continua* model.

See also C. L. M. Keyes and S. J. Lopez, "Toward a Science of Mental Health: Positive Directions in Diagnosis and Interventions," in *Handbook of Positive Psychology*, eds. C. R. Snyder and S. J. Lopez (New York: Oxford University Press, 2005), pp. 45–59.

P. J. Greenspoon and D. H. Saklofske, "Toward an Integration of Subjective Well-Being and Psychopathology," *Social Indicators Research* 54 (2001): 81–108; S. M. Suldo and E. J. Shaffer, "Looking Beyond Psychopathology: The Dual-Factor Model of Mental Health in Youth," *School Psychology Review* 37 (2008): 52–68. Studying children, Greenspoon and Saklofske proposed a similar model called the "dual factor system" (DFS). The researchers tested and verified the validity of the DFS on a sample of more than 400 schoolchildren (grades three through six). Next, Shannon Suldo and Emily Shaffer (2008) replicated and extended Greenspoon and Saklofske's findings. Using a sample 349 middle school students, they found that 57 percent of the children enjoyed "complete mental health" (high SWB, low psychopathology); 13 percent were vulnerable (low SWB, low psychopathology); 13 percent were symptomatic but content (high SWB, high psychopathology); and the remaining 17 percent were troubled (low SWB, high psychopathology). The researchers also found that children with "complete mental health" had a large number of favorable outcomes compared to others (for example, better reading skills, school attendance, academic success, social support).

Subjective well-being (or positive mental health), therefore, needs to be taken into account to understand optimal functioning in both children/adolescents and adults.

183   *(more than 95 percent of its budget goes to curtail illness)*: www.nih .gov/about/budget.htm. You can plow through it and try to make your own estimate. My plowing suggests that 5 percent to health as opposed to illness is conservative.

184   *"Is health a real thing"*: There have been numerous serious efforts to move medicine in the direction of a definition of positive health and away from a mere absence of illness definition of health. Health promotion, prevention, and the Wellness movement are examples. One article that reviews the history usefully is R. Manderscheid, C. Ryff, and E. Freeman, et al., "Evolving Definitions of Mental Illness and Wellness," *Preventing Chronic Disease* 7 (2010): 1–6.

184   *discovered "learned helplessness" in the mid-1960s:* M. E. P. Seligman, *Helplessness: On Depression, Development, and Death* (San Francisco, CA: Freeman, 1975). A comprehensive account and complete bibliography of the helplessness experiments in animals. See also S. F. Maier and M. E. P. Seligman, "Learned Helplessness: Theory and Evidence," *Journal of Experimental Psychology: General* 105 (1976): 3–46.

C. Peterson, S. F. Maier, and M. E. P. Seligman, *Learned Helplessness: A The-*

ory for the Age of Personal Control (New York: Oxford University Press, 1993); J. B. Overmier, "On Learned Helplessness," *Integrative Physiological and Behavioral Science* 37 (2002): 4–8. Debates about the theory of learned helplessness have continued up to this day. For a short introduction to the nature of these debates, as well as a list of relevant references, see Overmier.

184 *in the paradigm human experiment, carried out by Donald Hiroto:* D. S. Hiroto, "Locus of Control and Learned Helplessness," *Journal of Experimental Psychology* 102 (1974): 187–93.

See also D. S. Hiroto and M. E. P. Seligman, "Generality of Learned Helplessness in Man," *Journal of Personality and Social Psychology* 31 (1975): 311–27.

187 *this experiment—published in* Science *in 1982:* M. A. Visintainer, J. R. Volpicelli, and M. E. P. Seligman, "Tumor Rejection in Rats After Inescapable or Escapable Shock," *Science* 216 (1982): 437–39.

187 *the last time that I have been involved in an animal experiment:* S. Plous, "Attitudes Towards the Use of Animals in Psychological Research and Education: Results from a National Survey of Psychologists," *American Psychologist* 51 (1996): 1167–80. Plous conducted an interesting survey of members of the American Psychological Association and found that the majority of the four thousand respondents disapproved of studies that involve inflicting pain or death on animals. Plous quotes reasons given by respondents to disapprove of animal research, including reasons related to external validity: "I'm a neuropsychologist and have worked in rat and monkey labs. However, I'm increasingly convinced about differences between animal and human brains and behavior and think we should usually study humans"; "I used to conduct research with animals. I believe that much of the pain I inflicted on animals was *not* justified by the value of the data." Plous also quotes defendants of animal research, thus showing that this debate has certainly not been resolved.

188 *I have come to think that establishing external validity is an even more important but much more nettlesome scientific inference than establishing internal validity:* For additional comments on the relative importance of internal and external validity in psychological research, see M. E. P. Seligman, "Science as an Ally of Practice," *American Psychologist* 51 (1996): 1072–79; M. E. P. Seligman, "The Effectiveness of Psychotherapy: The Consumer Reports Study," *American Psychologist* 50 (1995): 965–74.

189 *It was that observation that led to the field called learned optimism:* M. E. P. Seligman, *Learned Optimism* (New York: Knopf, 1991).

189 *we looked systematically at the way that the people whom we could not make helpless interpreted bad events:* L. Y. Abramson, M. E. P. Seligman, and J. D. Teasdale, "Learned Helplessness in Humans: Critique and Reformulation," *Journal of Abnormal Psychology* 87 (1978): 49–74.

189 *we devised questionnaires to measure optimism:* C. Peterson, A. Semmel, C. VonBaeyer, L. Y. Abramson, G. I. Metalsky, and M. E. P. Seligman, "The Attributional Style Questionnaire," *Cognitive Therapy and Research* 6 (1982): 287–300.

189 *as well as content analytic techniques:* P. Schulman, C. Castellon, and M. E. P. Seligman, "Assessing Explanatory Style: The Content Analysis of Verbatim Explanations and the Attributional Style Questionnaire," *Behaviour Research and Therapy* 27 (1989): 505–12.

— 311 —

189   *We found that pessimists:* for a review, see G. M. Buchanan and M. E. P. Seligman, eds., *Explanatory Style* (Hillsdale, NJ: Erlbaum, 1995).

190   *Only optimism* [. . .] *predicted a second heart attack:* G. M. Buchanan and M. E. P. Seligman, "Explanatory Style and Heart Disease," in *Explanatory Style,* eds. G. M. Buchanan and M. E. P. Seligman (Hillsdale, NJ: Erlbaum, 1995), pp. 225–32.

191   *Men with the most optimistic style* [. . .] *had 25 percent less CVD than average:* L. Kubzansky, D. Sparrow, P. Vokonas, and I. Kawachi, "Is the Glass Half Empty or Half Full? A Prospective Study of Optimism and Coronary Heart Disease in the Normative Aging Study," *Psychosomatic Medicine* 63 (2001): 910–16.

191   *Death from cardiovascular disease was strongly influenced by a sense of mastery:* P. G. Surtees, N. W. J. Wainwright, R. Luben, K.-T. Khaw, and N. E. Day, "Mastery, Sense of Coherence, and Mortality: Evidence of Independent Associations from the EPIC-Norfolk Prospective Cohort Study," *Health Psychology* 25 (2006): 102–10.

192   *Pessimism was very strongly associated with mortality:* E. Giltay, J. Geleijnse, F. Zitman, T. Hoekstra, and E. Schouten, "Dispositional Optimism and All-Cause and Cardiovascular Mortality in a Prospective Cohort of Elderly Dutch Men and Women," *Archives of General Psychiatry* 61 (2004): 1126–35.

192   *if positive emotion worked through optimism:* K. W. Davidson, E. Mostofsky, and W. Whang, "Don't Worry, Be Happy: Positive Affect and Reduced 10-Year Incident Coronary Heart Disease: The Canadian Nova Scotia Health Survey," *European Heart Journal* (2010). Retrieved August 2, 2010, from doi:10.1093/eurheartj/ehp603.

B. Pitt and P. J. Deldin, "Depression and Cardiovascular Disease: Have a Happy Day—Just Smile!" *European Heart Journal* (2010). Retrieved August 2, 2010, from doi:10.1093/eurheartj/ehq031.

193   *The optimists (the top quarter) had 30 percent fewer coronary deaths than the pessimists:* H. Tindle, Y. F. Chang, L. Kuller, J. E. Manson, J. G. Robinson, M. C. Rosal, G. J. Siegle, and K. A. Matthews, "Optimism, Cynical Hostility, and Incident Coronary Heart Disease and Mortality in the Women's Health Initiative," *Circulation* 118 (2009): 1145–46.

193   *Something Worth Living For:* The three Japanese studies of *ikigai* are T. Sone, N. Nakaya, K. Ohmori, T. Shimazu, M. Higashiguchi, and M. Kakizaki, et al., "Sense of Life Worth Living (*Ikigai*) and Mortality in Japan: Ohsaki Study," *Psychosomatic Medicine* 70 (2008): 709–15; K. Shirai, H. Iso, T. Ohira, A. Ikeda, H. Noda, and K. Honjo, et al., "Perceived Level of Life Enjoyment and Risks of Cardiovascular Disease Incidence and Mortality: The Japan Public Health Center–Based Study, *Circulation* 120 (2009): 956–63; K. Tanno. K. Sakata, M. Ohsawa, T. Onoda, K. Itai, and Y. Yaegashi, et al., "Associations of *Ikigai* as a Positive Psychological Factor with All-Cause Mortality and Cause-Specific Mortality Among Middle-Aged and Elderly Japanese People: Findings from the Japan Collaborative Cohort Study," *Journal of Psychosomatic Research* 67 (2009): 67–75.

See also P. Boyle, A. Buchman, L. Barnes, and D. Bennett, "Effect of a Purpose in Life on Risk of Incident Alzheimer Disease and Mild Cognitive Impairment in Community-Dwelling Older Persons," *Archives of General Psychiatry* 67 (2010): 304–10.

195   *they report fewer symptoms:* This phenomenon has been described in the following articles: D. Watson and J. W. Pennebaker, "Health Complaints, Stress, and Distress: Exploring the Central Role of Negative Affectivity," *Psychological Review* 96 (1989): 234–54; S. Cohen, W. J. Doyle, D. P. Skoner, P. Fireman, J. M. Gwaltney, and J. T. Newsom, "State and Trait Negative Affect as Predictors of Objective and Subjective Symptoms of Respiratory Viral Infections," *Journal of Personality and Social Psychology* 68 (1999): 159–69; S. Cohen, W. J. Doyle, R. B. Turner, C. M. Alper, and D. P. Skoner, "Emotional Style and Susceptibility to the Common Cold," *Psychosomatic Medicine* 65 (2003): 652–57.

197   *None developed sores, leading to the conclusion that they must have already been infected:* The story is told in E. Kraepelin, "General Paresis," *Nervous and Mental Disease Monograph* 14 (1923).

199   *People with high positive emotion before the rhinovirus develop fewer colds:* S. Cohen, W. J. Doyle, R. B. Turner, C. M. Alper, and D. P. Skoner, "Emotional Style and Susceptibility to the Common Cold," *Psychosomatic Medicine* 65 (2003): 652–57.

200   *The higher the positive emotion (PES), the lower the interleukin-6 (IL-6):* W. J. Doyle, D. A. Gentile, and S. Cohen, "Emotional Style, Nasal Cytokines, and Illness Expression After Experimental Rhinovirus Exposure," *Brain, Behavior, and Immunity* 20 (2006): 175–81.

200   *Sheldon replicated this study with flu virus as well as cold virus:* S. Cohen, C. M. Alper, W. J. Doyle, J. J. Treanor, and R. B. Turner, "Positive Emotional Style Predicts Resistance to Illness After Experimental Exposure to Rhinovirus or Influenza A Virus," *Psychosomatic Medicine* 68 (2006): 809–15.

200   *"if a crane falls on you, optimism is not of much use":* M. E. P. Seligman, *Learned Optimism* (New York: Knopf, 1991). The same point is made in Chapter 10 (p. 176): "If you are hit by a Mack truck, your level of optimism is not going to make much difference. If you are hit by a bicycle, however, optimism could play a crucial role. I do not believe that when a patient has such a lethal load of cancer as to be deemed 'terminal,' psychological processes can do much good. At the margin, however, when the tumor load is small, when illness is beginning to progress, optimism might spell the difference between life and death."

201   *no measurable effect on prolonging life in patients with inoperable cancer:* P. Schofield, D. Ball, and J. Smith, et al., "Optimism and Survival in Lung Carcinoma Patients," *Cancer* 100 (2004): 1276–82; P. Novotny, R. Colligan, and B. Szydlo, et al., "A Pessimistic Explanatory Style Is Prognostic for Poor Lung Cancer Survival," *Journal of Thoracic Oncology* (forthcoming). Novotny and Colligan, et al., found that optimists survived six months longer than pessimists in a large sample of 534 adults.

201   *Ehrenreich recently published:* B. Ehrenreich, *Bright-Sided: How the Relentless Promotion of Positive Thinking Has Undermined America* (New York: Holt, 2009).

201   Smile or Die: B. Ehrenreich, *Smile or Die: How Positive Thinking Fooled America and the World* (London: Granta Books, 2009).

201   *seven years longer than those not smiling:* E. Abel and M. Kruger, "Smile Intensity in Photographs Predicts Longevity," *Psychological Science* 20 (2010): 1–3.

202   *Evidence is thin:* M. Shermer, "Kool-Aid Psychology," *Scientific American* 39 (2010): 39. Michael Shermer is founding editor of *Skeptic* magazine. Coming from a bias to skepticism, I like the premises of the magazine, but in this case, the skeptic-in-chief failed to underpin his skepticism by reviewing the primary literature.

202   *eighty-three separate studies of optimism and physical health:* H. Rasmussen, M. Scheier, and J. Greenhouse, "Optimism and Physical Health: A Meta-Analytic Review," *Annals of Behavioral Medicine* 37 (2009): 239–56.

For a heated exchange about this meta-analysis, see J. Coyne and H. Tennen, "Positive Psychology in Cancer Care: Bad Science, Exaggerated Claims, and Unproven Medicine," *Annals of Behavioral Medicine* 39 (2010): 16–26.

L. Aspinwall and R. Tedeschi, "Of Babies and Bathwater: A Reply to Coyne and Tennen's Views on Positive Psychology and Health," *Annals of Behavioral Medicine* 39 (2010): 27–34.

M. Roseman, K. Milette, Y. Zhao, and B. Thombs, "Is Optimism Associated with Physical Health? A Commentary on Rasmussen et al.," *Annals of Behavioral Medicine* 39 (2010): 204–6.

M. F. Scheier, J. B. Greenhouse, and H. N. Rasmussen, "Reply to Roseman, Milette, Zhao, and Thombs," *Annals of Behavioral Medicine* 39 (2010): 207–09. I will let the scholarly reader judge, but I believe the cancer outcome is still an unsettled empirical issue, and the huge army data set will likely settle it within the next three years.

202   *although the effect was smaller than for CVD:* H. Tindle, Y. F. Chang, and L. Kuller, et al., "Optimism, Cynical Hostility, and Incident Coronary Heart Disease and Mortality in the Women's Health Initiative," *Circulation* 10 (2009): 1161–67.

203   *Yoichi Chida and Andrew Steptoe [. . .] recently published an exemplary comprehensive meta-analysis:* Y. Chida and A. Steptoe, "Positive Psychological Well-Being and Mortality: A Quantitative Review of Prospective Observational Studies," *Psychosomatic Medicine* 70 (2008): 741–56.

See also J. Xu and R. Roberts, "The Power of Positive Emotions: It's a Matter of Life or Death—Subjective Well-Being and Longevity Over 28 Years in a General Population," *Health Psychology* (forthcoming).

205   *there exists only one in the optimism-health literature:* G. M. Buchanan, C. A. R. Gardenswartz, and M. E. P. Seligman, "Physical Health Following a Cognitive-Behavioral Intervention," *Prevention and Treatment* 2 (1999). Retrieved November 14, 2009, from http://proxy.library.upenn.edu:8457/prevention/volume2/pre210a.html.

See also M. Charlson, C. Foster, and C. Mancuso, et al., "Randomized Controlled Trials of Positive Affect and Self-Affirmation to Facilitate Healthy Behaviors in Patients with Cardiopulmonary Diseases: Rationale, Trial Design, and Methods," *Contemporary Clinical Trials* 28 (2007): 748–62.

206   *it was the optimists who gave up smoking:* G. E. Vaillant, *Aging Well: Surprising Guideposts to a Happier Life from the Landmark Harvard Study of Adult Development* (New York: Little, Brown and Company, 2003).

206   *happy people also sleep better than unhappy people:* A. Steptoe, S. Dockray, and J. Wardle, "Positive Affect and Psychobiological Processes Relevant to Health," *Journal of Personality* 77 (2009): 1747-75.

206   *people who have one person whom they would be comfortable calling at three in the morning:* G. E. Vaillant, *Aging Well: Surprising Guideposts to a Happier Life from the Landmark Harvard Study of Adult Development* (New York: Little, Brown and Company, 2003).

206   *lonely people are markedly less healthy than sociable people:* J. T. Cacioppo, L. C. Hawkley, L. E. Crawford, J. M. Ernst, M. H. Burleson, R. B. Kowalewski, W. B. Kowalewski, E. Van Cauter, and G. G. Berntson, "Loneliness and Health: Potential Mechanisms, *Psychosomatic Medicine* 64 (2002): 407–17.

J. T. Cacioppo, L. C. Hawkley, and G. G. Berntson, "The Anatomy of Loneliness," *Current Directions in Psychological Science* 12 (2003): 71–74.

207   *The blood of optimists had a feistier response to threat:* L. Kamen-Siegel, J. Rodin, M. E. P. Seligman, and J. Dwyer, "Explanatory Style and Cell-Mediated Immunity in Elderly Men and Women," *Health Psychology* 10 (1991): 229–35.

See also S. Segerstrom and S. Sephton, "Optimistic Expectancies and Cell-Mediated Immunity: The Role of Positive Affect," *Psychological Science* 21 (2010): 448–55.

207   *promote atherosclerosis:* See for instance S. A. Everson, G. A. Kaplan, D. E. Goldberg, R. Salonen, and J. T. Salonen, "Hopelessness and 4-Year Progression of Carotid Atherosclerosis: The Kuopio Ischemic Heart Disease Risk Factor Study," *Arteriosclerosis, Thrombosis, and Vascular Biology* 17 (1997): 1490–95.

A. Rozanski, J. A. Blumenthal, and J. Kaplan, "Impact of Psychological Factors on the Pathogenesis of Cardiovascular Disease and Implications for Therapy," *Circulation* 99 (1999): 2192–2217.

207   *women who score low in feelings of mastery and high in depression have been shown to have worse calcification of the major artery, the trunk-like aorta:* K. A. Matthews, J. F. Owens, D. Edmundowicz, L. Lee, and L. H. Kuller, "Positive and Negative Attributes and Risk for Coronary and Aortic Calcification in Healthy Women," *Psychosomatic Medicine* 68 (2006): 355–61.

207   *Helpless rats, in the triadic design, develop atherosclerosis at a faster rate than rats that demonstrated mastery:* G. M. Buchanan and M. E. P. Seligman, "Explanatory Style and Heart Disease," in *Explanatory Style,* eds. G. M. Buchanan and M. E. P. Seligman (Hillsdale, NJ: Erlbaum, 1995), pp. 225–32.

207   *less of a fibrinogen response to stress than those with low positive emotion:* A. Steptoe, J. Wardle, and M. Marmot. "Positive Affect and Health-Related Neuroendocrine, Cardiovascular, and Inflammatory Processes," *Proceedings of the National Academy of Sciences* 102 (2005): 6508–12.

208   *high heart rate variability are healthier, have less CVD, less depression, and better cognitive abilities:* J. Thayer and E. Sternberg, "Beyond Heart Rate Variability: Vagal Regulation of Allostatic Systems," *Annals of the New York Academy of Sciences* 1088 (2006): 361–72.

210   *Normative Aging Study:* See www.nia.nih.gov/ResearchInformation/ScientificResources/StudyInfo.htm?id=26.

214   *Dr. Darwin Labarthe:* Darwin Labarthe is also the author of D. R. Labarthe, *Epidemiology and Prevention of Cardiovascular Disease,* 2nd ed. (Sudbury, MA: Jones and Bartlett, 2010).

215   *people who walk ten thousand steps every day markedly lower their risk for heart attack:* See for instance P. D. Savage, and P. A. Ades, "Pedometer Step

Counts Predict Cardiac Risk Factors at Entry to Cardiac Rehabilitation," *Journal of Cardiopulmonary Rehabilitation and Prevention* 28 (2008): 370–77.

D. M. Bravata, C. Smith-Spangler, V. Sundaram, A. L. Gienger, N. Lin, R. Lewis, C. D. Stave, I. Olkin, and J. R. Sirard, "Using Pedometers to Increase Physical Activity and Improve Health: A Systematic Review," *Journal of the American Medical Association* 298 (2007): 2296–2304. A review and meta-analysis of the benefits of walking on health.

215   *As Nietzsche tells us, good philosophy always says, "Change your life!"*: see the introduction by the editor of F. Nietzsche, W. Kaufmann, and P. Gay, *Basic Writings of Nietzsche* (New York: Random House, 2000).

216   *the real epidemic, the worst killer, is the epidemic of inactivity*: D. C. Lee, X. Sui, and S. N. Blair, "Does Physical Activity Ameliorate the Health Hazards of Obesity?" *British Journal of Sports Medicine* 43 (2009): 49–51. Reviews Steve Blair's work on obesity and physical activity.

216   *Poor physical fitness correlates strongly with all-cause mortality, and particularly with cardiovascular disease*: X. Sui, J. N. Laditka, J. W. Hardin, and S. N. Blair, "Estimated Functional Capacity Predicts Mortality in Older Adults," *Journal of the American Geriatric Society* 55 (2007): 1940–47.

217   *Here is a representative one*: X. Sui, J. N. Laditka, M. J. LaMonte, J. W. Hardin, N. Chase, S. P. Hooker, S. P., and S. N. Blair, "Cardiorespiratory Fitness and Adiposity as Mortality Predictors in Older Adults," *Journal of the American Medical Association* 298 (2007): 2507–16.

218   *exercise will not make you much thinner*: J. Cloud, "Why Exercise Won't Make You Thin," *Time*, August 9, 2009.

218   *The surgeon general's 2008 report*: www.cdc.gov/nccdphp/sgr/index.htm (1999).

219   *(The real danger point is fewer than 5,000 steps a day)*: C. Tudor-Locke and D. R. Bassett, "How Many Steps/Day Are Enough? Preliminary Pedometer Indices for Public Health," *Sports Medicine* 34 (2004): 1–8. Based on previous evidence, Tudor-Locke and Bassett suggested the following indices to evaluate pedometer-determined physical activity: fewer than 5,000 steps a day indicates that individuals have a sedentary lifestyle (which, as noted before, is associated with a wide array of negative health outcomes). Individuals who take 5,000 to 7,499 steps a day are considered "low active." Those who take 7,500 to 9,999 steps a day are considered "somewhat active." The cutoff for classifying individuals as "active" is 10,000 steps a day. Those who take more than 12,500 steps a day are considered "highly active."

Chapter 10: The Politics and Economics of Well-Being

221   *When politicians run for office, they campaign about what they will do, or have done, for the economy*: For an interesting discussion of the role of the economy in the 2008 presidential election, see the symposium in *PS: Political Science and Politics* 42, no. 3 (2009), including the articles R. S. Erikson, "The American Voter and the Economy, 2008," *PS: Political Science and Politics* 42 (2009): 467–71; M. S. Lewis-Beck and R. Nadeau, "Obama and the Economy in 2008," *PS: Political Science and Politics* 42 (2009): 479–83.

222   *perhaps an overabundance, of goods and services:* as described by
G. Easterbrook, *The Progress Paradox: How Life Gets Better While People Feel
Worse* (New York: Random House, 2003).

222   *Ed Diener and I published an article:* E. Diener and Seligman, M. E. P.,
"Beyond Money: Toward an Economy of Well-Being," *Psychological Science in the
Public Interest* 5 (2004): 1–31.

223   *Life satisfaction in the United States has been flat for fifty years even though
GDP has tripled:* E. Diener and Seligman, M. E. P., "Beyond Money: Toward an Economy of Well-Being," *Psychological Science in the Public Interest* 5 (2004): 1–31.

See also E. Zencey, "G.D.P. R.I.P.," *New York Times,* August 9, 2009.

223   *Depression rates have increased tenfold:* The two major studies that found
the epidemic of depression are L. Robins, J. Helzer, M. Weissman, H. Orvaschel,
E. Gruenberg, J. Burke, and D. Regier, "Lifetime Prevalence of Specific Psychiatric
Disorders in Three Sites," *Archives of General Psychiatry* 41 (1984): 949–58; G. Kler-
man, P. Lavori, J. Rice, T. Reich, J. Endicott, N. Andreasen, M. Keller, and R. Hirschfeld,
"Birth Cohort Trends in Rates of Major Depressive Disorder Among Relatives of
Patients with Affective Disorder," *Archives of General Psychiatry* 42 (1985): 689–93.

223   *Rates of anxiety have also risen:* J. M. Twenge, "The Age of Anxiety?
The Birth Cohort Change in Anxiety and Neuroticism, 1952–1993," *Journal of
Personality and Social Psychology* 79 (2000): 1007–21.

223   *Social connectedness in our nation has dropped:* R. Putnam, *Bowling
Alone: The Collapse and Revival of American Community* (New York: Simon &
Schuster, 2001).

223   *trust is a major predictor of well-being:* J. F. Helliwell, "How's Life?
Combining Individual and National Variables to Explain Subjective Well-Being,"
Economic Modeling 20 (2003): 331–60.

223   *There is an enormous literature on money and happiness:* For a review,
see R. Biswas-Diener, "Material Wealth and Subjective Well-Being," in *The Science
of Subjective Well-Being* (New York: Guilford Press, 2008).

See also E. Diener and R. Biswas-Diener, "Will Money Increase Subjective
Well-Being?" A Literature Review and Guide to Needed Research," *Social Indicators Research* 57 (2002): 119–69.

Finally, for a discussion of the relationship between money and happiness
between nations, see E. Diener and S. Oishi, "Money and Happiness: Income and
Subjective Well-Being Across Nations," in *Culture and Subjective Well-Being,* eds.
E. Diener and E. M. Suh (Cambridge, MA: MIT Press, 2000), pp. 185–218.

223   *In the graph:* A. Deaton, "Income, Health, and Well-Being Around the
World: Evidence from the Gallup World Poll," *Journal of Economic Perspectives* 22
(2008): 53–72.

224   *This is the venerable "Easterlin paradox":* R. A. Easterlin, "Does Eco-
nomic Growth Improve the Human Lot?" in *Nations and Households in Economic
Growth: Essays in Honour of Moses Abramovitz* (New York: Academic Press, 1974);
R. A. Easterlin, "Will Raising the Incomes of All Increase the Happiness of All?"
Journal of Economic Behavior and Organization 27 (1995): 35–47.

224   *it has been challenged recently by my young colleagues at Penn, Justin
Wolfers and Betsey Stevenson:* J. Wolfers and B. Stevenson, "Economic Growth

and Subjective Well-Being: Reassessing the Easterlin Paradox," *Brookings Papers on Economic Activity* (2008): 1–87.

226   *Life Satisfaction for Various Groups:* See E. Diener and M. E. P. Seligman, "Beyond Money: Toward an Economy of Well-Being," *Psychological Science in the Public Interest* 5 (2004): 1–31.

227   *these two components, mood and judgment, are influenced differentially by income:* as shown by E. Diener, D. Kahneman, R. Arora, J. Harter, and W. Tov, "Income's Differential Influence on Judgments of Life Versus Affective Well-Being," in E. Diener, *Assessing Well-Being: The Collected Works of Ed Diener* (New York: Springer, 2009), pp. 233–46.

227   *There are fifty-two nations for which substantial time series analyses of subjective well-being (SWB) exist from 1981 to 2007:* R. Inglehart, R. Foa, and C. Welzel, "Development, Freedom, and Rising Happiness: A Global Perspective (1981–2007)," *Perspectives on Psychological Science* 3 (2008): 264–85.

227   *some very instructive anomalies appear:* R. Inglehart, R. Foa, and C. Welzel, "Development, Freedom, and Rising Happiness: A Global Perspective (1981–2007)," *Perspectives on Psychological Science* 3 (2008): 264–85.

227   *Poor people in Calcutta:* See R. Biswas-Diener and E. Diener, "Making the Best of a Bad Situation: Satisfaction in the Slums of Calcutta," *Social Indicators Research* 55 (2001): 329–52; R. Biswas-Diener and E. Diener, "The Subjective Well-Being of the Homeless, and Lessons for Happiness," *Social Indicators Research* 76 (2006): 185–205.

227   *Utah is much happier than its income suggests:* See P. J. Rentfrow, C. Mellander, and R. Florida, "Happy States of America: A State-Level Analysis of Psychological, Economic, and Social Well-Being," *Journal of Research in Personality* 43 (2009): 1073–82.

229   *"The Importance of What We Care About":* H. Frankfurt, "The Importance of What We Care About," *Synthese* 53 (1982): 257–72.

229   *"On Bullshit":* H. G. Frankfurt, *On Bullshit* (Princeton, NJ: Princeton University Press, 2005).

229   *"functional autonomy of motives":* G. W. Allport, "The Functional Autonomy of Motives," *American Journal of Psychology* 50 (1937): 141–56.

230   *My solution was "prepared" Pavlovian conditioning:* M. E. P. Seligman and J. L. Hager, eds., *Biological Boundaries of Learning* (New York: Appleton-Century-Crofts, 1972).

230   *This is called the Garcia effect:* J. Garcia and R. A. Koelling, "Relation of Cue to Consequence in Avoidance Learning," *Psychonomic Science* 4 (1966): 123–24; J. Garcia, B. K. McGowan, F. R. Ervui, and R. A. Koelling, "Cues: Their Relative Effectiveness as a Function of the Reinforcer," *Science* 760 (1968): 794–95.

230   *the sauce béarnaise phenomenon:* M. E. P. Seligman and J. L. Hager, "Biological Boundaries of Learning: The Sauce-Bearnaise Syndrome," *Psychology Today* 6 (August 1972): 59–61, 84–87.

230   *specific fears run in families:* See for instance I. Skre, S. Onstad, S. Torgersen, D. R. Philos, S. Lygren, and E. Kringlen, "The Heritability of Common Phobic Fear: A Twin Study of a Clinical Sample," *Journal of Anxiety Disorders* 14 (2000): 549–62.

230   *identical twins are more concordant for depression* [. . .] *than fraternal twins:* P. F. Sullivan, M. C. Neale, and K. S. Kendler, "Genetic Epidemiology of Major Depression: Review and Meta-Analysis," *American Journal of Psychiatry* 157 (2000): 1552–62.

232   *experiences bring more well-being than material goods of the same price:* L. Van Boven and T. Gilovich, "To Do or to Have? That Is the Question," *Journal of Personality and Social Psychology* 85 (2003): 1193–1202; L. Van Boven, "Experientialism, Materialism, and the Pursuit of Happiness," *Review of General Psychology* 9 (2005): 132–42.

233   *baseline statistics for other projects that resemble theirs:* D. Kahneman and D. Lovallo, "Timid Choices and Bold Forecasts: A Cognitive Perspective on Risk Taking," *Management Science* 39 (1993): 17–23; D. Lovallo and D. Kahneman, "Delusions of Success: How Optimism Undermines Executives' Decisions," *Harvard Business Review* 81 (2003): 56–63.

233   *"How Positive Thinking Destroyed the Economy":* See Chapter 7 in B. Ehrenreich, *Bright-Sided: How the Relentless Promotion of Positive Thinking Has Undermined America* (New York: Holt, 2009).

234   *(George Soros* [. . .] *calls it "reflexive reality"):* G. Soros, *The Age of Fallibility* (Perseus, 2006).

236   *Sandra Murray* [. . .] *has done an extraordinary set of studies on good marriage:* For a review, see S. L. Murray, J. G. Holmes, and D. W. Griffin, "Reflections on the Self-Fulfilling Effects of Positive Illusions," *Psychological Inquiry* 14 (2003): 289–95.

See also S. L. Murray, J. G. Holmes, D. Dolderman, and D. W. Griffin, "What the Motivated Mind Sees: Comparing Friends' Perspectives to Married Partners' Views of Each Other," *Journal of Experimental Social Psychology* 36 (2000): 600–20; S. L. Murray, J. G. Holmes, and D. W. Griffin, "The Self-Fulfilling Nature of Positive Illusions in Romantic Relationships: Love Is Not Blind, but Prescient," *Journal of Personality and Social Psychology* 71 (1996): 1155–80.

237   *"one damn thing after another":* A. J. Toynbee, *A Study of History* (Oxford: Oxford University Press, 1961). The historian Arnold Toynbee is credited for having said that history is not "one damn thing after another," a thesis he defended in his classic *A Study of History*, a twelve-volume opus describing and analyzing the rise, development, and decay of more than twenty civilizations.

238   *Huppert and Timothy So surveyed 43,000 adults:* T. So and F. Huppert, *"What Percentage of People in Europe Are Flourishing and What Characterizes Them?* (July 23, 2009). Retrieved October 19, 2009, from www .isqols2009.istitutodeglinnocenti.it/Content_en/Huppert.pdf.

See also E. Diener and W. Tov, "Well-Being on Planet Earth," *Psychological Topics* 18 (2009): 213–19; D. Bok, *The Politics of Happiness: What Government Can Learn from New Research on Well-Being* (Princeton, N.J.: Princeton University Press, 2009); C. Keyes, "Promoting and Protecting Mental Health as Flourishing," *American Psychologist* 62 (2007): 95–108.

239   *Notice that such criteria are not merely subjective:* The importance of correlating subjective measures with objective indicators is underscored by

A. Oswald and S. Wu, "Objective Confirmation of Subjective Measures of Human Well-Being: Evidence from the U.S.A.," *Science* 327 (2010): 576–78.

240   *how to weight income disparity within a nation:* M. Berg and R. Veenhoven, "Income Inequality and Happiness in 119 Nations," in *Social Policy and Happiness in Europe,* ed. Bent Greve (Cheltenham, UK: Edgar Elgar, 2010). This is an example in which political leanings and the data are at odds and are presently duking it out. The left holds that wide income disparity is unjust and that taxing the very rich to reduce it ought to make people happier. It points to Denmark, perennial number one nation in life satisfaction, as an example. Ruut Veenhoven, however, has actually gathered worldwide data on this. In his World Database of Happiness (worlddatabaseofhappiness.eur.nl), he correlates size of income disparity with happiness and finds zero relationship. So taxing Bill Gates even more heavily will likely not affect your mood or your life satisfaction.

241   *happiness turns out to be more contagious than depression:* J. H. Fowler and N. A. Christakis, "Dynamic Spread of Happiness in a Large Social Network: Longitudinal Analysis over 20 Years in the Framingham Heart Study," *British Medical Journal* 337 (2008): a2338. James Fowler and Nicholas Christakis recently showed that people's happiness depends on the happiness of those to whom they are connected. They followed 4,739 participants over twenty years and found that happiness clusters (that is, groups of happy people socially connected) could be explained by the spreading of happiness rather than by a tendency for happy individuals to associate.

See also J. Fowler and N. Christakis, "Cooperative Behavior Cascades in Human Social Networks," *Proceedings of the National Academy of Sciences* 107 (2010): 5334–38.

241   *Friedrich Nietzsche analyzed human growth and human history in three stages:* F. Nietzsche, *Thus Spoke Zarathustra* (Cambridge, UK: Cambridge University Press, 2006).

INDEX

ABOUT THE AUTHOR

Martin E. P. Seligman, PhD, the Zellerbach Family Professor of Psychology at the University of Pennsylvania, works on learned helplessness, depression, optimism, positive psychology, and comprehensive soldier fitness. His research has been supported by the National Institutes of Health, the National Science Foundation, the MacArthur Foundation, the Annenberg Foundation, the Templeton Foundation, Atlantic Philanthropies, and the Robert Wood Johnson Foundation.

He is the recipient of several Distinguished Scientific Contribution awards from the American Psychological Association. Dr. Seligman received both the American Psychological Society's William James Fellow Award (for contribution to basic science) and the James McKeen Cattell Fellow Award (for the application of psychological knowledge). He received the inaugural Wiley Award of the British Academy for lifetime contributions to psychology in 2009.

In 1996 Dr. Seligman was elected president of the American Psychological Association by the largest vote in modern history.